D0474422

arningcentre@duchy

The Changing Face of Further Education

What values and policies are driving the development of further education institutions?

The rapid expansion and development of the post-compulsory sector of education means that further education institutions have to cope with ever-evolving government policies.

This book comprehensively examines the current trends in further education by means of both policy analysis and research in the field. It offers an insightful evaluation of FE colleges today, set against the background of New Labour Lifelong Learning intiatives and, in particular, the links between college and community.

This timely investigation of FE and New Labour policy takes a unique community education perspective to determine whether the social objectives of current policy can be achieved by policy-makers, managers, staff and students in FE institutions.

For students, lecturers and educators in the post-compulsory sector, in addition to policy-makers and managers, this is an invaluable source of information on a subject which is still largely under-researched.

Terry Hyland is Professor in Post Compulsory Education and Training at Bolton Institute.

Barbara Merrill is Senior Lecturer in the Centre for Lifelong Learning at the University of Warwick.

The Changing Face of Further Education

Lifelong learning, inclusion and community values in further education

Terry Hyland and Barbara Merrill

RoutledgeFalmer
Taylor & Francis Group

LONDON AND NEW YORK

First published 2003 by RoutledgeFalmer
11 New Fetter Lane, London EC4P 4EE

Simultaneously published in the USA and Canada
by RoutledgeFalmer
29 West 35th Street, New York, NY 10001

RoutledgeFalmer is an imprint of the Taylor & Francis Group

© 2003 Terry Hyland and Barbara Merrill

Typeset in Times New Roman by
Keystroke, Jacaranda Lodge, Wolverhampton
Printed and bound in Great Britain by TJ International Ltd,
Padstow, Cornwall

British Library Cataloguing in Publication Data
A catalogue record for this book is available from the British Library

Library of Congress Cataloging in Publication Data
A catalog record has been requested

ISBN 0–415–26807–9 (hbk)
ISBN 0–415–26810–9 (pbk)

Contents

Introduction

Until the incorporation of further education (FE) institutions in April 1993 it was common to see references to the sector in terms of its 'Cinderella' or 'Invisible Man' status. In the years since then, the colleges have witnessed an impressive increase in student numbers at all levels, the implementation of new curricula and learning strategies, the expansion of provision in new areas in the 16–19, vocational education and training (VET), adult and higher education (HE) spheres; and the sector is now central to the current New Labour lifelong learning policies aimed at enhancing economic competitiveness and workforce skills, widening participation and challenging social exclusion at all levels of the education system.

However, the fact that Helena Kennedy in her highly influential 1997 policy report on widening participation was still able to trot out the old chestnut definition of the scope of FE activities in terms of 'everything that does not happen in schools or universities' (Kennedy, 1997, p. 1) demonstrates forcefully that clarity of purpose and definition of strategic mission for the sector have yet to be achieved. As Lucas (2001) commented recently, the sector is still very much 'in the shadows' (p. 38) in terms of national planning. Thus, in spite of the official government statement that the 'further education sector is at the heart of the revival in learning that we are witnessing in this country' (DfEE, 2000a, para. 95), Green and Lucas (1999b) – acknowledging the improvements and important developments in the sector since incorporation in 1993 – still wanted to conclude their investigation of recent FE trends by observing that:

> the sector is still very fragmented despite the centralised national system of funding – all in all it is still a long way from the promised national sector . . . In the effort to maximise funding, compete with other providers and survive the first five years of 'efficiency savings',

FE has lost any notion of having a distinctive national or regional role. The sector is not only facing a financial crisis, but is also in a state of strategic drift.

(p. 37)

In a similar vein, Hodgson and Spours (1999) argue that there is a 'considerable consensus both within and outside further education colleges that the sector will need reform and support if it is to fulfil its mission'. The main challenges, therefore, are:

to rescue the sector from its current financial difficulties; to clarify the regional and national roles which further education is expected to play in promoting and supporting lifelong learning now and in the future; and to provide the infrastructure within which the sector can carry out this role.

(p. 87)

On a more optimistic note, Smithers and Robinson (2000) suggest that, since incorporation, there is 'no doubt that the great majority of the colleges have relished their freedom'. Moreover, the colleges:

currently provide for nearly 4 million students compared with 2.9 million when the sector was born. With the inclusion of the sixth-form colleges the sector now has more A-level students than the schools . . . [and] continues to be the main provider for adults with 15% growth over five years . . . the colleges now have more degree students than did the universities at the time of the landmark Robbins Report in 1963.

(p. 3)

They go on to remind us, however, that the 'colleges are still in the making; once more they are being re-formed' (p. 11).

This 're-formation' of FE has proceeded apace since the New Labour administration entered its second phase of policy-making, and the whole post-compulsory education and training (PCET) sector has, from April 2001, been completely re-organised under the national Learning and Skills Council (LSC) and its forty-seven regional bodies (LSC, 2001a). Lucas (2000) argues that the setting up of the local learning and skills councils (LLSCs) 'nudges the post-16 system towards greater coherence, with an emphasis on planning' (p. 156). Referring to the fact already mentioned that the DfEE (now the DfES) currently views 'the further education sector as a key sector for developing lifelong learning', Lucas goes on to make the interesting observation that the colleges:

> are, despite incorporation, still embedded in local communities and historically have had good links with sectors of the community that are now seen as potential sites for the dispersed learning opportunities envisioned in The Learning Age . . . It would seem that until now the present drift of further education is positioning the sector towards the US community college mode.
>
> (pp. 156–7)

Gravatt and Silver (2000) similarly contend that 'community and partnership are two of the most powerful terms in the current further education lexicon' (p. 116), and Scott (1996) remarks that:

> For almost a quarter of a century FE colleges have been engaged in a long revolution, sloughing off their technical school past and evolving towards a broader community-wide comprehensive college future . . .
>
> (p. 52)

The reflection of local needs, as Cripps (2002) argues, soon emerged as central to the 'vision of the 1944 Act' (p. 35), and our own work on the sector has been influenced by this evolution towards a 'community-wide' culture, in particular, the ways in which the organisational and cultural ethos, approaches to learning and teaching, and the lives of learners and FE staff at all levels have been shaped by the interaction of colleges with all aspects of community life and its diverse agencies and stakeholders. The normative vision of community developed throughout – incorporating historical, philosophical and sociological perspectives – will interrogate developments in the sector against the background of the 'communitarian' ethics which underpin current policy (Levitas, 1998), 'social capital' notions (Schuller and Field, 1998; Winch, 2000) and the conception of the human economy which exists for 'the protection of gifts' and seeks 'to foster persons who will maintain and preserve the essential characteristics of community'(Rozema, 2001, p. 237).

All of this will be brought together in a final chapter wherein we outline a blueprint for a 'philosophy of further education' underpinned by values which, it is argued, are essential to the lifelong learning policy, theory and practice which currently inform and drive all developments in the PCET system, that is now part of the broader, newly defined and re-organised learning and skills sector (LSS).

Chapter 1

Further education –
past and present

The LSS and post-compulsory education and training (PCET) sector in general, and its largest component and chief vehicle – the further education (FE) sector – in particular, has, arguably, witnessed more radical change and development over the last few decades than any other sphere of educational provision. In the then Secretary of State's speech to the Association of Colleges for Further and Higher Education in 1989, Kenneth Baker was concerned to point out that FE was no longer 'just the bit between school and higher education'. There was an insistence that the FE sector was:

> not just the Cinderella of the education service . . . Over 1,750,000 attend further education colleges . . . taught by the equivalent of 63,000 lecturers. There are some 400 LEA-maintained colleges. The whole thing costs £1 billion a year. It is a big, big enterprise.
>
> (Baker, 1989, p. 3)

Given the sweeping and fundamental changes the sector has experienced since 1989 – the massive expansion of numbers, the growth of the new general and national vocational qualifications (G/NVQs), the incorporation of colleges under the 1992 Further and Higher Education Act, the funding and inspection regimes under the Further Education Funding Council (FEFC) and the recent re-organisation under the Learning and Skills Council (LSC), changes in staff contracts and conditions of service as well as the financial and management vicissitudes of a significant number of institutions – it could justifiably be said that the 'bit between school and higher education' has been changed out of all recognition over the last few decades.

Moreover, trends in FE need to be located against the background of fundamental changes in the PCET sector generally which are driven by

New Labour's 'lifelong learning' (DfEE, 1998a) policy (examined in more detail in Chapter 2). The key objectives of lifelong learning are the widening of participation in further and higher education to foster greater social inclusion and cohesion and the raising of skill levels to enhance Britain's economic competitiveness. Although the economic arguments always seem to have pride of place (Hyland, 2000, 2002), they are invariably twinned with the social inclusion aims which were raised in the Kennedy Report (1997) and officially endorsed in the government's response to DfEE (1998b). These key aims have been reinforced more recently in the DfEE policy document on the role envisaged for FE institutions after the re-organisation of the sector under the LLSCs in April 2001. The then Secretary of State, David Blunkett, made it clear that although he saw:

> further education as playing a key role in the economic agenda, it is also central to meeting the social objectives of our lifelong learning policy. Economic prosperity and social cohesion go hand in hand, and working with partners at local and regional level . . . I therefore look to further education to work with and support partners in the adult and community and the voluntary sectors; to play a key role in the delivery of information, advice and guidance for adults; and crucially to ensure that it is central to addressing the basic skills needs of adults, a task which is critical to both our economic and social agendas.
>
> (DfEE, 2000a, para. 4)

The role of partnerships – between FE colleges, higher education institutions (HEIs), schools, employers, voluntary agencies and other community stakeholder groups – is now a central feature of New Labour policy for the PCET sector as the new Secretary of State, Estelle Morris, noted in welcoming the LSC corporate plan (DfES, 2001a, pp. 1–2). Before examining this new, extended role for FE institutions in the twenty-first century, it is worth looking briefly at the past and recent history which have served to shape the present sector.

FE – origins and development

Pratt (2000) has suggested that it 'was in the last quarter of the nineteenth century that the system of further education as we know it today became established' (p. 13). In terms of social, economic and educational origins this is correct, though in strictly conceptual terms 'further education' did not enter the educational lexicon until it was first used to refer to post-school provision in Section 41 of the 1944 Education Act (Dent, 1968, p. 35) which required local education authorities (LEAs) to secure provision of adequate facilities for:

(a) full-time and part-time education for persons over compulsory school age;
(b) leisure-time occupation, in such organized cultural training and recreative activities as are suited to their requirements, for any persons over compulsory school age who are able and willing to profit by the facilities provided for that purpose.

In their interesting sketch of the historical development of those activities which have since been subsumed under the FE umbrella, Green and Lucas (1999a) present an outline based on five periods: the nineteenth century, 1900–1944, 1940s to 1970s, 1970s and 1980s and, finally, the 1990s. We intend to use these broad categories and – supplementing existing accounts with philosophical, historical, social and empirical studies, in addition to our own work on the sector (Hyland and Merrill, 1996, 2001; Hyland,1999; Merrill 2000) – to offer a broad outline of the evolution of the sector.

The nineteenth century

The main strands of development prior to the establishment of state systems were working-class 'self-help' movements, offering social and cultural enrichment through adult education activities, and the Mechanics Institutes which provided a diversity of technical and vocational education courses (Hall, 1994). The key aims of the former – the various workers and mutual improvement societies which grew out of the labour and co-operative movements – aimed to provide general literacy, scientific, cultural and political education to remedy the absence of state provision for working people in these areas. Clubs and circles were organised by Chartists, Owenites and Christian Socialists, an example of the latter being the establishment of the London Working Men's College in 1854 (Harrison, 1954). Simon (1969) suggests that many of these early movements were designed to counteract the impact of the more middle-class Mechanics Institutes which were developing apace in all regions throughout the nineteenth century.

The first Mechanics Institute was founded in Edinburgh in 1821, beginning a development which was to lead to the establishment of technical colleges later in the century which, in turn, provided a foundation for the birth of the FE sector. By the mid-nineteenth century there were 610 Institutes with a membership of more than half a million, although, as Green and Lucas (1999b) note, they 'did not gain credibility as genuinely mass adult education providers' since their 'increasingly middle-class ethos alienated potential working-class entrants' (p. 11).

The chief aim of the Institutes was to teach 'useful knowledge' but they 'failed in their purpose primarily due to the lack of literacy among those who needed such knowledge' (Musgrave, 1970a, p. 65). Moreover, in the development of programmes, the Institutes began a process of separating general, scientific and technical education (Evans, 1975) which – reinforced by the intense political and education debates about technical education later in the century – created divisions between vocational and academic studies that bedevil the system to this day.

The essentially voluntarist, *ad hoc* and fragmented nature of educational developments in the early nineteenth century was later questioned and criticised when Britain's position as the 'foremost industrial nation' (Musgrave, 1970a, p. 144) was threatened. This position had been displayed for all the world to see at the Great Exhibition held at the Crystal Palace in 1851 but – by the time of the Paris Exhibition of 1867 – a member of the Exhibition jury, Dr Lyon Playfair, was moved to write to the Taunton Commission (then considering the state of technical education) urging them to examine the health of 'scientific instruction' (ibid.) as part of their remit so as to help the country keep pace with foreign competition.

Following the report of the Royal Commission on Scientific Instruction in 1884, a Technical Instruction Act was passed by Parliament in 1889 which legislated for:

> instruction in the principles of science and art applicable to industries, and in the application of specific branches of science and art to specific industries or employments. It shall not include the teaching of any trade or industry or employment.
>
> (Musgrave, 1970a, p. 68)

The overt theoretical thrust of the Act reflected – in addition to the dominance of the ideals of liberal education (and distaste for the practical; Coffey, 1992) among leading educators and politicians of the time – both the territorial power of craft guilds to preserve the secrets of their occupations and also the state of the debate about the differences between technical education (principles) and technical instruction (practice). As Musgrave (1970a) notes, 'technical education for the upper levels of the labour force might still be seen in terms of general principles, but at the lower levels to teach the practice was now becoming the custom' (p. 69). This division of technical education into different levels and types was later to be reinforced and embedded in the state schooling system.

In the last decades of the nineteenth century the liberal voluntarist creed gave way to active state intervention in both general popular education and the public provision of technical education. The Elementary Education Act of 1870 which effectively established compulsory state provision had 'primarily an economic purpose' (Coffey, 1992, p. 50). Introducing the Bill in the House of Commons in February 1970, Forster (author of the 1870 Act) argued that upon 'the speedy provision of elementary education depends our industrial prosperity . . . if we leave our work-folk any longer unskilled . . . they will be overmatched in the competition of the world' (Maclure, 1973, pp. 99–100). As Pratt (2000) suggests, the nineteenth-century origins of FE can be located in that 'burst of state involvement and collectivism that, in contrast to some popular opinion, characterized the late Victorian period' (p. 13). Reinforcing this line of argument, Sanderson (1999) argues that the 'British system was so transformed between 1870 and 1914 . . . that it had become an impressive support for industry rather than a liability' (p. 26). He goes on to elaborate this perspective with the assertion that:

> Before 1890 English education was defective, lacking a proper structure of universities, state and local government finance, technical colleges, free and compulsory elementary education or popular secondary education . . . After 1890, however, the situation was transformed with free and compulsory elementary education, the restructuring of the secondary system . . . the elevation of civic university colleges into independent degree granting institutions with state grants from 1889, the spread of the polytechnics, municipal technical colleges and City & Guilds examinations.
>
> (p. 29)

Public examinations and qualifications had been established with the foundation of the Royal Society of Arts in 1856 and the City and Guilds of London Institute in 1879, the latter – in collaboration with the City of London Livery Companies – playing a leading role in establishing the colleges and polytechnics which spread to the regions throughout the 1990s. After the passing of the 1889 Technical Instruction Act, the funding of these new institutions was helped by the so-called 'whiskey money' released through the 1890 Local Taxation Act and used specifically to finance the expansion of public technical education (Musgrave, 1970b). However, in spite of all these positive developments, technical education in England at the end of the nineteenth century remained, according to Green and Lucas (1999b):

> intellectually narrow and institutionally marooned between school and work, it never acquired a status comparable with that achieved in certain other continental states. Its form became characterised by an historical absence – the lack of any legitimised notion of general culture and general education with which to frame technical skills. FE colleges would find it hard to break out of this mould and to rectify this absence.
>
> (pp. 14–15)

1900 to 1944

Pratt (2000) describes the period from the passing of the 1902 Education Act (giving county boroughs the responsibility for organising technical education) to the 1944 Education Act as 'one of considerable growth' when 'students in technical and commercial education more than doubled, from under 600,000 in 1910–11 to over 1.2 million by 1937–8' (p. 18). A key factor in this expansion was the establishment of public qualifications in the form of the National Certificates – later to become the mainstay of VET in FE colleges – awarded at ordinary (roughly equivalent to A-level) and higher (comparable to a pass degree) levels. The certificates were organised on a partnership model with colleges, industry and the professions all involved in the design of curricula and assessment (Venables, 1955).

The Fisher Education Act of 1918 made provision for a system of part-time education for all young people up to the age of 18 who were not in full-time education but – mainly because of the hostility of parents and employers to the day-release elements of the system combined with the economic downturn in the 1920s – the original plans were never fully implemented. Junior technical schools providing post-elementary VET did expand to cater for around 30,000 students by 1937, though they never achieved parity of status with academic secondary schooling (no more than the secondary technical schools founded after the 1944 Butler Education Act; McCullough, 1989).

It was during the immediate post-war years that, as Neary (1999, p. 91) expressed it, the 'modern condition of "youth" was invented . . .

as part of the Employment and Training Act (ETA)' passed in 1948. The ETA 1948 was a 'significant moment in the history of vocational education and training in Britain, representing the first co-ordinated response by the state to the disequilibrium' (ibid., p. 92) caused by the economic, social and cultural upheaval of the Second World War. It was a bold attempt at social and economic reconstruction – involving state-funded youth training, national manpower planning and systematic careers and guidance services (TUC, 1947) – and represented perhaps the first official government interest in easing the transition from school to work for young people. The fact that these ambitious goals were frustrated by social and economic developments is both typical of the so-called British malaise in the VET sphere and also a harbinger of subsequent ill-fated state initiatives in the 1970s and 1980s.

1940s to the mid-1970s

There was a large increase in training programmes throughout the war years – particularly linked to engineering, war production and the armed services – and day-release for young workers continued to expand (Evans, 1975). As mentioned earlier, the 1944 Education Act for the first time made it a legal duty for LEAs to provide FE. The so-called 'day continuation schools' planned after the Fisher Act were resurrected in the 1944 Act as County Colleges which school leavers would attend part-time up to the age of 18. However, for reasons similar to the historical failure of so many schemes in this sphere, 'county colleges joined day continuation schools among the might-have beens' (Maclure, 1991, pp. 7–8) of educational policy-making. This legacy of failure continues to influence the swings and cycles of policy in the PCET sphere as one initiative after another seeks to make up for the inadequacies of voluntarism in vocational education and training (VET) and – of special significance for the FE sector – the absence of a strong work-based learning route in Britain (Richardson and Gumbley, 1995).

By the end of the Second World War there were over 700 LEA maintained technical colleges (Smithers and Robinson, 1993, p. 28), a remarkable achievement in view of the education budget cuts in the inter-war years which – along with factors already mentioned – prevented the development of post-school part-time provision for young people. The Percy Report (Ministry of Education, 1945) – mainly as a response to the low national output of civil, electrical and mechanical engineers – recommended the selection of a number of technical colleges in which new degree-level technology courses could be developed (ten 'Colleges of Advanced Technology' had been established by 1956; Pratt, 2000, p. 21). This was the beginning of so-called 'advanced further education' which was to lead to the establishment of the polytechnics in the 1960s and 1970s (and also the creation of a binary divide between universities and polytechnics which the 1992 Further and Higher Education Act was meant to end).

The wartime debate about the future of FE and technical education which informed the policy-making leading to the 1944 Act provides some fascinating insights into public opinion and perceptions about the sector, in addition to highlighting the remarkably perennial nature of certain key themes, arguments and problems. In an article in the *Times Educational Supplement* (TES) in July 1943, Kenneth Lindsay MP made strong recommendations that there 'should be one ministry concerned with the directive control of the coming population. Basic education, vocational training and social selection are all aspects of one process' (in Dawn, 1995, p. 4). In a similar vein, the TES leader for the same issue speculated that:

> the expansion and improvement of facilities for vocational training and their marriage with those for cultural enrichment should do much to direct a strong flow of superior recruits into the industrial, commercial and artistic occupations upon which Britain's well being must always depend and thus enhance Britain's proud reputation for craftsmanship.
>
> (p. 6)

Although the merger of the Departments of Education and Employment with the creation of the DfEE in 1995 did go some way in responding to Kenneth Lindsay's plea, the curricular unification and rationalisation called for in the TES leader is still a problem awaiting a solution. Moreover, the dismantling of the DfEE in June 2001 – involving the creation of the Department for Education and Skills and the Department for Work, Family and Pensions (Educa, 2001a, p. 5) – seems to run counter to other general trends in the PCET sector which call for co-ordinated learning strategies linking schools, FE, HE, employers and community agencies (LSC, 2001a).

There is some justification in Maclure's critical comment that it 'is a matter of history how one half-hearted attempt after another to do something about industrial training and vocational education came to nothing during the 1950s and 1960s' (1991, p. 8), but this needs to be balanced against the substantial increase in numbers in the 700 LEA-controlled colleges in England and Wales. The White Paper on Technical Education published in 1956 built on the Percy Report and recommended the expansion of day-release students and proposed a new Diploma in Technology designed to enhance high-level technical and vocational education. The links between the work of the FE colleges and the generation of economic growth – raised in the 1945 Percy Report and the 1956 White Paper – was later reinforced in the 1959 Crowther Report on secondary education and the 1961 White Paper *Better Opportunities in Technical Education* (and, of course, it is a theme which has dominated the policy discourse on FE to this day).

Although there was an increase in student numbers in employment-oriented spheres in the 1960s – when FE colleges reached 'a high point of work-relatedness' (Green and Lucas, 1999a, p. 18) mainly through day-release and apprenticeships for technicians and craftspeople – there were many weaknesses in general VET provision. Most of these programmes were limited to a few employment areas, tended to exclude girls and women, and were often used by employers as a relatively cheap way of training their workers. In the attempt to remedy these problems, state intervention in VET came with the 1964 Industrial Training Act which established a regional network of Industrial Training Boards (ITBs) which, by 1966, covered 7.5 million workers. Training was financed through a grant/levy system imposed on firms which – though a constant cause of complaint by employers – did successfully expand employee training and FE day-release opportunities for workers throughout the 1960s and early 1970s (Evans, 1992).

In spite of a level of success, the 1964 Act never amounted to a national policy for VET and, over the years, was increasingly criticised on all sides of education and industry. Farley (1983, p. 53) summarised the main problem areas in terms of the system's lack of progress in avoiding shortages of skilled labour, criticisms from employers about the ITB financial sanctions, inadequate co-ordination of skills training in different occupations, and a failure to provide for the needs of young people in semi-skilled and unskilled jobs. The 1973 Employment and Training Act set out to solve these problems by setting up the Manpower Services Commission (MSC) which was designed to reform VET and bring together all the leading players and mechanisms within the PCET system and the labour market.

As the power of the MSC quango increased throughout the 1970s and 1980s, the work of the FE colleges – as 'academic drift' (Pratt, 2000, p. 21) caused certain institutions to concentrate on higher level work in the aspiration to polytechnic status – was for a time dominated by fairly low-level VET linked to the massive rise in youth unemployment following the 1973 oil crisis, economic recession and major de-industrialisation in the manufacturing sector.

1970s and 1980s

In summing up the state of the sector in the early 1970s, Green and Lucas (1999b) argue that:

> Despite the advances of the post-war years what had emerged was a highly uneven provision that varied substantially from one locality to another. Legislation had been permissive, allowing LEAs wide scope for interpretation. Vocational education and training remained low in status and apprenticeships were dominated by the engineering and construction industries which, by the 1970s, were in decline along with other traditional industries, such as shipbuilding and heavy engineering.
>
> (p. 20)

A number of factors influenced the evolution throughout the 1970s and 1980s of FE colleges from being predominantly VET or technical institutions to their present status as broadly based providers of general education and training. First, there was the growth of 'second chance' routes with post-16 learners wishing to pursue mainstream academic courses such as GCE 'O' (later GCSE) and A-levels, in many cases providing for school leavers who had failed to gain certification or for adults returning to study after a period of employment. Added to this was the factor which dominated PCET policy and practice in this period: the massive rise of structural youth unemployment. Various schemes for unemployed youngsters – Youth Training Schemes (YTS), Training Opportunities Schemes (TOPs) and later Employment Training – were established to remedy a chronic problem which left 2–3 million people unemployed throughout the 1980s. Most of this activity – typically low-level skills training – was organised and administered by the MSC but delivered through private agencies and post-school institutions and, by 1985, the MSC had taken control of 25 per cent of non-advanced work in FE colleges (Hyland, 1994).

This centralised control of the educational agenda was itself influenced by the 'new vocationalism' (Avis et al, 1996) which – through initiatives such as the Technical and Vocational Educational Initiative (TVEI) introduced into schools in the 1980s and early 1990s – sought to reconstruct the primary aims and purposes of education in terms of the preparation of young people for working life. In a similar vein, the establishment of the National Council for Vocational Qualifications (NCVQ) following a review of vocational qualifications in 1986 led to the introduction of National Vocational Qualifications (NVQs) designed to harmonise the system and establish national standards of competence derived from the needs of business and industry.

Much of the responsibility for effecting these radical changes devolved to the FE colleges which – during this same period – were being encouraged, as a result of government policy, to become responsive institutions, less producer-led and more sensitive to the needs of employers and other community bodies. This trend was reinforced by the 1988 Education Reform Act (ERA) which – in addition to confirming that FE was completely separate from the HE sector – instituted the process of the local management of colleges (as well as schools) by delegating greater powers to governing bodies. As Pratt (2000) observes, under ERA, local authorities:

> had to produce schemes of financial delegation and governing bodies had new powers and duties to manage their colleges to be more market-oriented, entrepreneurial and efficient. The local authority no longer had a majority on governing bodies.
>
> (pp. 23–4)

All of this paved the way for the full independence of FE institutions when they were granted corporate status through the 1992 Further and Higher Education Act.

1990s – incorporation and beyond

Under the 1992 Act the FE colleges became corporate institutions completely independent of local authority control with governing bodies dominated by representatives from business and industry. In addition to the political agenda which had led to this state of affairs the mission of the colleges was influenced by trends – emerging from the 'new vocationalism' of the 1980s that blamed education for not meeting the needs of industry – which 'placed FE at the centre of a national strategy for raising levels of skills and qualifications' (Green and Lucas, 1999b, p. 36), and also for raising participation and improving retention rates at all levels.

The mechanism for controlling and directing this national strategy was the funding regime introduced by the Further Education Funding Council

(FEFC) which – under the 1992 Act – was charged with administering the funding for all institutions in the sector. A degree of consistency of funding had been established under the local management arrangements of the 1988 ERA and this was intended to be reinforced through the FEFC regulations. As McClure (2000) argues, 'retention and achievement were at the top of the agenda' and this was realised through a system by which colleges were paid for three distinct stages of learning programmes: 'entry, on-programme and achievement' (p. 41). The vast majority of FE funding (90 per cent) under this regime was 'core' with the other 10 per cent dependent upon individual colleges' recruitment and growth figures and – when the funding is linked to the new FEFC audit and inspection systems – it is not difficult to locate the new regime against the background of the 1980s/90s *leitmotif* of 'value for money' in public sector spending.

Moreover, the primary objective appeared to have been achieved since – between 1993 and 1997 – student numbers increased by over a third as funding per student decreased in real terms by 21 per cent (Smithers and Robinson, 2000, p. 9). Although initially the national system of funding was welcomed as an improvement on the piecemeal and inequitable LEA model, subsequent experience has brought about less positive appraisals of incorporation changes. Financial deficits, mismanagement and outright corruption have resulted in public humiliation and disrepute for a number of colleges such as Bilston, Wirral, Derby and Halton (Smithers and Robinson, 2000, p. 7) and a recent estimate was that 40 per cent of institutions in the sector were experiencing financial difficulties (Baty, 2000).

Lucas (1999, pp. 54–61) has presented a detailed evaluation of the positive and negative aspects of the FEFC's model of incorporation in terms of a number of key themes and issues:

Positive

- general improvement (and expansion) of qualification achievements and service to students – greater attention paid to induction, tracking, learning difficulties and retention
- funding methodology has proved responsive to accommodation of issues such as widening participation and enhanced support for basic skills and learning disability
- award of funding in three distinct stages has improved colleges advice, guidance and counselling procedures and systems
- in spite of well-publicised failures, most colleges have proved to be flexible and responsive to new demands, and the new audit

and inspection systems have improved learning and teaching and enhanced public accountability
• despite the decline in non-vocational adult education caused by Schedule 2 funding anomalies, the overall picture (especially as 16–19 recruitment has levelled off) has been one of expanded adult recruitment based on flexible modes of delivery.

Negative

• notwithstanding its national profile, there is no national funding system for 16–19 year olds, and a confusion of diversified (often inequitable) funding streams for the FE sector in general – the struggle to maximise unit funding by colleges has marginalised the search for a distinctive national or regional role and a planned local curriculum
• the scramble for growth has emphasised quantity as against quality, resulting in larger class sizes, fewer class contact hours, students on the wrong courses and increasing numbers of drop-outs
• the unitised funding, tracking and audit systems have proved bureaucratically cumbersome, labour-intensive and costly
• the funding of learning programmes has been overly rigid and fails to recognise and reward partial achievements by students
• the combination of an output-related funding mechanism and outcome-based programmes has served to distort objective judgements of quality (FEDA, 1998), occasionally – in the case of NVQs – resulting in outright corruption and assessment abuse (Hyland, 1998)
• quality of teaching and staff-management relations have been damaged by the drive for efficiency savings, and staff development activity has declined
• franchising of courses to maximise funding units has sometimes resulted in low quality programmes of little value to either learners or employers (e.g. NVQ level 1 in 'shelf stacking'; Smithers and Robinson, 2000, p. 6)
• funding between sixth-forms, FE colleges and HE (provided by FE) has not been harmonised and most FE college provision is underfunded compared with similar provision in sixth-form colleges and HE institutions.

Post-1997 policies and developments

The appraisal of the FE sector's performance in the post-incorporation years – inevitably in view of the incredible diversity of post-school institutions – represents a mixture of positive and negative evaluations. Moreover, the experiences of institutions – even those with relatively similar provisions and funding arrangements – have proved to be different as, for example, between the London inner city and the Home Counties colleges researched by Ainley and Bailey (1997) and between the urban and rural colleges investigated by Leney et al. (1998). Our own work in the sector revealed similar disparities, for instance, between the mission statements of a primarily rural college – emphasising community, access and lifelong learning – and that of a predominantly urban college which was concerned mainly with skills for employment (Merrill, 2000, p. 9).

The challenges for the sector in the light of current research and policy analysis – particularly the spate of developments since New Labour came to power in 1997 – are examined in depth in subsequent chapters. As a way of concluding this chapter it might be worth taking note of what commentators regarded as the main problems and key issues for attention prior to the recent policy developments and re-organisation of PCET through the creation of the new learning and skills sector (LSS). It should then be possible to determine how the new LSC arrangements address these priorities, in addition to locating the role of FE within the general lifelong learning agenda (examined in Chapter 2) and in relation to community-wide interests and issues (Chapters 4 and 8).

Although, as Smithers and Robinson (2000) noted, it is 'difficult to separate out the effects of incorporation from the financial constraints under which the colleges have been operating' it is still abundantly clear that there 'has not been enough money to go round' (p. 193). However, Green and Lucas (1999b) urge caution in interpreting the general consensus about the 'crisis' in FE stemming from incorporation, and recommend marking distinctions between the 'methodological, political and organisational dimensions of incorporation' (p. 28). The Hodge Report (Education and Employment Committee, 1998) issued a clear statement that FE would need substantial reform and further support if it were to achieve the key objectives outlined in *The Learning Age*.

Against this background, the three challenges mentioned in the Introduction – funding issues, strategic regional and national identity and organisational infrastructure for the sector – which Hodgson and Spours (1999) saw as crucial to any FE reform programme, have all been tackled in varying degrees in the last few years. Moreover, in addition to the 'crisis of funding and a serious soul-searching about quality', the quasi-market competition in FE driving the obsession with quantity and growth at all costs has 'exacerbated its longer term crisis of positioning and identity' (Green and Lucas, 1999c, p. 227). This confused identity is, of course, largely a result of the historical evolution of FE outlined above, with the developments from a primarily technical and VET role to more diversified provision. In addition to the vast range of vocational programmes on offer – from NVQ/GNVQ level 1 to HNDs and franchised/validated and 2+2 degrees – there are GCSEs, A/AS, Vocational A-levels, access to HE, non-vocational adult programmes, plus the new VET sphere incorporating New Deal Welfare to Work courses, modern and graduate apprenticeships, national traineeships and foundation degrees (these recent course developments are examined in subsequent chapters). Moreover, although FE institutions are still the major providers of 16–19 education and training, they are now 'predominantly adult institutions with over 76% of FEFC-funded students over the age of 24, the overwhelming majority being part-time' (Green and Lucas, 1999c, p. 227) as well as delivering around 13 per cent of all HE courses.

Given this vast diversity, complexity and plurality, it is clearly a mammoth task to address the priorities and challenges for the sector mentioned above and – as explained in the next chapter – this is, perhaps, why the all-encompassing and flexible nature of the lifelong learning label appealed so much to the civil servants, educators and politicians faced with such a daunting challenge. On top of all this there are problems concerned with curriculum reform (and the vocational-academic divide), work-based learning, widening participation, the national skills agenda, staff development and staff-management relationships, college governance issues, and links between colleges, schools, HEIs, employers and the community in general.

It would be difficult to deny that the sector has come a long way in distancing itself from the former lower class image of the 'poor relation of the education system' stemming from 'its roots in the provision of technical and craft education for working-class men' (Leathwood, 1998, p. 256). However, the move to a broader, more diversified and pluralist base has been accompanied, Leathwood suggests, by a number of 'irrationalities' (ibid., p. 265) which include the following assumptions:

• that high-quality education can continue to be provided irrespective of the level of funding

- that learning will thrive in an environment devoid of emotions such as excitement, enthusiasm and passion
- that learning is all about being 'independent' and 'autonomous', with the interactive, social and emotional being insignificant
- that new technologies will solve all the problems
- that 'the market' is the only way to provide education
- that staff are lazy, inefficient and rebellious and so require constant surveillance and 'tough','hard' managers
- that by repeating the word 'diversity' often enough, we are demonstrating our commitment to equal opportunities.

The extent to which such 'irrationalities' have been addressed by FE institutions in the new LSS will turn on how successful they are in achieving the goals set for them by the present administration. The lifelong learning 'vision' for FE colleges was translated into four overriding objectives in the key policy document *Colleges for Excellence and Innovation* (DfEE, 2000a, pp. 4–5):

- to provide high and improving standards of education for 16–19 year olds, ensuring increased participation and achievement on broad and balanced programmes of study
- to play the leading role in providing the skills the economy needs at craft, technician and equivalent levels through initial technical and vocational education for young people and skills upgrading or re-training for adults
- to widen participation in learning, enabling adults to acquire the basic skills they need for employability, effective citizenship and enjoyment of learning
- to provide a ladder of opportunity to higher education, with a key focus on foundation degrees, built on partnerships and networks with higher education institutions, and with *Learndirect* to share and make widely available learning resources.

The impact of this FE mission on learning, teaching, curriculum, staff, students and the wider community that colleges serve will be examined in subsequent chapters. As a preliminary to all this, the next chapter looks at the development of lifelong learning policy and practice and the role of FE within the emerging structure of activity, reform and innovation in the emerging LSS.

Chapter 2

Lifelong learning and further education

The FE sector can be said to represent the heart and soul of New Labour's general lifelong learning policy for the PCET sector. As the former Secretary of State at the DfEE explained:

> Colleges are at the heart of our ability to respond to the rapid transformation in the world around us because it is skilled people, and their creativity, enterprise and ability to innovate, who drive economic and social change today
>
> (DfEE, 2000a, para. 2)

Later in the same document is the statement that:

> Colleges are vital in tackling inequalities within their local communities. They are proving their success in attracting women students and those from ethnic minority backgrounds . . . Equality of opportunity must be central to everything colleges do.
>
> (para. 66)

Not only do these policy statements sum up the central role of FE in government policy, but they also neatly encapsulate the twin pillars of lifelong learning: economic competitiveness and social inclusion. Lifelong learning conceptions, policy and practice – and related perspectives surrounding the 'learning society' – are, however, complex, wide-ranging and, as Young (1998, p. 193) suggests, deeply 'contested'. All these key concepts need to be unpacked, analysed and clarified before the role of FE in the new order can be determined.

The concept of lifelong learning, which figures prominently in all the government prescriptions (Fryer, 1997; Kennedy, 1997; DfEE, 1999b), has a long history. Although earlier conceptions tended to be couched in terms of lifelong *education* rather than *learning* (a shift of emphasis which, as observed below, is significant) – usually in terms of 'recurrent education' (Houghton and Richardson, 1974), *education permanente* (Schuller and McGarry, 1979) or the 'learning society' (Husen, 1974) – there was, as long ago as 1969, a symposium on 'lifelong learning' in Britain organised under the aegis of the Education Division of the Commonwealth and International Library (Jessup, 1969). According to Legge (1982), the central perspective is of an education that is:

> planned as something which will be experienced by people in an individually ongoing, though discontinuous way, over the whole of their lives – and which will correspond with their emerging vocational social and cultural aspirations.
>
> (p. 7)

Appropriated from this older tradition (Edwards, 1997) to prescribe a notion of learning from the cradle to the grave – or, as Henry Morris once put it, with the aim of 'raising the school leaving age to 90' (Kellner, 1998, p. 15) – the lifelong learning slogan is once again being used as a popular means of challenging the mainstream school-centred, so-called 'front leading' model of educational provision. However, apart from this opposition to the mainstream schooling model, contemporary incarnations of lifelong learning are rather different from those associated with the older adult education tradition of 'recurrent education' and *education permanante* (Lawson, 1998).

Contemporary versions of lifelong learning – though retaining the learning throughout life connotations – tend to view the nature and purpose of learning primarily in terms of skills updating and the 'training and development needs' (Stephens, 1990, p. 51) of employees. In a recent issue of the *International Journal of Lifelong Education* (IJLE), the editors – although welcoming the fact that 'lifelong education' was now at the forefront of educational policy – went on to regret that the concept was 'increasingly being equated with continuing education and related rather specifically to vocational updating for which academic qualifications are awarded' (IJLE, 1998, p. 69). Tight (1998) suggests that the concept has become part of a trinity – lifelong learning, the learning organisation, and the learning society – aimed at 'articulating the importance of continuing learning for survival and development at the levels of the individual, the organisation and society as a whole' (p. 254).

The idea of a trinity does provide some interesting insights though it does raise problematic issues, such as – whereas the notion of the learning organisation applied to industry and business does have a legitimately vocationalist/economistic thrust – why the other two items concerned with individuals and society come to be interepreted in this rather circumscribed way.

Lifelong learning – increasingly linked in recent government policy documents with skills training and development for economic success in the global market – does not, as Strain (1998) points out, naturally carry such instrumental and technicist connotations, and it is worth marking the re-programming of these new educational shibboleths. What also needs to be noted is the subtle shift of emphasis from lifelong *education* to lifelong *learning*. As Field (2000a) observes, education suggests a formal system of provision provided for and funded by the state, whereas learning implies something much more informal and less dependent upon government organisation and finance. Thus, the key learning age vision of building a new culture of learning and aspiration can be seen, Field argues, as essentially, a 'soft objective' (p. 223) which places most of the responsibility for its achievement on individuals, communities and partnerships of various stakeholders. Moreover, the primary economic thrust of current policy is also in line with the 'new governance' strategy which 'places the responsibility on citizens to plan and develop their capacity for earning a living' (ibid., p. 222).

The policy slogan which immediately preceded lifelong learning – the 'learning society' that dominated educational discourse, research and policy-making for many years throughout the 1990s (Coffield, 1999, 2000a) – serves to illustrate how the process of 'vocationalisation' (Avis *et al.*, 1996) has transformed the whole ethos of PCET provision in which FE colleges play a central role.

Conceptions of the learning society

Barnett (1998, pp. 14–15) examines four different interpretations of the learning society in his critical analysis of the 1997 Dearing Report on higher education:

    (i)   the continuing replenishment of human capital so as to maintain and strengthen society's economic capital;

    (ii) the maintenance of cultural capital and the quality of life of individuals and the collective;

    (iii) the inculcation of democratic citizenship;

    (iv) an emancipatory conception aimed at fostering self-reflexive learners who can respond to change in a rational and creative manner.

Barnett concludes that the:

> Dearing conception of the learning society is the *economic* conception . . . but with a human face. Individual learning and development are to be welcomed but principally for their contribution to the growth of economic capital.
>
> (p. 15; original italics)

Dearing's preference for an economistic model – on the grounds that 'in the future, competitive advantage for advanced societies will lie in the quality, effectiveness and relevance of their provision for education and training' (Dearing, 1997, para. 34) – though some way short of the most extreme utilitarian conceptions of the learning society, reflects perfectly the culture shift in educational aims and values that has occurred in Britain over the last few decades. Indeed, as Field (2000b) has noted, there is now a 'global policy consensus' on the need to embed lifelong learning in modern industrial states, and this new emphasis can be seen as the 'natural outcome of the dramatic economic and technological changes that have overwhelmed the world system since the 1960s' (pp. 2–3).

In earlier times, the economic function of education was merely one – and not necessarily the principal one – of many formal requirements and aims of state systems. The Robbins Report (1963) on higher education, for example – though alluding to vocational preparation –was concerned chiefly with the intellectual, cultural and social purposes of education. Similar values informed the Russell Report (DES, 1973) and adult education and – going even further back – were paramount in the post-First World War report of the Adult Education Committee of the Ministry of Reconstruction (1919) which saw adult education as a 'permanent national necessity, an inseparable aspect of citizenship, [which] therefore should be universal and lifelong' (p. 5).

All this is a long way from current conceptions of the aims and purposes of lifelong learning which are neatly summarised in the then Secretary of State's comments on the 1998 Green Paper *The Learning Age*. David Blunkett observed that:

> the ability to manage and use information is becoming the key to the competitive strength of advanced economies. With increasing globalisation, the best way of getting and keeping a job will be to have the skills needed by employers . . . For individuals who want security in employment and a nation that must compete worldwide, learning is the key.
>
> (Blunkett, 1998, p. 18)

However, as mentioned earlier, economic competitiveness is twinned with social inclusion in almost all official policy statements and – when subjected to deeper scrutiny – finer nuances of contemporary conceptions of lifelong learning can be discerned.

Recent policy analyses in the field have ranged from accounts that label the learning society as a 'myth' which has 'no real prospect of coming into existence in the foreseeable future' (Hughes and Tight, 1998, p. 188), to 'idealist educational discourse' which is 'utopian' and 'unhistorical' (Rikowski, 1998, pp. 223, 226) or, alternatively, as a project which 'redefines educational needs and refurbishes the institutional forms by which these are provided within the polity' (Strain and Field, 1998, p. 239). The complex and contested nature of lifelong learning is clear and, in order to get closer to core elements, it is worth examining in more detail three leading 'contestants' – elaborated typologies that supplement the accounts already sketched – which present deep analyses of the principal perspectives in the field.

Edwards' Typology (1997, pp. 176–84)

(a) An educated society, drawn from the adult, liberal democratic, education tradition, this conception 'supports lifelong learning within the social policy frameworks of post-Second World War social democracies'.

(b) A 'learning market enabling institutions to provide services for supporting the competitiveness of the economy'. The primary objective is to 'meet the demands of individuals and employers for the updating of skills and competences'.

(c) A learning society is one in which 'learners adopt a learning approach to life, drawing on a wide range of resources'. Both the liberal democratic conception and the learning market are 'displaced by a conception of participation in learning as an activity in and through which individuals and groups pursue their heterogeneous goals'.

Young's Typology (1998, pp. 194–99)

(a) The schooling model emphasises 'high participation in post-compulsory schooling as a way of ensuring that the maximum proportion of the population reach as far beyond a minimum level of education as possible'.

(b) The credentialist model gives 'high priority to ensuring that the vast majority of the population have qualifications or certificated skills and knowledge and that the qualifications people achieve are related to their future employment'.

(c) The access approach represents a 'vision of a learning society of the future in which learning, after the phase of compulsory schooling, is increasingly freed from its ties with specialized educational institutions such as schools, colleges and universities'. This model stresses learner choice and autonomy, credit transfer and access to a wide range of information and communication technology (ICT) resources.

(d) Young's preferred perspective is what he calls the 'educative' model which 'starts with a recognition that all social life involves learning, whether conscious or planned or not'. Within this framework the 'learner questions and begins to transform the context of community of practice in which the learning takes place'. The ultimate end is the fostering of 'expansive learning' which can 'enable schools, colleges or training programmes to help students, teachers and people in the community to design and implement their own futures, as their prevailing practices show symptoms of crisis'.

Ranson's Typology (1998, pp. 2–10)

(a) A society which 'learns about itself and how it is changing' in order to cope with structural social, political and economic change and temper the 'dynamic conservatism' of modern societies in a way which allows for transformation 'without intolerable disruption'.

(b) A society which 'needs to change the way it learns' so as to support schooling/VET reforms which can accommodate 'massive expansion in participation' and keep pace with 'technological, communication and epistemological change'.

(c) A society in which 'all its members are learning' is one which 'recognizes that learning cannot be separated from society and is not just for the young but for all, throughout their lives'. The upshot is that 'diversity, accessibility, transferability, partnership and accountability become the defining characteristics of a comprehensive system of continuing education'.

(d) The final stage is a society which 'learns to democratically change the conditions of learning' and is informed by the notion that the task of 'reforming education from an elite (selective) to a socially just (comprehensive) system can never be a purely educational or pedagogical problem, but has to be conceived as a social and political one'. Such radical reform requires 'open public discourse'

CORNWALL COLLEGE
LEARNING CENTRE

since the 'process of reasoning in public discourse helps to uncover common ends and thus to transform different groups into sharing a sense of the community, to become a public'.

Ranson's typology represents a stage-development model of how a learning society might be fostered, developed and organised; until the conditions of one stage are met, it is not feasible to try to construct the elements of the subsequent stage. In fact all three perspectives – to a greater or lesser degree – can be characterised in stage-developmental terms, and the key themes, features and directions may be illustrated in terms of the continuum shown in Figure 2.1.

This could be described as an 'ideal' model – distilled from emerging policy trends and developments – though it is not completely fanciful or utopian since all the incorporated elements are either present in the theoretical discourse of lifelong learning or they have actually been implemented in some form in the PCET sector. The general direction of policy and programme development is from narrow skills training for individuals (perhaps through NVQs) towards a broader vocationalism (through GNVQs/Vocational A-levels), to wider, social, cultural and moral objectives linked to a socially just community (examined in greater depth in the final chapter). Against the background of this model, it is now possible to attempt a characterisation of recent policy-making and implementation in the PCET sector in general and in relation to FE institutions in particular

Schuller and Field (1998) have demonstrated the importance in educational policy-making of 'social capital' which is located in the 'kinds of context and culture which promote communication and mutual learning as part of the fabric of everyday life' (p. 234). Social capital is, indeed, of the first importance in achieving the key aim of fostering a learning culture and – as mentioned already – it is a major ingredient

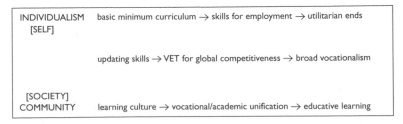

INDIVIDUALISM   basic minimum curriculum → skills for employment → utilitarian ends
[SELF]

updating skills → VET for global competitiveness → broad vocationalism

[SOCIETY]
COMMUNITY   learning culture → vocational/academic unification → educative learning

Figure 2.1 A developmental continuum for the learning society

in New Labour's general lifelong learning policy for the PCET sector. However, it is also clear that economic capital – admittedly always located within the social agenda – has pride of place. The economistic interpretation of lifelong learning is dominant throughout the various *Learning Age* policy documents. In the introduction to the *University for Industry: Pathfinder Prospectus* (DfEE, 1998c), for example, we are told that 'learning is the key to individual employability and business competitiveness' (p. 1), a notion which is reinforced in the principal *Learning Age* document which emphasises 'learning as the key to prosperity, for each of us as individuals, as well and for the nation as a whole' (DfEE, 1998a, p. 7). The document then moves on to rehearse the familiar arguments about investment in human capital linked with the 'knowledge-based global economy of the twenty-first century', and the need for a 'well-equipped and adaptable labour force' before urging us all to 'develop and sustain a regard for learning at whatever age' (ibid.). This policy remains substantially the same – with a special emphasis on the leading role of the FE sector – under the new regime of the recently established Learning and Skills Council and officially endorsed by the Department for Education and Skills (LSC, 2001b).

Thus far, at the level of avowed policy, this fairly basic account could be classified – using the models outlined earlier – in terms of Edwards' 1(b), learning for economic competitveness, Young's 2(b), a credentialist strategy concerned mainly with employability qualifications or Ranson's 3(b) which recommends learning as a way of keeping pace with technological change. At this level there seems to be little evidence of any broader concern with learning implied in the educated society based on learning networks (favoured by Edwards), nor is there much reference to the access model of extending educational opportunities for all kinds of learning (not just employment-related ones) which Young's account advocates. Ranson's radical vision of a learning democracy, which recognises that a learning society needs to re-think the fundamental social, political and moral conditions which contextualise all forms of learning, is also difficult to discern within the broad and primary thrust of the official policy vision.

On further inspection, however, and particularly in looking at the practical implementation and *wider implications* of the main policies, other features of the learning typologies linked to social and cultural objectives gain prominence. A large part of New Labour policy on education has had to be forged by active engagement with (and reaction to) the policies of the former Conservative administration. Hodgson and Spours (1999) have examined these issues in some depth and offer some interesting comparative perspectives. They suggest that the difference between New Labour policy and that of the previous Conservative government:

> is largely one of tone and emphasis; it relies on stressing certain aspects of policy and downplaying others. For example, New Labour policy documents on education, training and lifelong learning stress equity and social cohesion rather than 'personal competitiveness'
> ... They emphasise the role that education and training play in citizenship formation as well as their role in skills formation and economic competitiveness. The documents also minimize the role of the market in stimulating demand for learning and highlight the importance of strategic regional and local planning and co-operation.
>
> (p. 26)

This analysis appears to be on the right lines though – simply in terms of the policy features referred to – the differences surely go beyond matters of 'tone and emphasis'. One key difference between the former Conservative and current New Labour perspectives, for example, concerns the ultimate purposes of the learning society. For the Conservatives, learning for economic competitiveness seems to be an *end in itself* (DTI, 1995) – justified purely in terms of a self-sustaining and successful market – whereas New Labour policy (though informed by broadly similar economic priorities) almost always connects economic objectives with the *further end* of promoting social justice and cohesion. Many of these issues have been located within the wider discourse about the role of so-called 'third way' values and politics in recent policy-making.

Third way values and PCET policy

The election of the Labour government in 1997 (reinforced by its re-election in June 2001) has not only brought about a new political administration but also, as Fairclough (2000) has observed, a whole new:

> vision of the world, partly actual, partly potential. It includes representations of the economy, of work, of crime, of the family, and so forth. It also includes representations of politics and government as ways of changing the world – specifically of what is claimed to be the 'new politics', the politics of the 'Third Way'.
>
> (p. 21)

The attempt to steer a course between 'a neo-liberal model and a social capitalist model' of politics is forming itself as the 'intellectual bedrock' (Hodgson and Spours, 1999, p. 8) of the New Labour project. Halpin (1999) has argued that the new 'third way' politics offers real opportunities for transcending the old discredited polarities and generating genuine political alternatives.

Giddens (1998) is one of the chief architects and proponents of the third way and begins his exegesis of the concept by explaining that 'it is of no particular significance in and of itself' and 'has been used many times before in the past history of social democracy' (p. vii). Kellner (1998) accepts the social-democratic origins and claims that the basic strategy can best be captured by the idea of 'mutualism' which 'offers a way out of the sterile argument between state ownership and private enterprise' (p. 15). In a similar vein, Leadbetter (1998) argues that the 'central ethic of the Third Way is simple and traditional: co-operative self-improvement'. He goes on to elaborate the approach in terms of a politics which:

> encourages people to recognise their shared needs and the potential for shared solutions. It promotes co-operation and collaboration, as well as ambition and striving. This is not wishy-washy political correctness. The most knowledge-intensive sectors of the economy, software and bio-technology, thrive on a mix of competition and collaboration.
>
> (p. 15)

For Giddens (1998), the 'overall aim of third way politics should be to help citizens pilot their way through the major revolutions of our time: globalization, transformations in personal life and our relationship to nature'; third way politics 'looks for a new relationship between the individual and the community, a redefinition of rights and responsibilities' (pp. 64–5). This is followed by helpful lists (the listing of positive and favourable concepts and values – such as 'justice, fairness the equal worth and dignity of all', often without further clarification or elaboration – is, as Fairclough (2000, pp. 46, 53) notes, a key characteristic of New Labour discourse) of leading third way values and principles. Values include 'equality, freedom as autonomy, no rights without responsibilities and no authority without democracy', all supporting a 'third way programme' which incorporates the 'radical centre, an active civil society, the democratic family, the new mixed economy, positive welfare and the cosmopolitan nation' (Giddens, 1998, pp. 66, 70). The ultimate aim of the programme is the 'social investment state' which 'defines equality as inclusion and inequality as exclusion' (ibid., p. 102).

More recently, in response to a host of criticisms of his original thesis – chiefly that the third way is an 'amorphous political project, difficult to pin down and lacking in direction', that it 'fails to sustain the proper outlook of the left and . . . lapses into a form of conservatism', that it 'accepts the basic framework of neoliberalism, especially as concerns the global marketplace', and that it 'has no distinctive economic policy, other than allowing the market to rule the roost' (Giddens, 2000, pp. 22–5) – Giddens re-iterates the 'fundamentals of third way politics' (ibid., pp. 50–4). The key defining features are expressed in terms of:

   (i)   an acceptance of the 'logic of 1989 and after' that the old left–right divisions are no longer feasible or useful;

  (ii)   a belief that the 'three key areas of power – government, the economy and the communities of civil society – all need to be constrained in the interests of social solidarity and social justice';

 (iii)   the construction of a new social contract based on the theorem 'no rights without responsibilities';

 (iv)   the development of a 'wide-ranging supply side policy which seeks to reconcile economic growth mechanisms with structural reform of the welfare state';

  (v)   the creation of a 'diversified society based upon egalitarian principles';

 (vi)   taking globalization seriously by seeking to 'transform existing global institutions and supporting the creation of new ones'.

The last point made by Giddens concerning globalisation requires special emphasis and attention since it is a central theme in New Labour's general lifelong learning policy. A distinctive feature of third way discourse is that – whether the subject is education, health, crime or welfare – the agenda is always determined by economic considerations generally and the global market in particular. Thus, although political points may ostensibly be about health, welfare, crime, the family or community, the debate sooner or later returns to the impact of the global economy on all aspects of life in Britain. Education policy statements provide excellent examples of the ordering of priorities in this respect.

The original *Learning Age* blueprint, for example, refers to 'investment in human capital' as the foundation of 'success in the knowledge-based global economy' (DfEE, 1998a, p. 7) and this so-called 'new' economy figures prominently in the former DfEE's responses to the work of the National Skills Task Force. In the 'new economy it is education and skills which shape the opportunities and rewards available to individuals' (DfEE, 2000b, para.1); and in the Secretary of State's final statement on the work of the National Skills Task Force (DfEE, 2001a) we are told that:

> The combined resources of Government, business and individuals are poised to achieve the goal of a highly-skilled, inclusive economy. This is essential if we are to grasp the opportunities of a new learning age.
>
> (para. 56)

The use of the term inclusive *economy* rather than inclusive *society* is worth noting here; and when we are told that 'equality of opportunity is not simply a moral objective – it is an economic imperative' (DfEE, 2000b, para. 2), there can be little doubt that references to moral or social values are clearly subordinate to economic priorities.

In the vision of society outlined here people seem to relate to each other – not primarily as neighbours, citizens or community members – but as (potential) owners/recipients of employability skills striving for survival in the harsh climate of the global market. Fairclough (2000, p. 155) talks about the 'reality-rhetoric dichotomy' in New Labour language, and it is at this excessively utilitarian level of economic imperatives that the gap is at its widest. There are two main areas of weakness and ambiguity: the nature and extent of the so-called knowledge economy and the reality of the global market. Avis (1996) has described the fallacies in this sphere in terms of 'post-Fordist mythology'.

The demand for high-level knowledge and skills in modern economies, though real, tends to be grossly exaggerated. The majority of workers in post-industrial or post-Fordist economies require (and will probably continue to require) only basic literacy, numeracy and employment-related skills to function effectively in most jobs. As Sieminski (1993) puts it, it 'will only be sectors of core workers who will need opportunities to acquire new skills'; for the majority of workers, fairly basic competence-based VET will suffice and will have 'more to do with maintaining social control and compliance' from 'those who will occupy an uncertain future being assigned to the periphery of the labour market' (pp. 98–9). In a similar vein, Coffield (2000b) argues that:

> Government rhetoric about developing a competitive edge by building the knowledge driven economy is overplayed . . . Reich

reports that only 7% of American workers can be called 'symbolic analysts' or knowledge workers. The knowledge economy is a myth whose main function is to feed fears of future mass unemployment and so spur millions of learners on to new and still higher levels of attainment.

(p. 241)

As former director of the massive *Learning Society* project, Coffield's views carry weight and, clearly, provide much food for thought. However, we would want to say at this stage that – even though there does seem to be some evidence, simply in terms of the large numbers of people employed in low-grade service industry jobs, to support aspects of this 'mythical' view of the knowledge economy – it does not necessarily follow that higher levels of learning are irrelevant to the promotion of social inclusion and the just community (this point is followed up in Chapter 8).

The other feature of the economic thesis which needs to be challenged is the idea that globalisation is either a necessarily permanent or inevitable feature of modern industrial production or that it is something which nations must react to passively as opposed to responding proactively (this is taken up further below). The importance of social capital and the values associated with a just community are emphasised throughout the book (and elaborated in detail in Chapter 8), and their acceptance sometimes involves challenging the policy discourse or revealing its failure to live up to its own avowed social inclusion agenda. As Green (1997a) observes in discussing globalisation issues, the prime task for educators is to 'construct cultures of citizenship and nationhood in ways appropriate to modern conditions' (p. 186). Similarly, Giddens (2000) argues – in even stronger terms – that 'globalization creates favourable conditions for the renewal of communities' and that 'civil society is fundamental to constraining the power of both markets and government' (pp. 63–4).

Linked to this agenda is the crucial business – already referred to in a number of places – of ensuring that the full lifelong learning continuum (outlined in Figure 2.1) is available to all learners, and that both social and economic capital are given equal weight within the framework of a socially just society. Proponents of lifelong learning have a sort of moral duty to 'police' the uses and constructions of the concept in this respect, with the aim of ensuring that the relentless vocationalising trends in the system do not completely submerge the social, cultural, spiritual and citizenship elements of the process. As long ago as the 1969 symposium on the topic, Jessup (1969) was warning educators not to give 'undue emphasis' to the 'vocational element in lifelong learning' on the grounds that it was 'a mistake to stress too much the economic significance' (p. 20) of the process. If caution was needed then, it certainly is needed now in an age when the 'vocationalisation of everyday life' (Avis *et al.*,1996, p. 165) and the 'McDonaldisation of education and training' (Hyland, 1999, p. 11) seem to be immutable and dominant features of educational provision at all levels.

All these values and sentiments – in addition to informing the practical challenges for proponents of lifelong learning – will contribute to the moral framework within which policy and practice for the PCET sector has to be ultimately located and evaluated.

Lifelong learning and further education

Referring to the fact that the incorporation of FE colleges in 1993 was partly determined by emerging trends over the previous few decades, Green and Lucas (1999b) concluded that 'incorporation is best under-stood by examining the points of continuity between the past and present rather than . . . a clean break with the past'. Yet the examination of the implications of the recent policy trends since 1997 at the end of the previous chapter does seem to point to something more like a new agenda rather than a continuation of past policy, even if the new agenda is driven by a fierce tension between what Cripps (2002) calls the 'market coding and caring coding' (p. 263) which still operates in the sector.

Until recently, however, the consensus – as mentioned earlier, typically arising from debates about globalisation and the third way – seemed to be that New Labour education and training policy was essentially a continuation of the former Conservative strategies. Esland *et al.* (1999), for instance, argue that the 'neo-liberal promotion of free market economic globalisation has continued to provide the overarching framework for Britain's political economy as it enters the new millen-nium' (p. 2). Similarly, Whitfield (2000) asserts that New Labour's 'third way modernisation project is based on a minimum reversal of Tory legislation . . . the continuation of the Conservatives' transformation of public services' (p. 82); and Rikowski (2000a) argues that the reliance on human capital notions in current policy is 'embarrassingly close to the position taken within many education reports flowing from previous Conservative administrations' (p. 6).

A good deal of this criticism seems to be – at least in some respects – on the right lines but it requires further inspection and elaboration. The importance of globalisation in relation to education and most other areas of policy-making has already been mentioned, and the centrality of the concept warrants a special mention. Certainly many features of current policy – including the national skills agenda and the reform of FE – are often justified in terms of the need to respond to global market pressures. But does it always make sense to speak of such pressures as simply something to which all states and governments have to respond? Ball (1999) suggests as much in his argument for:

> the need to see the policy continuities between the Conservatives and Labour in an international context and . . . that in a sense Labour's policies are not specific to Labour at all; they are local manifestations of global policy paradigms.
>
> (p. 195)

Fairclough (2000) similarly suggests – in accounting for the rhetoric/ reality in current political debate – that New Labour is seeking 'to achieve rhetorically what they cannot achieve . . . in reality . . . a reconciliation of neo-liberal enterprise with social justice' (p. 16).

Whether such a reconciliation – particularly in terms of the social inclusion and community values side of the lifelong learning agenda – is realistically possible or not is a matter which will be taken up in later chapters. What can be said for now is that the standard view that modern states are helpless in the face of globalisation forces has been seriously questioned in recent years. As mentioned earlier, both Green (1997a) and Giddens (1998, 2000) envisage reconstructed concepts of citizenship, community and nationhood in order to counter the excesses of the global economy. Symes and McIntyre (2000) have pointed to the 'dark sides' (p. 4) of the new global economics, and Gray (1998) presents a graphic illustration of this side of the picture in reminding us that:

> In every country the new and more volatile strain of capitalism is transforming economic life. The impact of anarchic global markets on the economic cultures of continental Europe institutionalises high levels of structural unemployment. In these societies the principal source of social division is unequal access to work.
>
> (p. 74)

The impact of global economics on Third World countries has been even more disastrous for working people (Rikowski, 2000b), and Bales (2000) has shown how globalisation processes have increased new forms of slavery and child prostitution throughout the world.

Some of these excesses run directly counter to the aims of social cohesion espoused in recent educational policy documents. Indeed, the Prime Minister's aim – in specifically linking New Labour educational policy with the Human Rights Act – of constructing a synthesis 'between collective action in the pursuit of social justice and the liberal commitment to individual freedom in a market economy' (Blair, 2000, p. 21) would be very difficult to achieve if globalisation could not, at least in some degree, be countered by national policy initiatives. What needs to be emphasised, therefore, is that the mechanisms and machinations of the global economy are not inevitable and immutable 'givens' that states have to respond to in the best way that they can but corporate constructions the power and status of which can be challenged.

There are a number of fundamental misconceptions about the connections between nationhood, neo-liberalism and global markets which Gray (1998) seeks to remedy in the suggestion that the contemporary 'model of globalization errs badly in writing off sovereign states as marginal institutions'. He goes on to argue that:

> For multinationals, sovereign states are not marginal actors in the world economy whose policies are easily circumvented. They are key players whose power is well worth courting. The leverage of sovereign states may actually be greater in some respects today than it has been in the past.
>
> (p. 69)

A number of myths about the so-called 'free market' are responsible for many of the misunderstandings in this sphere. As Gray explains, this market:

> is not – as today's economic philosophy supposes – a natural state of affairs which comes about when political interference with market exchange has been removed. In any long and broad historical perspective the free market is a rare and short-lived aberration. Regulated markets are the norm, arising spontaneously in the life of every society. The free market is a *construction of state power*.
>
> (p. 211; italics added)

There are, in fact, only two periods when a genuinely *laissez-faire* regime within the world market existed: in Britain between the 1840s and 1870s, and in the USA, Britain and, significantly, New Zealand in the 1980s and early 1990s. Moreover, as Gray explains, even these markets could not have been constructed without active state intervention in the fields of industrial relations, the deregulation of the labour market and a generally proactive fiscal policy. It was mentioned in the previous chapter that, in the last quarter of the nineteenth century, Britain witnessed a spate of educational reforms – typified by what Taylor (1972) called the 'patently interventionist 1870 Education Act' (p. 57) – which represented a response to foreign competition and had the aim of 'limiting market freedoms for the sake of social cohesion' (Gray, 1998, p. 14).

There are clear parallels between this end of the nineteenth century state interventionism in education and New Labour's lifelong learning policies implemented at the end of the twentieth century. In spite of the lack of hard evidence about general social – as opposed to individual – rates of return to national investment in education and training (Dore, 1997), such investment is once again being proposed as a panacea for all kinds of economic and social ills. There is always, of course, the fact that – whereas the educational system is relatively amenable to reform with the possibility of immediate and tangible results (e.g. improvement in reading standards, increase in numbers of FE learners, more New Deal leavers placed in sustainable jobs, etc.) – the economy and general social order are not quite so malleable and susceptible to manipulation. Nevertheless, the pace of educational reform between 1997 and 2000 has been formidable and can only be described in terms of its centralist and interventionist tendencies (Selwyn, 2000; Avis, 2000).

Hodgson and Spours' (1999) analysis of these recent trends concluded with a criticism of New Labour for 'its reliance on voluntarist initiatives which, while practical and focused on the needs of the excluded, may not in the final analysis work effectively because of system barriers' (p. 136). In terms of government interventions, a distinction is made between 'weak frameworks' which 'place responsibility on individuals to access the type of learning opportunities they require to improve employability and enter the labour market', and 'strong frameworks' which 'provide structures within the education and training system which support genuine individual empowerment' (ibid., p. 137). The UfI and voluntary employer training initiatives are cited as instances of the 'weak' approach, whereas a unified post-16 funding system, a unified curriculum and a strengthened national framework for Modern Apprenticeships, are offered as examples of 'strong' strategies.

This is an interesting analysis, particularly in view of the fact that the three examples of strong government strategies cited by Hodgson and Spours are, to some extent, part of New Labour's current development plan (and will be examined further in later chapters). The New Deal for

Young People (NDYP) is not mentioned specifically in this context but, on any reading, this and the other Welfare to Work (WtW) schemes which have been operating since 1997 can only be characterised as strong interventionist policies designed to remedy social exclusion and disadvantage (Hyland, 2000, 2002). Moreover, it could be argued that the Curriculum 2000 proposals aimed at the reform of post-16 qualifications and the wholesale re-organisation of the PCET sector under the LSC are also clear cases of strong centralist policies. Similar claims could be made about recent policies aimed at helping the most disadvantaged students to participate in further and higher education (Educa, 1999).

Different interpretations of current government education policy could be explained in terms of the fact that – for critics of neo-liberalism – state interventionism is almost never enough whereas – for critics of statist strategies – any government interference in education smacks too much of centralist control. Green's (1990) investigation of the role of education systems in state formation demonstrated that there is no such thing as a state which does not manipulate its education system in the pursuit of certain ends; there are only relevant degrees of manipulation and control. The third way policies mentioned earlier can, perhaps, serve the additional purpose of charting a middle way between voluntarism and centralist intervention. However, there is always likely to be a tension between different political strategies here, and it is instructive to reflect on the question of just how much state direction and control is required to enable educational institutions to fight social exclusion and promote community participation and equality of opportunity at all levels.

Thus, it could be argued that the third way strategy which seeks a mean between social justice and the new economy does require a strong and determined national plan which – whilst acknowledging global pressures – seeks to mitigate their worst excesses in the interests of fostering the just community. Moreover, the influence of such an approach can be clearly discerned in recent flagship projects such as the UfI and the New Deal initiatives. The UfI, for instance, was specifically designed against the background of Giddens' main ideas. In the original blueprint devised by Hillman (1997), three broad strategies to meet the challenges of lifelong learning were considered: *laissez-faire* (free market), *dirigisme* (state direction) and *animation* (partnership between the state and relevant stakeholders). Unsurprisingly, the 'third option' was chosen by planners because, as Hillman explains:

> It is less expensive than *dirigisme* but entails more role for govern-ment than *laissez-faire*. It creates expectations and political liability

but is much less risky than *dirigisme*. At best it can realise the flexibility and responsiveness of the market while making sure that things happen faster and that commercially marginal groups are not excluded.

(p. 33)

All the dominant and distinctive characteristics of current policy-making are present in this explanation: public–private partnerships, social inclusion (interpreted mainly in economic/employment terms), prudent handling of the public purse and the regulation of the market in the interests of all members of society. Moreover, this intervention in the market through the establishment of UfI *Learndirect* centres is – in spite of the 'brokerage' metaphors (Milner, 1998) – quite unlike the market-isation of education and training through the Training and Enterprise Councils (TECs) under the Conservatives (Evans, 1992) and much more like the old statist forms of 'supply-side' initiatives (Robertson, 1999).

A broadly similar strategy informed the organisation of the New Deal WtW schemes which allowed for consortia – involving the regional employment services, local authorities, careers services, FE colleges, TECs, voluntary and private agencies – to collaborate in planning and delivering provision (Hyland and Musson, 2001). There was a commit-ment to flexibility and an expectation that 'arrangements for delivery would vary from area to area in accordance with the views of the local partners and the needs of the young people in the area (DfEE, 1997, p. 3). Although there are now a number of New Deal schemes in operation – for lone parents, people over 50, communities, and so on – the principal flagship NDYP scheme for 18–24 year olds in receipt of Job Seekers Allowance (JSA) has now been operating for five years with some success. The role of FE colleges in this and other flagship programmes will be taken up again in later chapters. At this stage we need to examine – against the background of the policy priorities in New Labour's first term – more recent policy trends, in particular the plans for FE and PCET under the new LSC regime.

Learning, skills and the LSC

Just as 'training' came either to replace or to assume parity of esteem with 'education' to describe *processes* during the new vocationalism of the 1970s and 1980s, so 'skills' (and later 'competences', Hyland, 1994) came to replace the traditional aims and purposes of the educational task in terms of *content* during the same period. By the late 1970s Hart

(1978) was noting that 'you cannot dip much into educational writings without realising that the ambit of so-called skills is growing' (p. 205), and a decade later commentators were observing that the word 'skill' is 'ubiquitous in educational discourse' (Barrow, 1987, p. 188) to the extent that 'skills are now officially seen as an essential part of the curriculum' (Griffiths, 1987, p. 203). In the twenty-first century educational discourse skills are not just *part* of the curriculum, they *are* the curriculum, at least as far as the PCET sector is concerned. Almost all recent policy documents have 'skills' in the title. The main funding and co-ordinating body for the post-school sector, the LSC, has a title recognising learning and skills but not education or training; and more recently the Department for Education and Employment has become the Department for Education and Skills (carrying with it the tacit implication that there are no problems of employment any more, just problems of skills!). In addition, 'key skills' dominate policy initiatives at both school and post-school levels, they figure prominently in all national learning targets, and are at the heart of the LSC vision that 'by 2010, young people and adults in England will have knowledge and productive skills matching the best in the world' (LSC, 2001a, p. 5). More recently the pervasive influence of 'skill-talk' has been revealed in the reconstruction and re-badging of NTOs as Sector Skills Councils (SSCs) whose chief objective will be to 'identify and tackle skills gaps in industry' (Kingston, 2001, p. 37). Shortly afterwards, the Secretary of State at the DfES, Estelle Morris (2001), in response to the fact that 'industry is being undermined by a skills shortage', declared that the newly created SSCs 'must work with schools and with the further and higher education sectors' to ensure that 'the connections between learning and employment are strengthened' (p. 39).

Is the concept of skill being used metaphorically here as a shorthand way of referring to current educational objectives, or is the intention to make the enterprise of education and training synonymous with the acquisition of skills? In any case, there are sound reasons for objecting to the wholesale and indiscriminating use of 'skills' to describe the outcomes of education and training. The principal ones are as follows:

1   The concept is neither well-founded nor clearly articulated, and there is no common agreement or shared understanding about whether it applies to the cognitive, affective or psycho-motor domains. As Jonathan (1987) argues, when faced with lists which include 'life skills, reasoning skills, survival skills, etc.' (p. 93) we are bound to ask questions about whether the same concept of skill is being used

in all cases and, indeed, whether the concept has not become entirely vacuous as a result of attempts to make it bear far more weight than it can possibly carry. A common error in this sphere involves making the false move from identifying features common to *different skills* and, from this, inferring the existence of a *common skill*. As Dearden (1984) observes in this respect:

> there may indeed be features common to all skilled perfor-
> mances in virtue of which we call them skilled, but it does not
> follow that it is the *same* skill which is present in each case: in
> the skater, the juggler, the flautist, the chess player and the
> linguist.
>
> (p. 78; original italics)

Moreover, if relatively low level activities such as 'taking orders' (MSC, 1977) are to be labelled as skills alongside 'considering others' views' (DES, 1985), 'enterprise skills' (Training Agency, 1990) and 'improving one's own learning performance' (NCVQ, 1992), it is not obvious how the conceptualisation of such varied accomplishments as skills adds anything at all to the basic description of learning programmes or educational content.

2   More importantly, the indiscriminate use of 'skill-talk' (Hyland and Johnson, 1998) serves to belittle the role and status of knowledge and understanding in education thereby seriously impoverishing learning of all kinds. Such reductionism may also cause us to overlook the fact that skills (and competences) require a foundation of knowledge and understanding just as education requires an infrastructure of training which can lead to 'the confident deployment of skill and technique in a wide variety of situations' (Winch, 1995, p. 324). Similarly, as Holland (1980) notes, in 'wrestling with the problems that are important in a field of study, ideas not skills are what count, and the problems get solved or transformed by the [person] with the profounder conception' (p. 23). Thus an over-emphasis on skills can easily lead to a descent into the impracticable since those who possess only techniques or knacks are unlikely to fully understand the basis of practice.

3   There is a more sinister aspect of skill-talk which separates theoretical and practical performance and which, according to Johnson (1998), 'places under threat rich and deep conceptions of teaching, knowledge and the person' (p. 211). What is being criticised here is not just the tendency to transmute complex human agency into

measurable bits of behaviour but also the idea that the whole educational endeavour can be reduced to skills training. It is also worth noting that personal qualities – qualities of character such as temperance, industry, loyalty, affability, patience, and so on, which are crucial to education and training at all levels – are fundamentally constitutive of persons (almost definitive of what people are) in the sense in which skills are not. As Smith (1997) has observed, you 'learn nothing about what sort of individual I am if you discover that I have or lack some skill or another' (p. 198). The notion of a good surgeon, or good chef, plumber, nurse, teacher, airline pilot etc., is not synonymous with the idea of a person who possesses a range of skills. Knowledge, understanding and moral qualities are intrinsically linked to personhood, whereas skills are only contingent.

In addition to all this, it has to be said that the claims about the general transferability of core or, as they are now called, key skills, are suspect on both empirical and logical grounds. The principal claims about domain-independent transferability have been rejected in a number of studies (Singley and Anderson, 1989; ED, 1993) and Halsall's (1996) conclusion that 'there is little empirical or philosophical evidence that core skills are transferable to all contexts and learning activities' (p. 78) is well justified by the available evidence. Moreover, the idea that putative skills such as 'problem solving' or 'critical thinking' can exist independently of domains of specialised knowledge does not pass philosophical inspection (Gardner and Johnson, 1996). Clearly, the idea of generally transferable skills – connected with the much vaunted 'flexibility' and 'multi-skilling' required of post-Fordist workers – has proved too attractive to resist, leading to much wishful (though wholly irrational) thinking. As Hyland and Johnson (1998) put it, key skills are 'simply too good *not* to be true!' (p. 170).

However, notwithstanding the opacity and nebulosity surrounding skill-talk, its language, concepts and principal themes – as mentioned earlier – pervade current debate and feature prominently in DfES policy and the LSC blueprint for the PCET sector. The establishment of the LSC in April 2001 represents the most radical re-organisation of the post-school sector since the incorporation of colleges in 1993. The central LSC (and its forty-seven regional councils) inherits the functions of the TECs and the FEFC, has some 4,500 staff, a budget of £5.5 billion annually, and has oversight of around 5 million learners (Twining, 2001a). The central and regional councils will have responsibility for the funding and provision of FE and sixth-form colleges, work-based training for young people, workforce development, adult and community learning, education–business links and advice and guidance for adult learners.

The 'key tasks' of the LSC outlined in the 2001 corporate (LSC, 2001a, p. 4) plan are listed as:

- To raise participation and achievement by young people.
- To increase demand for learning by adults, and to equalise opportunities through better access to learning.
- To engage employers in improving skills for employability and national competitiveness.
- To raise the quality of education and training delivery.
- To improve effectiveness and efficiency.

Achievement in undertaking these tasks will be measured against the key objectives and targets for 2004 (ibid., p. 1) shown in Table 2.1.

Such targets are clearly derived from the audit and accountability culture which inspired the initial establishment of national education and training targets (NACETT, 1998) and there are direct links with the agenda of the National Skills Task Force. As Twining (2001b) has commented, most of the LSC measures can be described as a 'worthy

Table 2.1 Key objectives and targets

Key objectives	Targets for 2004
1. Extend participation in education learning and training	80 per cent of 16–18 year olds in structured learning (2000: 75 per cent); set baseline and targets for adults in next year's plan
2. Increase engagement of employers in workforce development	Develop measure of employer engagement in next year's plan
3. Raise achievement of young people	85 per cent at level 2 by age 19 (2000: 75 per cent) 55 per cent at level 3 by age 19 (2000: 51 per cent)
4. Raise achievement of adults	Raise literacy and numeracy skills of 750,000 adults per cent of adults at level 2: target to be set in next year's plan 52 per cent of adults at level 3 (2000: 47 per cent)
5. Raise quality of education and training and user satisfaction	Set baselines and targets in next year's plan

statement of good intentions in the abstract, and not a detailed plan of how it will proceed and what funds will be allocated to each activity' (p. 9). Such a lack of specificity – resulting in an enabling rather than a prescriptive framework – can be connected with the third way policies mentioned above in relation to the UfI and the New Deal. Whilst stressing the fact that the LSC is a 'major player controlling substantial budgets', there is an insistence that it 'cannot act in isolation' and that all its 'decisions and actions will need to have regard to the interests of partner organisations which can help us achieve our aims' (LSC, 2001a, p. 23).

In charging each of the forty-seven regional LLSCs to draw up strategic plans by March 2002, the distinctive features of centralised advice were the emphasis on bridging the national/local divide by concentrating on regional needs and targets involving – as in New Deal, UfI and new FE strategies – collaboration and partnerships between all the relevant stakeholders (such as Regional Development Agencies, LEAs, Employment Services, Employers Organisations, Trade Unions, *Connexions* and Adult Guidance Services, QCA and voluntary/community agencies, in addition to regional educational institutions). The suggested model which – though not intended to be a 'straitjacket' (ibid., p. 15) for regional LLSCs clearly involves stronger guidelines than the animistic model which informed UfI *Learndirect* developments – involves three interconnected local components: a skills strategy, a participation strategy and a learning strategy for each region. Final versions will represent LSC 'partnership with a complex interlocking set of private and public agencies' with an increasing emphasis on 'cross-agency strategic planning' (ibid., p. 17).

FE, LSCs and beyond

Even though the LSC is in its infancy – with the FEFC still technically in charge of post-school funding mechanisms and regional councils currently drawing up their local strategic plans – the new quango is not without its critics (Twining, 2001b). The autocratic nature of LLSC planning, and the increasing systemic complexity and bureaucratic red tape (Tysome, 2001) are concerns expressed by college principals over the last year. Such concerns and related problems and areas of weakness have been linked to the incredibly wide and diverse roles that LSCs will have to play, the fragmented nature of the strategic planning and funding mechanisms in the sector, and the continuing voluntarist role of employers' participation in the PCET education and training enterprise

(Evans *et al.*, 2002). However, as Twining concludes, it is far 'too soon to judge the effectiveness, potential or actual, of the LSC and the local LSCs' (ibid., p. 10).

What can be done, however, is to evaluate the LSC corporate plan – and other recent general PCET policy initiatives – against the background of what commentators have suggested are the principal issues and problems for the FE sector after New Labour's first term in office. Hodgson and Spours (1999, pp. 93–4) referred to four such issues:

(i) an over-emphasis on 'supply-side measures' such as access and participation which fail to address the widening social, economic and cultural causes of educational disadvantage;

(ii) the dominance of the goals of widening participation and improving basic skills has marginalised the discussion of key strategic goals such as 'how further education relates to higher education, employers and the world of work'.

(iii) in spite of an ostensibly common (though actually fragmented) FEFC funding system, FE does not constitute a national sector because of the 'considerable autonomy of individual colleges'. What is required is a 'strong national framework of inspection and quality assurance, common post-16 funding and a common national qualifications system to underpin the concept of a tertiary system at local and regional level'.

(iv) clarity of mission and strategic partnerships will have to overcome the problems of the multiplicity of different agencies involved in PCET provision and the 'plethora of funding streams'.

In a similar vein, the research by Lucas *et al.* (1999) indicated that – in spite of the recent attempts to temper the often wasteful competitive and marketised nature of the FE sector brought about by the worst excesses of incorporation – there is still too much unprofitable competition in many regions due to *de facto* competition between local providers (schools, sixth-form and FE colleges, TECs and community agencies) because of the pressures and vicissitudes of post-school funding. More recently, Lucas (2001) has pointed to the ways in which the 'haphazard' development of FE colleges in the 1990s, has left them with 'no clarity of mission or distinct function that sets them apart from competing institutions'. He goes on to explain how the mission confusion underpinning recent trends:

has left 'modern' further education colleges in an ambiguous position. They have become institutions caught half way between catering for 16 to 19 year olds and adult returners; full-time students and part-time students. They offer vocational and academic courses, provide programmes such as higher national diplomas as well as those geared to adults needing basic skills, and cater for New Deal students and those wishing to gain access to higher education.

(p. 38)

However, the restructuring of the sector under the LSC does hold out the hope of solutions to such problems (Lucas, 2000) just as, for Hodgson and Spours (1999), the problems of diversification, multiplicity of objectives and fragmentation of strategic role and mission may be eased through 'regional and local collaboration' which forces colleges to 'define what they are really about' (p. 95). This process of development, definition and the emergence of strategic roles under the regional LLSCs – particularly in relation to the key themes of learning teaching, curricula, the developing roles of staff and students, and the significance of community-wide policy and practice – will inform and guide our investigations of the changing face of FE in the following chapters.

Chapter 3

Who is further education for?

As mentioned in the first two chapters, FE colleges are now characterised by a diverse student population, and are no longer the preserve of largely young, mostly male apprentices and A-level students. Different groups of students – 16–21 year olds, adults, part-time, full-time students – contest for space in colleges. The refectory is no longer divided into camps with an 'us' and 'them' situation with the apprentices located at one end and A-level students at the other. The post-compulsory sector of FE is open to all, yet certain groups may be more dominant than others if colleges choose to target particular groups. Since incorporation colleges have to compete in the market place for the more attractive and lucrative 'customers' in industry. At the same time HE work offers status, some funding – particularly those receiving direct development funding from the Higher Education Funding Council for England (HEFCE) – and a growing group of adult students. Such students may, through course progression, remain in the same FE college for a number of years. In contrast, disadvantaged and community groups may find themselves further marginalised from learning because of their lack of economic power in an era of marketisation, particularly as 'efficiency' comes to replace 'social responsibility' (Cripps, 2002, p. 139) in the FE mission.

The process of a changing student population – part of what Cripps calls the post-1944 'chameleonic policy process' (ibid., p. 23) – has been taking place since the late 1960s driven by a diverse range of internal and external drivers and levers. These include the decline in apprenticeship training due to changes in the economy, the expansion of HE causing a demand for more A-level students as well as the introduction of the delivery of HE programmes in FE, increased youth unemployment and the need for training schemes and, more recently, a policy focus on lifelong learning and widening participation. Colleges are multi-functional, multi-agency institutions offering courses ranging from basic education through to higher education, at either vocational or academic levels. The changing of the name from technical colleges to colleges of further education during the 1970s to the 1980s reflected the transformation and the new diversity of the curriculum and the student population. Further education's student population is pluralistic, reflecting the diversity not only of its local communities but also society in general in terms of age, class, gender and ethnicity. In this sense they are cosmopolitan institutions:

Colleges appear to be meant to cater for everyone, 16–19 year olds, both academic and vocational, adult returners, access students, HE students, those with special needs, the socially excluded and those not involved anywhere else. As part of the growing ethic of lifelong learning, if you are not in a school sixth form, at work or at university, then you should be involved with the local college.

(Green and Lucas, 1999b, p. 35)

FE colleges can be described as postmodern institutions with pluralistic, fragmented and diverse interests. Further education not only serves the interests of students but also local communities, employers, stakeholders, its governing body, regional agencies and the government. Unlike other education sectors it is difficult to define, at a national level, who FE is for, as the sector itself is not homogeneous. Each college has been shaped and defined by its own history and the influence of local education authorities, its governing bodies and local communities and employers. As Ainley and Bailey point out, 'there is no such thing as a typical college' (1997, p. 9).

Misperceptions of FE

Today colleges are overwhelmingly adult institutions, and the majority of FE students are over the age of 26. (Recent statistics indicate that 72.8 per cent of the 2.35 million students in LSC-funded FE provision in November 2001 were adults; Educa, 2001c, p. 5). This contrasts with the 1960s and 1970s when colleges were largely the domain of young working class, mostly males, learning an apprenticeship on either sandwich, day-release or full-time courses. Various government reports (1959 Crowther Report, 1961 White Paper, *Better Opportunities in Technical Education*) helped to establish colleges as technical institutions providing vocational education and the vehicle for promoting the country's economic health and growth. Employers assumed a role as stakeholder in FE. This image of FE as being the preserve of young apprentices continues to be a powerful one. As our English FE study reported, there is:

> a mismatch between what colleges are providing and what industrial organisations, community groups and local government bodies perceive further education to be doing. Colleges are changing faster than perceptions of them. This is almost certainly unavoidable, though there is much that colleges can do to raise awareness of their new role and functions.
>
> (Merrill 2000, p. 18)

This misperception of FE was highlighted in both the Scottish and English studies. The English study, funded by the Further Education Development Agency (FEDA), now the Learning Skills Development Agency (LSDA), looked at FE colleges and their communities. The Scottish study, undertaken jointly with Glasgow Caledonian University and funded by the Scottish Office, focused on the participation and non-participation of marginal groups of learners in FE. In both studies many adult participants stated that colleges 'was not for the likes of me' as it was 'just a place for young kids to go to'. The following comments were typical:

> I would not have thought that it would have been meeting the needs of the middle aged – the people of the estate. My perception of it is that it is a place for kids to go to after they have finished school and to do their further education, be it A-levels or whatever.
>
> (Member of a playgroup association)

This participant also added that parents living on the estate regarded FE as 'just a place for young kids to go to'. In the Scottish study many participants were learning at FE outreach centres, yet they did not perceive themselves to be FE students. Young working-class people also sometimes do not envisage college as either being a place for them or an option: 'Never really thought of college. I'm 18 and just want to enjoy myself just now.'

Those in employment also held out-of-date views about FE:

> In the main further education colleges carry on from where schools left off if youngsters have the feeling that they want to go on – if they are going to do A-levels. The second aspect of a technical college is

where you have youngsters who are sent on day release from companies and that sort of thing.

(Travel company employee)

One employer was aware of the outdated image of colleges:

> I think probably what would put people off . . . I think FE colleges have got an image of being for people of the 16+ age group. It takes a bit of bottle for an older person to go in if you have not done anything for years. I tried to get my neighbour to go – she thinks college is not for her.

Misperceptions were not just the preserve of adults only. One 16-year old male described FE as the place you go to 'if you cannot find a job and you did not do very well at school'. Many lecturers were conscious of the public image of FE:

> I think there's a lack of awareness in the local community and at the societal level. Getting the message to the local community is a big problem and I'm not quite sure how you should do it and whether there is a secret solution to get the message through . . . Local people don't even know where the college is, which is amazing.

Over the past years colleges have undergone considerable changes at a fast rate and this may be why people hold such misperceptions about FE. Alternatively, it may mean that FE is not doing an efficient job in informing the public about its role and functions, a shortcoming which itself may be partly a reflection of the mission conflicts and coding tensions in the sector noted by commentators (Green and Lucas, 1999b; Cripps, 2002).

Who are the students?

Learning is considered essential in post-capitalist societies as a tool to cope with social and economic changes. In order for the UK and Europe to compete economically in a globalised world individuals need to acquire/update their knowledge and skills. In the information society, as Castells (1996) points out, new social inequalities based on knowledge have emerged between the 'haves' and the 'have-nots' – the socially excluded. This creates a dualisation of society characterised by 'a sharp divide between valuable and non-valuable people' (Castells, 1996,

p. 161). For Bauman (1998) those without knowledge have become the new poor. Kennedy argued that 'FE is the key to widening participation' (1997, p. 28) and an essential player for realising the government's policy on lifelong learning and widening participation. Contradictions in the government's lifelong learning policy – the tensions between economistic and social inclusion aims noted in the policy analyses in Chapter 2 – are, however, making this objective increasingly difficult to achieve (particularly in the light of recent figures indicating a decline – from 29 per cent to 23 per cent – in the number of adults willing to participate in learning of any kind; NIACE, 2002).

In recent years FE colleges have become more flexible in terms of both delivery and the curriculum, as well as more diversified in the range of courses offered to all post-16 age groups. Yet at the same time, incorporation, the moves towards marketisation and competition between colleges, have meant that certain student groups are more appealing economically than others (Hodgson, 2000). Marginalised groups continue to be largely excluded from lifelong learning as work-based learning and skills-based VET become central within FE and accorded more value than courses to attract non-participants and those without qualifications (Lucas, 2001). Who further education is for is wider in terms of potential student groups at the level of rhetoric than in practice. While FE has, to a large extent, been forced along this road by government policy, there are some colleges which have struggled to maintain a community focus in their philosophy and practice. Two of the nine colleges in the FEDA study see themselves as having a strong community mission. Colleges located in areas of urban social deprivation in the Scottish study tended to have a closer relationship with their local communities and the socially excluded:

> Several of the teaching staff responded that social inclusion was what colleges had always done (and should be doing) and another responded that he felt the social inclusion agenda was bringing the college 'back to its roots'.
>
> (Gallacher et al., 2000, p. 59)

Several FE staff in the West Midlands colleges (FEDA study) expressed the view that the marketisation of colleges and the funding mechanism inevitably excluded marginalised groups from all but a minority of colleges committed to equal opportunities and community education. Most colleges cannot afford the costs of having such students. Policy changes have led to a restructuring of the colleges' internal community and a reassessment and realignment with its external communities. As one college lecturer reflected:

There was still a feeling, although under challenge, that the college could be instrumental in righting wrongs and would continue to work against inequalities. We never thought much about how we might have to compete really hard.

Other lecturers expressed regret and disappointment that they felt themselves under pressure from college management to attract profitable students. One college bluntly stated that 'there is a problem with community links – there is little or no money in it'. Johnston (1993) is critical of the dominance of marketisation in FE:

If further and higher education is to engage more positively with local communities, institutions need to move beyond the loaded language of the market and an over-reliance on top-down funding mechanisms like franchising. If a mission to serve the community and to foster equal opportunities is to be more than rhetorical window-dressing, colleges must have an institutional commitment and a theory of educational practice which informs college action, performance and staff development and so guards against an all too easy economic and market reductionism which says 'of course, we'd like to but we can't afford to'.

(p. 34)

Surveying communities

Different communities, businesses, local government organisations, community groups and individuals, were approached in the FEDA study for their views on FE: whether or not they considered FE to be relevant to their organisation or to themselves as individuals and what they wanted from FE. This information was collected through a questionnaire and follow-up interviews with a smaller sample. Not surprisingly, contrasting views between community/voluntary organisations and industry were very much apparent. Business organisations perceived the purposes of further education in largely instrumental and vocational terms, whereas voluntary/community groups expressed more collective and social purpose views. Colleges continually face the difficult task of catering for the needs of industry, voluntary/community groups and individuals in the local community. Some institutions are better than others at achieving a balance:

Colleges should . . . position themselves to respond both to employment-related demand and the individual and group learning needs of community residents. The strength of the college is that it is one of the few local public sector organisations that has the facilities to respond to both.

(Powell and Buffton, 1993, p. 46)

The nine colleges in the FEDA project serve diverse communities in terms of geography, economies and social structures. A few engage wholly or partially with rural areas and others with urban areas, from inner-city areas to the wealthier suburbs. A large part of the West Midlands has, in recent years, experienced severe economic decline and with it high rates of unemployment, particularly among men. Whereas some of the college catchment areas have witnessed the loss of apprenticeships and manufacturing industries, others have lost local coal mines, while those in rural areas are characterised by rural poverty and isolation. The West Midlands is, however, enriched by a multi-ethnic community. Nationally, the area has a very low participation rate in post-compulsory education, and, within this context, encouraging those who lack, using Bourdieu's (1977) concept, 'cultural capital' to participate in learning is a major task for the nine colleges. A college, or any other educational institution, is, therefore, not unsurprisingly, viewed by many people as not being a place for them.

All colleges share a history of strong links with local business companies, but the nature of these links has changed since incorporation. There is evidence that many employers believe that there is now greater interaction, negotiation and partnership between FE colleges and local firms than previously as a result of colleges having to compete on the market:

Further education has changed very much from where it was 20 years ago – tremendously changed. In fact now much more looking to what business wants rather than laying on courses and saying 'here they are, this is what we are offering'.

(Employer)

One college admitted that its relationship with employers had improved over the past few years:

In general there is a sense of a greater variety and number of links with outside organisations now than before. The quality of the

contacts we have with employers is better now. There is more understanding between employers and the college. We are more responsive
even though circumstances are more difficult for all. We are doing
more for small companies – they are more important in the economy
but working with them is more complicated and time-consuming.

Several employers explained that it is essential that colleges listen
to what their needs are if an FE/industry partnership is going to be
successful. Good communication and interaction at staff and student level
between the two organisations were also viewed as essential. One hotel
manager outlined what he considered to be a good partnership:

I think that it is important that they are prepared to listen to
what local businesses require. I deal with certain people at further
education colleges quite closely and they have been prepared to
listen to what we wanted and what we need in terms of students
coming to us to work and what sort of things they can do to help
prepare the students better for the workplace. There is a college that
I do a work experience paper for – a GNVQ student. The organisers
of the course came to speak to me and discussed what sort of person
I was looking for and what sort of requirements I would need. We
actually developed a relationship in that I went to the college and
talked to them and I talked to the students about the career path I had
taken and that was great because it was a representative from an
industry that they were interested in.

Some employers expressed the view that there was a lack of communication between colleges and local firms while others felt that FE could not
only cater for their training needs but also provide future staff through
ex-students though regretted that little of this was currently taking place:

Colleges should actually involve themselves in talking to local
business and discovering their needs to match training and job prospects to what is actually available after college, and create courses
around improvement of the businesses they are involved with.

Similarly:

I think colleges ought to make a determined effort to actually send
people out into various industries and get a feel for them and their
requirements because some people do need specialised skills
provided and, therefore, I will commit myself here – when I was at

college X I felt that a lot of the tutors would not have lasted five minutes in industry.

(Personnel officer)

Another employer was exasperated with the further education sector after contacting three local colleges to offer them work experience placements and jobs for their students and not receiving any reply from the relevant college departments. A director of an electrical firm was also frustrated over the lack of communication from a local college:

I know if there are courses at X college connected, for instance, even slightly with what we are doing we never get contacted to see if we have got anybody who we might want to attend those courses so I think that it is a bit lacking . . . They have not contacted us about anything . . . We have had six months when we have been struggling to get extra employees and we would like to take on . . . people who are just coming out of college. We have had nobody come forward and say, 'Could we possibly be helpful to your business?' or they have not asked us to go into the college and put our case forward . . . I am sure a lot of businesses would do that. We should perhaps be contacting colleges as well – both ways – and general information needs to be sent out . . . I do not think that a lot of people are aware of a lot of the courses. I do not think a lot of my friends or colleagues are aware.

The majority of employers do believe that FE has a role to play in relation to their needs, but some argue that colleges do not appear to respond adequately, a view which is increasingly being endorsed through current LSC strategy and the DfES transformation of the FE sector to make 'post-16 learning more responsive to local employers and communities'(DfES, 2002b, p. 1).

Employers continuously expressed the necessity for colleges to take into account the local economic structure, context and needs by offering vocational qualifications relevant to local industry (a current LSC priority). Besides delivering vocational qualifications to local people the other main role of FE in relation to industry is the provision of training for employees. This can be a lucrative source of income for colleges, although not all employers made use of this service. Small firms, for example, stated that cost and the size of the workforce made it difficult for them to take the opportunity of training provided by FE:

One of the problems with small, local businesses is that you are spending so much of your time trying to make the business work. It is very difficult to look over your shoulder and say, 'Right, we'll chuck half or one-fifth of your time away to worry about re-educating yourself and the people who work for you'. The expenditure is the problem. You have got to increase your turnover to cover the loss because it is a dead loss as far as your investment goes. OK you might get investment back in the first throw after they have had the education – to make them better employees, more useful employees. The only way you can do that is if you get grants for the industries concerned where they will get some type of pay back for taking on further training.

(Industrial services business manager)

Larger companies outlined different issues. Many of them have no need for training provision provided by FE colleges as they have their own in-house training facilities. Other large firms were sceptical that colleges have the appropriate knowledge or up-to-date technology for skills training:

Availability of up-to-date equipment to learn on is essential. For example, the Morris Minor is no longer relevant in today's vehicle technology. Some, indeed many, colleges suffer from out-of-date equipment.

(Motor manufacturer)

However, other employers did not agree:

You come to the phrase 'updated skills' and there is a huge necessity because of the training shortage about ten years ago. Older people in businesses are having to update their skills in regards to electronics, computers, communication and the like and I think that it is vitally important for businesses to use the college because again the colleges have got the equipment and the skill and the ability to show people how to do it.

A few employers were critical of the increasing competitive and marketised behaviour of colleges in recent years:

I would like all three colleges in X to complement rather than compete . . . Encourage people to return to work and help in the process of linking employers with potential employees.

Competitiveness was particularly criticised in urban areas where there were two or more colleges in the same city. Local government organisations indicated that further education should rationalise and return to more co-operative approaches, partly to reduce duplication but also to avoid competition. There was also criticism from a range of employers of 'the smarmy salesman side of having to compete for students and funding'. Although employers compete in the market it was not considered to be suitable behaviour for colleges.

Another employer remarked:

> I do not know what colleges are doing at the moment, either it is for money or what, but you all seem to be out with your little nets trying to get people. I have calls from different colleges like, 'Can I come and see you?' 'Would you be interested in this, that and the other?' I have people calling in from colleges trying to sell their courses or trying to persuade you to go to this college rather than that college. I do not know quite what it is – you all seem to have these marketing people now marketing the college. I appreciate that marketing plays a big part in everything now but there seems to be this – as I said – throwing out the net trying to catch a few more people for that particular college.

Lecturers were also critical of the competitive behaviour of colleges. One lecturer explained that his college competed for students from industry from a wide radius of towns with FE institutions up to twenty-five miles away:

> I think we'd have a much greater impact if we were working together than working separately . . . it must be quite confusing for potential students to have all these people saying, 'Well, you should be doing this.' I think that if we adopt an approach where we try and sell things together and do things together it would be much more successful. All the colleges are trying to get the same students and it's just not working. There's not enough students out there to go round all the colleges and we're all competing for the same areas. I wonder whether the colleges are putting an awful lot of effort into competing for those cuddly four-to five GCSE students who are really nice and cause no trouble when if they gathered their efforts together they could have those students for less effort and use some of that effort elsewhere for students who wouldn't normally be so ready to come into colleges.

A poor experience at one FE college coloured their judgement of all colleges to the extent that they no longer used them. For some employers their experiences were mixed within the same college from being positive to negative. One Mental Health NHS Trust explained that the 'variance between lecturers was too extreme. They were either very good or very bad and in some cases, did not turn up'. One District Council was particularly scathing:

> Today most FE colleges are inefficient, disorganised and use more and more lecturers who are no more qualified in the subject area than the students – their expertise being out-of-date or in another area.

It is clear that colleges nationally have a lot of work to do to improve their image and quality if they want the majority of employers to view FE as an institution for them and their company's needs.

In contrast, the voluntary and community sector was critical of FE for different reasons. A large number of voluntary and community organisations strongly felt that colleges were ignoring them and, as a consequence, were not serving the needs of certain groups in society such as the disabled and those with mental health problems:

> There should be a wider provision of courses integrated for people with disabilities, closer working with organisations such as ourselves and disability training for staff – this is the greatest barrier to disabled people.
>
> (Care centre)

> Provide enabler support to people with learning disabilities to enable them to access mainstream courses. Provide more care assistant support to enable people with profound disabilities to access college. A wider range of courses accessible to people with learning disabilities.
>
> (Care centre)

Disabled groups were, therefore, perceived to be excluded by colleges:

> What is required is an attitudinal change. Although the FE college has become accessible in the physical sense, it is not so in respect of actively promoting and encouraging disabled people to become involved in courses.

Many community organisations argued for the inclusion of non-participants and excluded groups not only in terms of courses but also the use of premises:

> Be more receptive and provide specific provision to meet the diverse needs of the community, especially those who are at a disadvantage such as women, youths and under-educated adults.
>
> (Asian Youth Association)

Although, on the whole, colleges are contacting employers about catering for their training needs it does not appear to be happening, or very little, in relation to voluntary and community organisations. Most colleges, partly because of the funding structure, are focusing their attention on students from the sectors that can afford to pay the most. Several college lecturers expressed concern, and in some cases, anger, that the funding mechanism and market forces restricted them from working with marginalised groups. However, a minority of colleges have successfully maintained their community mission and commitment. This works in colleges where there was strong support from the principal. A manager at an FE outreach centre described the strategy they employ:

> What's been new for us during the past year is that we received a grant from the Community Education Councils . . . which enabled us to employ community development workers and their brief was to go out into the community – not necessarily looking to transfer people in the communities into students in classes. The brief was very clear and backed by the principal, that it was to empower people in the community to look after themselves, and to enable them to access facilities on college sites wherever they may be.

Voluntary and community organisations also pointed out that courses should be provided free to excluded and marginalised groups. They would also like colleges to offer them the use of their resources and facilities, such as rooms for printing, particularly in the evenings and at weekends either for free or at a low cost. They felt that they had the right to access what they consider to be public space, a view which accords with the recommendations of the Tomlinson Report (1996b) on inclusive learning in FE and, indeed is now enshrined in legislation through the Special Education Needs Disability Act (SENDA, 2001).

Some small businesses and voluntary and community organisations would like to take advantage of training courses for their staff but do not have the resources to do so. Not all the comments from this sector were negative:

> We have a high regard for the college but have not really made use of it – mainly because we are under-funded and therefore wary of costs involved in sending staff on training, but also we only have three paid staff and therefore find it difficult to find the time. From my perception the college has made remarkable progress in recent years and many of my volunteers have benefited from its courses, particularly women returners. The college, including the excellent Access Centre, already offers the local community a great deal.
>
> (Volunteer centre)

Colleges need to develop institutional policies and strategies covering all aspects, admissions and publicity, teaching and learning, at departmental and institutional levels, to promote the inclusion of marginalised groups in the community. As McGinty and Fish (1993) point out:

> Increased participation should be a concern of the whole college. All departments should make their programmes accessible to the widest possible range of students and increase participation through supporting the learning of less confident students. Increased participation is not simply a matter of providing for more separate specialist groups.
>
> (1993, p. 83)

Not everyone chooses FE: young people

FE colleges have always catered for younger students in the 16–19 age group. Although young people still participate, the 'student type' has changed. Vocational courses are expanding while A-level teaching is in decline. Staff in the FEDA study felt that colleges are now seeing more disaffected 16–19 year olds, as teaching that age group is now perceived to be more difficult. In the days of apprenticeship training lecturers were able to use the threat of losing their apprenticeship if students did not conform. Some staff stated that the increase in disaffected young students is partly attributable to issues of competition with schools and sixth-form colleges:

> On the secretarial side the students that come in now – even the secretarial girls – are nowhere near the sort of students we used to get

years ago. I think the schools keep the better students. The schools have taken over a lot of the courses that were initially college-oriented – NVQs, GNVQs . . . FE colleges are picking up the bits that schools don't want and that has had an effect, that the students we get are nowhere near the quality educationally.

(Business administration lecturer)

Similarly, another lecturer declared:

I think the role is at the moment – apart from trying to find courses for mature students – we tend to be mopping up people from schools who aren't very successful and that I'm not happy with. I'm not very happy with the present system.

Not all FE students are there by choice, a state of affairs likely to be increasingly experienced in colleges as the plans for 14–19 re-organisation bring younger school students into the sector (DfES, 2002a). Changes in the labour market and government policy associated with this has led some college lecturers to feel that 'further education has become a dumping ground for young people, and that standards are falling':

Years ago you had a choice – you could either go to college or you could get a job if you particularly wanted to earn money at 16. If you were fed up with education you could do that. If you wanted to make a career for yourself, you could stay at school or you could go to college, whereas now they don't have that choice. They've either got to come to college, stay on at school or go into youth training, so for some it's 'Oh well an FE course is better than training'.

(College lecturer)

The motivation is not there a lot of the time. I think it is also the fact that jobs are not available for students when they leave school, and what they do is come to college because there is nothing else.

(College lecturer)

Ainley and Bailey's (1997) study found a similar situation in the colleges they studied, and such views were also echoed by young people in the Scottish study:

I think going to college is in fashion at the moment. Well it's like there is nothing else to do because you can't get work.

(Male young student)

New Deal students were identified by lecturers as being particularly problematic and the ones most likely to display behavioural problems. For certain groups of young people in receipt of Job Seekers' Allowance (Hyland and Musson, 2001), New Deal is compulsory, just like school. Although government policy intentions behind New Deal may appear on the surface to be about social inclusion and improving employability, young people view it as a form of coercion and social control. Financial incentives through, for example, European Social Funds (ESF), and Skillseekers allowance, tipped the balance for some young non-participants into viewing college as being a possibility for them. Without the funding many stated that they would not be able to afford to go to college.

Some young people chose to reject college at the age of 16 as they assumed that college would be the same as school: 'I just feel that college would be the same as school. I hated most of the teachers and they hated me so it just didn't work' (female, non-participant). Negative experiences of school resulted in this group disliking learning. Many did not want to repeat a pattern of failing again. Other young people did not see the point of gaining qualifications when they lived in an area of high unemployment;

> One of my mates did go. He went for a year doing a trade I think, but after the year he came out and still couldn't get a job. So when you see that happening you do think, what's the point of it. I just wouldn't want to go.

While many adults perceive FE to be a place for young people this is not a view shared by all young people; particularly marginalised groups.

FE as a space for adults

Adults attending courses, from return to learn through to higher education, now form a large share of the FE student market. As Tuckett (2002) remarked recently, 'Adult participation is the main business of many colleges' (p. 38) and, with the exception of vocational courses for employees and special needs groups, adults attend college through choice. FE lecturers recognise that adult learners are committed and motivated to studying and have become a favoured group to teach:

> Most of the students we have here at the moment are actually mature students. To start with, when you have mature students they are generally of a different nature because they're committed and they

generally want to get on and progress. They're very much more capable of working on their own. They don't need much guidance. I find it's much more of a tutorial process. It's much calmer and a big contrast between teaching GNVQ Intermediate and the HNC.

(College lecturer)

Yet colleges generally do not have the feel of being institutions designed for adults. Although the majority of colleges have some form of HE in FE provision, either directly or indirectly funded, not all of them have specific teaching rooms or facilities for adults to create an HE environment. A recent evaluation of HE in FE undertaken by the National Institute of Adult Continuing Education (NIACE) and the University of Warwick (2002) revealed that colleges were split in terms of their policy and practice in relation to provision of facilities for HE in FE. Some colleges feel that it is better to integrate HE students with other students using the same facilities as non-HE students, recognising that they could not offer the same environment as an HE institution but instead a different one. Other FE colleges provide separate HE facilities, often in a separate building to try to create an HE environment. For some of the larger colleges, HE students form their biggest group of students. Through a consortium arrangement one college even contributed to approximately a third of a university's undergraduate numbers. Nationally by 1998–9, 888.8 (thousands) students were taking a first degree (full and part-time) in FE. Again some of the larger colleges offer postgraduate programmes including at PhD level. Statistics from DfE (1991) and DfEE (2000c) reports indicate that postgraduate students have increased from 1.9 (thousands) in 1989–90 to 3.1 (thousands) by 1998–9. Provision of HE programmes is particularly important in geographical areas which lack a HE institution such as Suffolk. In such areas the local FE institution becomes the HE institution having to offer progression opportunities at this level.

Foundation degrees constitute the latest HE in FE government initiative. A two-year qualification, foundation degrees were introduced to meet New Labour's target of 50 per cent of 18–30 year olds participating in higher education by 2010. Following on from the Dearing Report recommendations it expands the delivery of sub-degree work in FE. Foundation degrees are vocational to address the government's concern with an intermediate level skills deficit among the workforce and are, therefore, aimed at a particular group of young people and adults in employment, although the type of employment is wide-ranging; for example, classroom assistants, engineers, voluntary and community workers:

. . . to meet the shortage of people with technician level qualifications, to develop in students the right blend of skills which employers need, and to lay the basis for widening participation and progression – we need a new qualification.

(DfEE, 2000c, p. 6)

Work-based learning is core to this type of degree, enabling students to be 'earning and learning':

> For many young people entry to Foundation Degrees will take place after successful completion of Modern Apprenticeships, so that, for the first time, we have a robust, high-standard ladder of progression in work-based learning. Full-time study will suit some young people, whilst others will want to take the degree part-time, staying in employment. In this way, Foundation Degrees will provide an accessible and flexible building block for lifelong learning and future career success, drawing together further and higher education and the world of work.
>
> (Blunkett, 2000, p. 5)

Further education colleges were chosen as the location for the delivery of foundation degrees because of their accessibility in local areas for working adults and the flexibility of colleges in relation to teaching hours and a students' family and work commitments. Blair (1999) had hinted earlier in a speech in Oxford who the foundation degrees would be aimed at: 'the middle third of achievers' who lacked progression routes to 'worthwhile' vocational higher education programmes.

Access courses were an earlier lifelong learning/widening participation initiative (1978) attracting adults into FE with the aim of encouraging more people into higher education. At first Access courses focused on employment areas where there was a staffing shortage such as teaching and social work and targeted specific minority and non-participant groups (women and ethnic minorities). Access courses have grown in popularity and diversified into a wide range of discipline areas. After completing an Access course some adults choose to stay on at the FE college to study for a degree, either for part or whole of it, franchised and validated by a university. Access provision forms part of the government's widening participation, lifelong learning and social inclusion agenda, although Access courses were initially introduced under the Conservative government. Return to learn courses also fall under this umbrella and again have contributed to the significant rise in the adult student population at FE level. One admissions tutor stated that this was one of their main and easy-to-target groups compared to others:

> I think the big success story of the last few years has been the adult returners. It's increasing in numbers and there's still a lot to do in that area. I wonder about the older age groups – the early retirement and post-retirement. I'm not sure about the 16+ – it's a very competitive area . . . I think it needs a lot more thought. I suppose the low response sorts of areas tend to be the low income areas or the disadvantaged groups and the unemployed, possibly, who tend not to respond. Trying to increase participation rates of the lower social economic groups is one of the big issues that we need to probably address.

As this admissions tutor recognises, there are many adults who do not view college as a place for them, often because it is thought of as being too much like school. Initial schooling, for them, was a negative experience which they do not want to repeat as an adult:

> Well, if I think back on it the reasons I am apprehensive to go to college or a classroom situation must be based on past fears or experiences. I don't seem to do too well in the classroom situation
>
> (Non-participant, male)

These views are demystified and changed if adults are confident enough to try a course at an FE college. As one student revealed:

> You're not just sitting there and somebody's just standing up the front dictating to you like they did in school. I thought it would be like that here (college) but it's not.
>
> (Male returner)

Outreach centres run by FE colleges are a positive attempt to attract such students, as many adults, particularly working-class, or the unemployed, are tentative and uncertain learners (Gallacher *et al.* 2000). Taking the step to return to learn either at a community outreach centre or at an FE campus is a major decision. Such adults often opt for the smaller, more informal and approachable environment of an outreach centre compared to the FE campus, as the latter is perceived as belonging to the social space of other groups outside of their milieu and cultural capital:

I think it would be off-putting to be honest. I don't think I would have gone to a college. The fact that this was where it was kind of thing, and I knew that there was going to be people like myself. What I'm trying to say is I wouldn't go into a class of students who are in their 20s, because I would feel out of place and to my mind people in their 20s will pick up things quicker . . . I wouldn't be happy at any college. If I had a general knowledge and confidence to do what I was attending to do, kind of thing, the basic knowledge, I would maybe consider attending a college. I would need to be knowledgeable before I would even consider anything like that. What I'm trying to say is I would never have entered a beginners course in a college because I would feel stupid.

(Male participant at an outreach centre)

FE outreach centres in local communities possess a different ethos and structure to the main college, largely to attract those who have been out of education for a long time: the excluded, marginal groups. In many ways the approach in outreach centres is closer in nature to community development/education work than it is to mainstream FE. It is less affected by the ideology and practice of marketisation, focusing instead on empowering and changing individuals and communities. As Martin (1996) explains:

This construction of community education held out a vision for the development of education as a locally delivered public service that was the antithesis of the fragmentation and competition of a marketised system. It also sought to engage policy development with the local context in a systematic way, recalling Henry Morris's concern to ground education in the community.

(1996, p. 138)

One outreach tutor describes her centre's way of working to attract the uncertain adult learner. It also highlights the narrow geographical perception which some people feel to be their local area:

The kettle was always on, and that was important to encourage people back who lacked courage or self-esteem and want to get back into education but want to do it in a gentle way so that they are less threatened . . . I've been to a X town which is one-and-a-half miles away from Y town centre. If you talk to a lot of people in X they feel that Y college is not for them because it is not in their community. We've endeavoured to put classes on for them in their locality.

The outreach centre manager identified two main groups who participated at the centre:

> We have those that come in during the day and they might either be
> unemployed or they are looking to update their skills to go back into
> work, or they come along for the social side. Then there are the
> students who come in during the evenings, who work during the day
> and know exactly what they want. There is still a domination of
> women students but there are differences among age groups,
> minority groups, young people. The men that we recruit have either
> taken early retirement and come to do a leisure course like Art and
> Design . . . or they come to do the computer courses. The female
> students − I would say the majority are thirtysomething − the
> children have gone to school and they are looking to update their
> skills or change direction altogether, and so they come to us for
> qualifications.

Another outreach centre manager outlined a more diverse range of
adult students who used their centre. This college's outreach centre is also
not just confined to a physical building:

> The communities we serve − for us it's anybody, anywhere at any
> time, so it ranges from people in isolated rural communities where
> people find it very difficult to get to the main site. The communities
> range from single parents, adult returners to the unemployed.
> Increasingly we are working with older groups. We're doing a lot of
> reminiscence work in old people's homes and sheltered accom-
> modation. We work with a whole range of minority ethnic groups
> − Sikhs, Muslims, Hindus, Afro-Caribbeans − offering a range of
> training. We're looking at supporting parents who are volunteers in
> schools . . . if people come to us with an idea or things they want,
> then we would look to provide them with the service they need.

Outreach centres play an important role in providing a non-threatening
learning environment for adults who are unsure of themselves as learners
and who want a social and physical space for learning which does not
remind them of school. Unfortunately not all colleges have this facility.

Another category of adult students, not often associated with or
discussed in relation to FE, are those with learning difficulties. The
Tomlinson Report (1996b) was the first national report to look at adult
students with learning difficulties or disabilities in FE. It advocated a

more radical and humanistic practice by concentrating on the individual learner and starting with their learning needs and requirements based on the concept of inclusive learning, thereby taking it a step beyond mere integration. As Florian (1997) argues, the Act posed a challenge to the FE sector to offer a meaningful learning situation for adults with learning difficulties. FE has had to provide a range of courses to meet the needs of this group. In the Scottish study, one group of adults with learning difficulties were interviewed (see Chapter 5). In this particular case they were participating on a course which aimed to move them towards greater living independence and self-reliance.

FE, therefore, serves several communities of adults. While some may participate for only a few weeks on an employment training scheme, for example, others may stay for several years progressing from return to learn through to degree; and for a minority, to postgraduate level. The attraction for adults is the fact that it is local, accessible and flexible in its delivery of programmes. However, for some with negative memories of school, the FE campus remains threatening and 'not a place for them', despite the recent efforts by FE to attract non-participants. For this group, an FE experience has to be in something even more local, such as an outreach centre.

Stakeholders in FE

The technical and vocational origins of FE colleges have ensured that employers have always been a key stakeholder. Over the last decade higher education institutions have emerged as other major stakeholders and, with the introduction of the foundation degree, employers and higher education institutions are now joint stakeholders/partners in one initiative. All such developments reflect the key government policy of encouraging industry and education to work together through partnerships/consortia – a favoured way of working by New Labour at local and regional levels (LSC, 2001a). Developing and maintaining effective partnerships was one of the conditions for the institutions involved in the proto-type foundation degrees in 2001–2002. Some FE colleges may feel that this is not an equal partnership as the criteria stated that higher education institutions had to be the lead institution. In total sixty-eight FE colleges participated in a consortia with HEIs to deliver forty prototype programmes.

Longer-standing consortia/partnership arrangements between FE and HE have centred on first degree courses through a range of collaborative structures, such as franchised degrees, 2+2 degrees, validation. Greater collaboration between FE and HE and the provision of a broader HE curriculum available outside of higher education institutions stems partly from government policy as outlined in the Green Paper, *The Learning Age* (DfEE, 1998a). The Green Paper indicated that universities should work more closely with FE colleges. At the same time HEFCE was advocating the same policy:

> Further education colleges have a crucial role to play in the development of a higher education system that meets the growing needs of the learning society and increases the opportunities for students from disadvantaged backgrounds to participate.
>
> (HEFCE, 1998, p. 1)

FE/HE consortia have moved towards a more regional basis with a few being led by an FE institution as in the north-west. However, the issue of equity is sometimes an issue for FE colleges. For partnerships to be successful there has to be something in it for both sides; and for FE colleges it forms part of their widening participation strategy and importantly endows them with status through higher level teaching. Higher education institutions use such consortia to address their widening participation strategies, and for some new universities it provides much needed student numbers.

Summary

Who further education is for is not a straightforward question to answer. Since incorporation colleges are facing conflicting demands of having to compete in the market on one hand while, on the other, having to address the government's lifelong learning policy of reaching out to and including the disadvantaged. Colleges need to provide a more even balance between profitable courses and social purpose type courses. Pleasing all communities and being available for all is a difficult task, especially for the smaller colleges. Colleges are now multi-faceted, multi-purpose institutions or 'community service stations' as Ainley and Bailey (1997) describe them.

Numerically FE colleges are now dominated by part-time adult students, and increasingly becoming adult colleges; yet catering for the 16–19 age group remains important. The strengths of FE lie in its diversity and comprehensiveness; its weakness resides in the fact that it is a jack of all trades. Should FE colleges try to cater for all community groups or should colleges, at least those in highly populated urban areas, specialise in certain areas? In adjusting to incorporation, the colleges' internal and external communities are still being worked out. It is important that the less powerful voices in the community are not forgotten in the emerging further education as it competes to establish an influential role within the new LSS and in the lifelong learning/social inclusion agenda. As one college principal has pointed out:

> But further education has to be given its chance, because it is the only genuinely comprehensive bit of the entire system. The agenda for the future is the Kennedy agenda: social inclusion; widening participation; wiring the world . . . We can refresh the parts other sectors cannot reach. Only further education can do that.
>
> (Flint, 1998)

Whether the sector is able to achieve such ambitious goals and the necessary synthesis of conflicting aims and interests will, to a large extent, depend upon college staff, and it is to their experiences over the last few years that the next chapter is addressed.

Chapter 4

Colleges and staff

A college's community is not confined to outside its walls in the geographical area surrounding the college. Holistically the college itself forms a community of people internally differentiated into staff and students. Like all social institutions, FE colleges have a social system that operates at the meso and micro levels. These broad internal communities can be broken down again into smaller groups of staff distinguished by hierarchy, status and pay (management, lecturers, technicians, support and guidance, cleaners, etc.), while students are differentiated by age and mode of study. Each individual and level within the hierarchy has clearly defined roles with social behaviour and interaction governed by rules, regulations and policies. All institutions work towards the integration and cohesion of their members through either democratic or authoritarian means. Experiences of staff (and students) will, therefore, vary according to the culture and context of a particular institution. In using the concept of culture, Clarke *et al.* provide a useful working definition in their idea that:

> We understand the word 'culture' to refer to that level at which social groups develop distinct patterns of life, and give expressive forms to their social and material life-experience. Culture is the way, the forms, in which groups 'handle' the raw material of their social and material existence ... A culture includes the 'maps of meaning' which make things intelligible to its members.
>
> (Clarke *et al.*, 1976, p. 10)

Within the dominant culture of an FE college as a whole there are a number of subcultures (teaching departments, support departments, advice staff, technicians, etc.), each with its own values, attitudes and ways of behaving. As Clarke *et al.* explain:

Subcultures are smaller, more localised and differentiated structures, within one or other of the larger cultural networks . . . A subculture, though differing in important ways – in its 'focal concerns', its peculiar shapes and activities – from the culture from which it derives, will also share some things in common with that 'parent culture'.

(p. 13)

Harper (1997, pp. 45–6) also talks about 'power culture' (senior management authority), 'role culture' (bureaucracy or structural organisation) and 'person culture' (how organisations serve individuals), and concludes that, since incorporation, many FE principals have explicitly sought 'culture changes' involving the overt attempt to 'change the normally accepted values shared by employees of the college' (ibid., p. 44). Such culture changes in staff relations since 1993 have changed the face of FE in recent years and form a backdrop to our snapshot of perspectives offered by college staff in the late 1990s.

Staff, culture change and mission codes

The changes in governance stemming from the 1992 Act led, in a significant number of cases, to the 'confrontational' (Shattock, 2000, p. 90) style of management which in more recent years has resulted in changes to the membership of governing bodies and moves to a more co-operative ethos (DfEE, 1998b). From a teacher union perspective, the impact of incorporation on college lecturers has been – according to Taubman (2000) – 'largely retrograde', with the 'story of staff relations' in recent years described as a 'narrative of almost unrelieved gloom' (p. 82). From a wider research and policy perspective on the sector, there are broadly similar observations about FE teachers being a 'profession in crisis' (Robson, 1998, p. 585), with plenty of evidence about the 'intensification of labour with lecturers consistently working over hours' leading to the 'sense of an over-burdened profession' (Avis et al., 2001, p. 61).

References to the new 'managerialist' culture that followed incorporation have been made in other chapters, and there are clear links between this new culture and the changes in professionalism and in learning, teaching and the curriculum (examined in more detail in Chapter 7). As Robson (1998) puts it, the 'disparate and fragmented cultures of the sector' (p. 597) were, in the years following incorporation, obsessed with business and commercial concerns. A combination of the new funding mechanisms, new management styles and an intensely competitive ethos forced colleges:

> to increase levels of student participation and to improve quality in a market situation in which they compete for students. This was clearly in line with government ideology and thinking with regard to all social services and was based on the belief that in the past the FE sector had been less efficient and effective than it could have been. It was also designed to create a new culture and philosophy in FE colleges.
>
> (pp. 597–8)

Moreover, as Cripps' (2002) analysis of government policy discourse and its impact on different forms of provision demonstrates, the 'theme of derision' (p. 146) was simply constructed by government as a means of attacking all public sector professionalism for the purpose of introducing a marketised and outcome-based audit culture. All of this resulted in a conflict between rival missions and between the 'caring' and the 'market' language codes referred to in the previous chapter. The impact on staff was uneven and highly differentiated, depending on type of college, prevailing ethos, management style, and the degree of resistance to or acceptance of the new marketised climate. Staff in general 'academic' departments still felt that they had a fair degree of autonomy within the new system, whereas 'vocational' lecturers spoke of an obsession with financial targets. Themes and perspectives common to all the colleges resarched by Cripps, however, revealed some common themes: top-down strategic planning, input/ouput targets and an obsession with financial targets and budgets. As one lecturer put it:

> Money is what drives the institution; the government has shifted from seeing education as a public service to education as a product and we have to keep our heads above water financially.
>
> (p. 247)

A broadly similar range of perspectives emerged from the staff interviewed for the FEDA research. Staff who participated in the project (lecturers, support staff, clerical) mostly spoke about feeling part of a community within an FE college. In a postmodern sense some talked about a greater fragmentation and a greater range of communities within institutions since incorporation, with individuals only interacting with a small number of those communities. Their day-to-day life in college is experienced within the cultures of small communities rather than the community of the college as a whole. Life is largely restricted to within the boundaries of departments despite the increase in cross-departmental initiatives:

I think there's a problem because I don't feel that the college is a community. It feels quite fragmented to me. It doesn't feel like a whole college. Every department is fairly separate from the other.

(College lecturer)

Another lecturer felt that she did not have a full picture of life in all areas of the college:

Not enough. I understand certain things because of the staff room I'm in, where different curriculum areas meet – so you can understand a little bit. It's not a big college, but even so there are areas that I've never really been into and I don't know what goes on there. So yes, I do tend to live in my little world. I don't necessarily want it to be that way. There seem to be certain perimeters.

(College lecturer)

As you move up the college hierarchy to middle and senior management the more individuals have an overview of the college community as a whole. The college community is also divided in other ways. Teaching HE in FE now forms a significant part of the curriculum in many colleges, particularly the larger ones. Some of the latter have opted for separating their FE provision from their HE provision both in terms of physical buildings and facilities and teaching staff. Lecturers teach only FE or HE. Managerial, curriculum and administrative meetings are held separately, so the two sides of FE never meet, except at senior management level. In some cases pay and conditions of service are different for those teaching HE compared to those involved in FE work as HE work is given higher status. There is little research to indicate what the attitudes of the two groups of staff are in this situation and whether or not it results in divisions and resentment. Colleges who have a separate HE system argue that it helps to create a better and more realistic HE environment for its students. In effect they are two colleges and communities in one.

FE as outreach

FE outreach centres, are essential sites of learning for adults who may be uncertain learners. However, from the staff perspective those who teach in the community are marginalised (as are students) and isolated from life at the main campus: it is a separate community. Exceptionally a minority of colleges do have strong community links with community education and other agencies with a high proportion of teaching situated in community settings. For outreach staff the knowledge that they are considered peripheral to the institution may not be a problem as they have chosen to teach in such an environment and favour this approach to teaching. However, tutors interviewed in outreach mentioned that college and heads of departments did not always understand or value the work they did. One centre manager stated that 'people (at the main site) tend to treat you like an outsider if you work in outreach – sometimes you feel very much like you are imposing if you walk into an office'. This was even the case in colleges where community outreach is a key strategy. As a result it can also be difficult to persuade lecturers based on the main campus to teach in a centre for a few hours a week. This was a situation which a head of an outreach centre in the Scottish study commonly faced. She felt this reluctance was partly about being in a place which they considered marginal and lower status compared to the main campus but was also tied up with having to change their teaching approaches from didactic to a student-centred one.

Some staff were aware that adult students who attend outreach centres often do not realise that the facility is part of the FE college (see also Chapters 2 and 5). As one member of staff outlines:

> B used to be an old secondary school. It's about a mile and a half away from the main site. Groups like Age Concern meet down there so in many ways B acts as the community centre of the college . . . My impression would be that the local community would view it as a separate provision from the college. They would talk of it as B Community Centre as opposed to the main college.

Senior management interviewed believed that this area of college work would grow in the future influenced by the social inclusion agenda – something that they were in favour of. Outreach centre workers also felt that their working conditions had been affected by incorporation:

> Before incorporation and the merger – I suppose you could say in the good old days – outreach – there was obviously a lot less staff then

and I believe that there was very much a community. We had regular team meetings and there wasn't the pressure that there is now. We had things like fun day at the end of the year. We would see each other socially out of work. I think it was more of a community then than it is now. I think outreach has grown. We have less time to get together. We still have a team meeting once a month but it's often very fraught. There's a lot on the agenda. The meeting finishes at 5.30 pm and everybody is keen to get away and we tend not to see each other socially now. We all knew each other very well and we don't any more. There's a lot of staff in Y that we never see – they don't always go to the meetings and that's sad I think . . . it is sad.

Over the past decade since the 1992 Act, the staff structure and conditions of service have changed significantly and have still not completely stabilised in some colleges. Severing links with LEAs following the Further and Higher Education Act gave institutions and their governors new financial, management and administrative responsibilities. Colleges were asked to produce a mission statement and strategic plans by the FEFC – previously this had been under the control and prerogative of the LEA. The mission statements now reflect the individual colleges' principles and ethos. The mission statements of the 1990s assumed the new language of incorporation: cost-effectiveness, training and customers with some reference to lifelong learning.

Incorporation also brought with it a new type of management, based, like college mission statements, on market principles. Not surprisingly, college staff interviewed for this project talked overwhelmingly about the impact of incorporation and marketisation on their working life. Marketisation of college life together with the new style of management introduced a new working relationship between managers and lecturers: in the early days of incorporation this was occasionally a conflictual one as lecturers resisted the new working conditions being imposed on them. Managers had to adopt a more business-like style to survive the realities of a market economy.

> The greater range of responsibilities of management are primarily that of curriculum and academic leadership towards the managing of quality and funding mechanisms, responding to outside pressures.
>
> (College manager)

In some colleges appointments at senior management level were filled by people from a managerial or industrial background rather than from within FE as their skills were perceived as being more relevant for the changing FE environment. Managers expressed the view that there is now more to manage.

The FEDA project looked at how the management structures had changed over a ten-year period and what this meant for staff in terms of the way they worked. Lecturers and managers who had worked in a particular college for over ten years were asked to describe the management structure before incorporation. Internal documents were also referred to for evidence. Most colleges stressed that the management structure in that era was traditional, formal and hierarchical. One college explained that 'the hierarchical nature of the management structure allowed strict demarcation of budgets, areas of responsibility and centralised control'. Colleges were highly departmentalised with heads of departments playing an active role in the curriculum decision-making process. In contrast to the structure today, 'there was little integration between departments – it was empire building' (college lecturer). Boundaries between departments were broken down as there is now greater inter-departmental, cross-curricular initiatives. Lecturers had to adjust to working with other 'tribes' within their colleges. One person who now works across the curriculum in the area of key skills reflected:

> Now I'm getting to know people who were just names before and actually beginning to know more about other things that go on in other departments . . . I mean if we become very insular within our own department you kind of know what's going on there but you don't really know what's going on across college but I do have some ideas of some of the initiatives that are going on across college now.

Several mentioned that they would like departments to be less isolated and to develop a stronger sense of community to develop within colleges. This they felt was the responsibility of senior management. One person cited the example of a college newsletter as a positive step in this direction, others wanted a common staff room. Opportunities to meet as a whole staff were perceived to be fewer or of a different nature post-1992:

> I know it sounds rather simple but we don't even have now the end of year get together that we used to have and OK that may be a fairly simple thing and quite pathetic but at least that was a time when everybody got together in the courtyard and we had a Bar-b-Q. We moaned and groaned about everything but we all went away for 2–3 weeks holiday and came back and thought 'well that was quite nice'

or 'remember so and so'. At least it got you together at a certain time but now the only time we get together are during staff development weeks when we have to forcibly sit in the library and listen to people like the principal telling us what we've got to do, you will do it in this way . . . I think we've lost a lot in that way.

In working across departments one lecturer became aware of a culture of resistance to change in relation – particularly from older staff – to introducing key skills across the curriculum because he feels lecturers see it as 'something extra to what we originally had to teach'.

Incorporation prompted significant transformations to the staffing structure. The numbers of part-time staff increased dramatically for reasons of cost-effectiveness so that in some colleges part-time staff now outnumber full-time staff. For example, one college in the study employed 600 part-time staff compared to 200 full-time following incorporation. This can bring with it particular problems and issues; communication being one of them as part-time staff generally only attend college for teaching sessions. Often they do not attend department meetings or staff development courses. Only a minority of colleges pay them to attend such events. In many ways their involvement in college life is marginal and, as one college explained, it is difficult to establish a good relationship with part-time staff: 'this (the employment of part-time staff) enables greater flexibility for the college and reduces its fixed costs but we need a good relationship with part-time staff'. Another lecturer elaborated further:

> We have to rely on part-time members of staff which obviously causes a great deal of problems for students who are having perhaps problems with a particular unit or an assignment as they've got to wait until the following week until that lecturer comes in, so that holds up processes. It's also difficult for a Team Leader like myself if you're having meetings. They very often can't make a meeting because they are part-time, they're perhaps working at another college, they don't get funded for coming in for meetings so they only get part involved in the course which is a great shame as you do need the support of every member of the team and it's difficult if they are not there. I think a lot of people in the college tend to be very dissatisfied now because we feel as if we don't have any say in what's going on. We don't know what's going on half the time.

For teaching staff one of the most resented effects of incorporation was the introduction of new employment contracts in 1994. It rapidly became a very divisive issue among staff as some lecturers refused to sign the new contract. At the same time the power of the teaching union NAFTHE was reduced. The new contracts significantly increased and broadened the workload of lecturers both in terms of teaching hours and administration. 'Ten years ago the main duties of a lecturer grade 1 were teaching, taking registers, marking and preparation' (college lecturer). Promotion was viewed as automatic after the appropriate time of teaching. Increased workload, especially in terms of teaching, was felt to have raised levels of stress amongst staff. Other lecturers noted a change in ethos and atmosphere between pre- and post-incorporation. Ainley and Bailey (1997) found similar evidence in their study of lecturers' attitudes and experiences. One lecturer reflected:

> There was a greater buzz around the place, stress was not in people's vocabulary, there were fewer student problems and student retention was not perceived to be a problem.

Other differences were noted, such as increase in administrative duties, having to teach courses in less time and a feeling that there is more work to do, making for a decline in the quality of life and an increase in stress for staff:

> When I first started in the Travel and Tourism, the students were all averaging 29/30 hours on their programmes and you had sort of a three hour slot to deliver a unit. Now we are being pushed further and further to get more and more done in less and less time. So that's the biggest problem . . . We are constantly being pressured to give added extras, added value on top of whatever we are offering on a basic course – simply for funding so there's lots and lots of pressures I feel on tutors . . . You are involved mainly in paper work with teaching as a sideline issue which is a great shame.

Some recognised that marketisation had impacted upon managers as well and that since incorporation they were also working under constraints. The feeling of being pressurised to do more work for less time changed some tutors' attitudes towards undertaking college work at home in the evenings and during holidays:

> I made the decision some time last year. I thought that if I am doing extra hours then I am going to utilise every single solitary hour that I'm here in this college and I make a point now that I do not work at

weekends. I think that's the time for myself and my family and I refuse to do work at weekends. Whereas before I used to take it home, I used to work over the holiday but now I don't – I won't do it. I think they get enough value for money out of you while you are here, never mind impinging on your personal life as well.

The break from LEAs led to increased competition for competing markets. The 1992 Act resulted in greater internal control, isolation and fragmentation of services. Many lecturers viewed the move towards competition for markets and students as a detrimental step, particularly in urban areas where there is often more than one FE college. Occasionally it affected a wider geographical catchment area. One lecturer at a college in a Midlands city stated that his college competed for students from industry in two local towns, one sixteen miles away, the other twenty-two miles and both with FE colleges of their own. Another explained:

I think we'd have a much greater impact if we were working together than working separately . . . it must be quite confusing for (potential) students to have all these people saying, 'Well you should be doing this'. I think that if we adopt an approach where we try and sell things together and do things together, it would be much more successful. All the colleges are trying to get the same students and it is just not working – there's just not enough students out there to go round all the colleges and we're all competing for the same areas. I wondered whether the colleges are putting an awful lot of effort into competing for those cuddly four-to-five GCSE students who are really nice and cause no trouble . . . when if they gathered their efforts together they could have those students who wouldn't normally be so ready to come into colleges.

A head of a department in discussing competition between colleges for students reflected about the past and present:

It is in my opinion a very bad thing [competition]. When I started we weren't allowed to run identical courses within the catchment area of the college and that was very good as it meant that the resources could be sometimes shared and now certainly we can be operating the same courses as X college. We are chasing a limited piece of the market with three times the resources. It really is very, very inefficient. If people had got together right at the start and said 'OK well look Y college the bulk of your work is catering, X college will give you so many students – which it used to be. Now the market is thrown open. I spent three years training lecturers from Y – who came along and actually took all my notes so we're in competition. It is just a game of poker. At the start of the year you just hold onto your hand until somebody folds and then you get those students that enrolled at Y or if we decide to close our course they go to X.

Under LEA control in cities or towns where there is more than one FE college institutions tended to specialise in certain areas to avoid competing against each other. While such colleges have kept their identity in relation to a particular discipline they have also been forced economically to compete against each other in other subject areas such as training for industry. In some areas this has led to mergers between colleges as a means of survival. Lecturers also talked about internal competition for students and a lack of coherence and collaboration across a college both before and after incorporation:

> I can remember going to a careers convention and I was there to try and encourage women returners but there was also somebody else from hairdressing doing the same thing and somebody else from somewhere else doing the same thing and it wasn't co-ordinated at all. You had this department which was meant to be the community education department but all the other departments were trying to do their bit for the community as well and I think it was very much the situation we have now where different departments are vying for the same people.
>
> (Curriculum Project Leader for Key Skills)

Economic pressure was very evident in the college lifeworld of the lecturers we spoke to. Many felt alienated from their work as market forces changed the nature and ethos of what they considered to be fundamental to the role of teaching in FE. Lecturers lamented that teaching was no longer about putting the students' needs first but simply about bringing in money by getting students to complete courses to ensure that funding is received. As one learning resources administrator explained:

> Ultimately it still comes down to money and hard economic realities – a sort of 'how can we get these people to learn what we want them to learn at the cheapest possible cost' and 'which corners can we cut?' . . . I do worry about that a bit really.

The focus on economic effectiveness concerns all aspects of college life, not only teaching departments. A library manager at one college explained that previously different types of libraries worked co-operatively with each other. Now:

> We have to be very accountable for everything that we do both in terms of staff development and training . . . where we're going . . . evaluating the service that we're offering people, making sure that we are targeting their needs and meeting it in the most effective way we can.

Some stated that they were no longer able to sustain offering programmes for marginalised learners or community groups as they are not profitable. For this group of staff economic rather than pedagogical and equity issues dominated their life as an FE lecturer, undermining their professional identity:

> The big change has been the fact that we're so market driven now. If you create a market, that's not going to promote a community . . . the market has been here for quite a while now but it's more emphasised in further education. If you are driven merely by market forces you're not going to create the same type of community. The staff are not going to feel the same way about the role that they have. If they don't deliver the market will gobble them up and a lot of people do feel that way that there's too much of a competitive edge emerged rather than honing people to improving them and ensuring that they deliver quality. They could actually end up doing the reverse. I personally think that they've become totally money-orientated, which is understandable. They're now in business and they have to make a profit. The profit side is now all-important, to the loss of the students. Years ago the most important thing in the college was the students and I think they've lost it. They think the student – getting a student through the course – is all-important now only because they get money for it whereas years ago there was some kudos in getting a student qualified and through a course.
>
> (College lecturer)

Another lecturer explained that when he first started lecturing he worked in a Department of Community Education but this did not survive in the new FE world:

To me it's changed an awful lot because when I came in there was a whole department there for community education and we worked with schools, there were Saturday workshops for children to come in and all those things went. All the things we perhaps didn't get much money for and I think a lot of the change is the fact of incorporation in having to raise a lot of our income, or a lot more of the income than we used to have to raise. There's a lot of things that went because they didn't produce much profit or any profit.

The move towards marketisation and the change in working conditions undermined the morale of many staff and their willingness to work proactively with groups in the local communities:

A lot of things have changed since incorporation and since contracts have changed. I think that to get out into the community then we need to go during unsociable hours to access different groups of people. Staff have been very much more unwilling to do that sort of thing since changing the contracts. They say: 'Well, I've done this,' and 'I'm not going up to such and such to do this'. I think that this has had a big effect. Staff are not so willing to make those links because it is something extra; they have to find the extra time to do it. I think that the college has to do a lot to change relations within the college with its staff before they can actually make big steps into the community because we need co-operation within the college for us to be able to go out and do that.

Another lecturer felt that staff were previously 'more devoted to that sort of thing'. With long teaching hours there is little space left for community development type work yet it is essential for attracting marginal, non-traditional learners into FE. Several lecturers we interviewed made a plea for senior management to provide them with more time to address what they saw as a priority; reaching out into the community. Many interviewees stated that they would like to work more with the socially excluded, but feel constrained by the need to bring money into the college. Powerless, low income groups cannot offer this. Barrow (1991), in fact, predicted this scenario in speculating that:

The Act may increase the preponderance of full-cost courses at the expense of the less financially attractive, with management perhaps concentrating their energies on the development of full-cost courses rather than seeking to meet minority needs.

(p. 124)

The social inclusion and widening participation policy agenda is helping to counter this, especially in areas where there is special funding available (Thomas, 2001). Incorporation has resulted in colleges re-organising the institutional structure – in some cases more than once. Often this was carried out with minimal consultation with teaching staff. Some lecturers despised the fact that they were suddenly told that they were no longer teaching X but Y together with an increase in teaching hours with little time left for preparation. One lecturer, for example, who teaches on a degree programme for non-traditional adults, recalled how in the past he was given time during the summer period to talk to people in community centres, local shopping centres and other places to encourage adults back into education and was successful in achieving this. In recent years his teaching load has increased significantly and, as he is no longer given time to go out into the community, he no longer carries out this role. Recruitment is now viewed as being the preserve of the marketing department only and as a result of these changes the number of adult students entering the degree programme has declined dramatically.

The economic realities of competition in the post-1992 Act era has meant that some colleges, particularly the smaller ones, have had to merge with other colleges perhaps in a nearby town. One of the colleges in our study merged with a smaller college situated in a town about ten miles away. Historically there have been divisions between people in the two towns. There was resentment by local people at being taken over by the larger college as the two communities see themselves as being separate. When colleges merge, the community of the college itself is changed. In many ways the structure becomes more impersonal as a library manager located at one of the smaller sites explains:

I think when we were a single site I knew more of the teaching staff . . . now staff work across both sites. A lot of staff will return to their main site rather than using the support facilities on a site they may be visiting so I'm aware of the names of teaching staff who are running some courses or options on courses but I don't know them personally. In the past I would have gone out and found those staff but it becomes more difficult when you've got more sites to actually know people face to face.

Talking about students

Colleges consist of two student communities in terms of time; a day time community and an evening one. As a library manager observed:

> I often find that evening students are unaware of the culture of the day time students and vice versa. Many day time students are totally unaware and taken aback when they find the car park is full to brimming in the evenings . . . obviously they're people who are at work in the day and they're a different type of student but the two communities are really quite ignorant of each other . . . maybe there's something we could build on.

Several lecturers talked about increasing behavioural problems among the 16–19 year old group who now have to attend some form of education and training as a result of government initiatives such as New Deal. One lecturer described his experiences:

> With my course this year three particular students – not coping with the work and because they can't cope with the work then behavioural problems come out. You have them storming out of class and very immature behaviour which then reflects on the other students. Really it can cause quite a lot of difficulties . . . I think a lot of the problems stem from when the Benefit rule changed and that you have this group of 16–18 year olds who really do not want to be in education and they have to do some sort of training or full-time education to progress.

Mature students were viewed in a much more positive light as they are assumed to be committed and want to progress. However, many lecturers were concerned about government policy which advocates lifelong learning without financial support. They were also aware that many students, like university students, are now taking on part-time jobs for financial reasons. One lecturer, although critical of the financial situation of students, felt it also offered an opportunity for providing local HE in FE provision but was aware that the college would have to be careful to avoid competition with local universities as he felt that 'the universities have the ability to crush us without mercy if we touch on their well established territory'.

Support staff in colleges have links with students, but this aspect is rarely looked at in research. One librarian explained how she views it as her role to help students with their work when they are in the library yet students find it difficult to grasp that staff are there to help them with their learning. She would like to see the divisions between teaching and support staff ended:

> We try to communicate with the teaching staff about the needs of individual students because it's in our best interests to know why a student is working in the library – what we can do to help them. If they are causing problems we need to perhaps alert the tutor and things like that. Students never seem to think of us in the same terms as they think of teaching staff and I would like to try and alter that perception of the support staff ability so that students wouldn't see different groups – they would just see everybody as helping them in different ways.
>
> (Librarian)

Summary

In comparing pre- and post-incorporation institutions, the majority of staff, both teaching and non-teaching, believed that life had been better before the 1992 Act, a finding which is echoed in other research on the sector (Ainley and Bailey, 1997; Cripps, 2002). While some of this may be the result of a romanticised collective memory rather than reality, it clearly shapes the attitudes, culture and behaviour of FE staff today. Ten years on, much of the disquiet and opposition has acquiesced but underneath the surface there is still some resistance to the new working conditions and the marketisation of education. The lecturing community, however, feels that it is largely powerless and has been undermined as a profession with little control over working lives and conditions in colleges:

> Life as a lecturer is now felt to be driven by values that espouse competitiveness, individualism and marketisation in a culture wanting more of its labour force . . . With increasing workloads, teaching and administration, staff feel that they no longer have time for extra-curricular work, particularly making contacts with the local community. Discontent with and conflict over working conditions have been redirected from the LEA to internal senior management, who are perceived by staff as having internalised the values and practice of new managerialism. While communication has improved between departments/faculties, the dominant management structure

remains hierarchical; incorporation does not appear to have resulted
in a democratisation of the college community.

(Merrill *et al.*, 2000, p. 48)

Only a minority of participants in our study were at all positive about
life after the 1992 Act and incorporation. For some, although there is
increased workload, they feel that colleges are now livelier places and
that market forces have focused lecturers' activities on ensuring that
students remain on courses and pass qualifications:

> There's been a great change in the culture overall. Quite positive in
> the sense that every student that comes through these doors, we've
> got to make sure that they achieve something by the time they leave
> and that's focused people's energies and minds very considerably.
> There may, though, be a tendency to become overwrought where
> everybody is just reacting to everything and there's not much time to
> be reflective. However, the college is growing. The results are
> improving and so we all have to say on balance there's been more
> positive than there has been negative.
>
> (College lecturer)
>
> I think the role of FE colleges is growing. It's more important than
> it ever was . . . we've grown outwards to sort of fill needs – more
> than any other sector has. Schools can't really . . . and we're catering
> for everybody else. I think we try pretty hard. I don't think we always
> get it right all of the time. I think there's people who walk in and
> walk out again.
>
> (College lecturer)

Widening participation, social inclusion and lifelong learning policy
initiatives have enabled colleges to recapture some space to work
with marginalised learners as well as expanding, significantly in some
colleges, their HE community. Whether all of this has been converted
into stronger links between FE institutions and the communities they
serve – translating economic into social capital (Hyland, 2002) – is
examined in greater depth in the next chapter.

Chapter 5

Colleges and students

Discussing students' experiences of FE is complex as the FE student body is not homogeneous: it is diversifying and changing. What little research has been undertaken tends to focus on a specific age group such as post-16 (Bloomer and Hodkinson, 1997, Bates and Riseborough, 1993, Furlong, 1992); young adults (Harkin *et al.*, 2001); or mature adults (Gallacher *et al.*, 2000). A minority of studies cut across both age groups (Ainley and Bailey, 1997; Green and Lucas, 1999d) or include FE students as part of a wider study (West, 1996). As mentioned in earlier chapters, the traditional image of FE college students as mostly white, working-class youths taking apprenticeship courses, is no longer true although this image remains today in people's consciousness. Adults now constitute a significant proportion of college students to the extent that they can be described as an adult college rather than a young person's college. College students are a microcosm of society as a whole in that all groups of people (post-16) are reflected in the student population. Relationships between colleges and its students have changed as a result of incorporation. The new language of marketisation means that students have become transformed into clients or customers with a more contractual type relationship. At the same time, students as fee payers are expecting more in terms of facilities, quality and standards.

This chapter offers an insight into the student world of FE with the caveat that it looks at several different groups of students and, therefore, is more of a snapshot offering a particular perspective and a flavour of student life in FE. It is also important to remember that similar groups of students, for example, adults on degree courses, may have different student experiences as colleges vary tremendously by ethos, structure, practice and policies. Interviews and, in recent years, life history/ biographical interviews are increasingly the favoured research methods employed for understanding the student experience (Gallacher *et al.*,

2000, Bloomer and Hodkinson, 1997, West, 1996) as they provide more depth than questionnaires and give the participant subjectivity by placing her/him at the centre of the research process. Participants are able to reflect upon, interpret, give meaning to and construct past events and experiences within a social context; it is their voices that are heard. As Denzin (1989) explains: 'People live lives with meaning, interpretative biography provides a method which looks at how subjects give subjective meaning to their life experiences' (p. 14). Life histories are particularly valuable in looking at why adults decide to return to learn in FE as they connect past, present and future lives. As Reinharz (1992) stresses: 'Interviewing offers researchers access to people's ideas, thoughts and memories in their own words rather than in the words of the researcher' (p. 19). Although focused on individuals, such approaches illustrate shared life experiences among groups of learners in relation to initial schooling, family life and work, as a result of class, gender and/or race, for example, as well as the interaction between agency and structure. The life history approach was used in the Scottish study. Adult learners' and non-participants' attitudes towards and experiences of (or not) were strongly shaped by both class and gender and the socio-economic context of, for many, disadvantaged urban and rural areas.

Conceptual developments

Recent conceptual developments in understanding learners' experiences and trajectories in FE includes the use of 'learning careers', initially by Bloomer and Hodkinson (1997) in their study of young people entering FE, and Gallacher *et al.* (2000) in relation to adult returners and non-participants in FE. Historically the concept of career in the sociological sense can be traced back to the Chicago School and symbolic interactionists who used the concept of career to a range of social contexts such as deviance (Becker, Shaw), work organisations (Hughes), educational institutions (Becker) and the mentally ill (Goffman). Hughes (1937) defined career in the following way:

> A career consists, objectively, of a series of statuses and clearly defined offices . . . subjectively, a career is the moving perspective in which the person sees his life as a whole and interprets the meaning of his various attributes, actions, and the things that happen to him . . . Careers in our society are thought of very much in terms of jobs . . . But the career is by no means exhausted in a series of business and professional achievements. There are other points at

which one's life touches the social order . . . it is possible to have a career in an avocation as well as in a vocation.

(p. 413)

Symbolic interactionists, therefore, broadened the use of career 'to refer to any social strand of any person's course through life' (Goffman, 1961, p. 119). For Goffman, career is closely tied to ideas of role and identity, thus linking social interaction and the reproduction of social structures. This connects career to a person's biography as career implies a sequence of changes in a person's self and life history. It makes visible the interaction between structure and agency, the private and public spheres and subjectivity and objectivity through the biography of a learner. For Goffman, these transitions mark a changing point in the way a person views the self and social world. He argues that the 'the value of the concept of career is its two-sidedness as the concept of career, then, allows one to move back and forth between the personal and the public, between the self and its significant society' (1961, p. 119).

In applying the concept to young people making the transition from school to FE, Bloomer and Hodkinson (2000) define the learning career as:

A career of events and meanings, and the making and remaking of meanings through these activities and events, and it is a career of relationships and the constant making and remaking of relationships, including relationships between position and disposition.

(p. 590)

Bloomer and Hodkinson focus almost entirely on the role of agency in shaping learning careers, while Crossan *et al.* (2003) argue:

for a model of learning careers that acknowledges the objective socio-economic positions in which actors are located. For us, the concept of learning career is used to shed light on the complex interplay between the social and economic structures which shape people's lives, the educational institutions which determine the processes of engagement with learning, and the learners themselves.

(2003, forthcoming)

A learning career does not have to be linear in pattern. For many adult learners, who may initially be uncertain about returning to learn for example, their biographies illustrate a discontinuous attachment to learning. In engaging in learning, both young people and adults in FE frequently undergo transitions and transformations in their life as a result of the learning process. In this situation the concept of 'learning biography' is also appropriate.

Young people and FE

Students (both young people and adults) hear about courses at colleges in a variety of ways: open days, schools, careers officers, word of mouth from friends or relatives and media publicity. Some young people ended up in FE through choice, others because parents or employers sent them or through a youth training scheme. It was often viewed as a better option to being in a low paid job or staying on at school. Several, when asked why they had opted for college at the age of 16, rationalised it by saying that they 'wanted a better education' and a better job:

> You've got more of a chance of getting what job you want if you've got good qualifications to back you up.

> But I need the money – I still need the money, but I'm just getting qualifications to get a job that will give me a bit more money.

One person felt there was no choice if you wanted a good job – almost in a coercive way: 'You're forced to be here in the sense that come here or not get such a good job'. The young men in this group of GNVQ students admitted that some of their peers at school did not share these attitudes and in a male, macho way had ridiculed them for continuing with their education:

> I haven't seen them. Well it's different actually. At the start they thought it was a joke – like they said 'what are you doing now?' 'I'm at college' and this led to some male bantering. Now they sort of realise as they have got really boring, uninteresting jobs. If they had a few more qualifications they could have put themselves to good use because they've got brain power they're just lazy . . . and you think 'well I don't like the idea I want to get somewhere'.

Others were persuaded to go by friends already at college:

> My mate is doing the NC and he told me about it. He told me you got paid and that, and I thought 'not bad', getting paid to go to college and I know another couple of folk that are coming.

Like those in Bloomer and Hodkinson's (1997) research, many young people in this study had little notion of what FE would be like or what to expect, but all assumed that it would be better than school. In comparing college to school all the 16–19 year olds shared a consensus regardless of whether they were students with learning difficulties, taking GNVQs or A-levels. College for them was a place that treated them as adults with fewer imposed rules and regulations, giving more freedom. Once the compulsory element of learning was removed studying became 'OK' as it was perceived differently, that is, learning was about achieving their own goals and not those of teachers. As one A-level student remarked: 'You're doing it for yourself'. Others similarly stated that:

> Because at school you think, 'Oh I don't really bother about the work' and then you come to college and it suddenly becomes important to you in your work.

> You haven't got the pressure on you to do the work. If you haven't finished it – tough. It goes against you at the end of the year.

Relationships with tutors were valued for being more informal and friendly: 'You don't have to call them sir or miss'; or 'We're sort of like first names which is actually better'. Tutors, they feel, in colleges 'Do not talk down to them'. Those taking A-levels had made a conscious decision that they did not want to stay on at school for further study but the choice of which FE college to attend was often made pragmatically. Frequently it was because it was the nearest one geographically rather than for the type of course or reputation of the college even in areas where there are a choice of colleges: 'I just knew that I wanted to do A-levels and I didn't want to stay on at school and so like this was the nearest college'. School for many was viewed as a negative experience, described as 'horrible' by many participants. Being pragmatic about which FE college to go to was common among all the groups of young people interviewed. School was viewed as a place where freedom was taken away from the self – almost equated to being a prison:

> You can't go out of the school property and you have to stay in school unless you have permission whereas at college you can go when you want to.

In contrast: 'I was allowed to do more things at college and if I wanted a fag we didn't have to hide round the back of a block'. Another participant continued: 'The doors open and you're locked in from 9.00 am until sort of 3.30 pm at school aren't you?'; with another participant concluding: 'You're here of your own free will. You don't have to go to classes. You choose to'. Being different to school and being treated like an adult were viewed as very important factors by all participants. Comparing school to college formed a dominant part of the interviews. A-level students felt that college was good preparation for university as it acts as a stepping stone.

A minority mentioned that family members had taken courses at the same FE college and that this had also been a positive factor for choosing FE rather than staying on at school. The competition for students between schools and colleges was revealed by the A-level students as all except one stated that their school did not provide them with any information about studying at local colleges and actively tried to discourage individuals from leaving to take A-levels elsewhere. A few reported that teachers at school had told them 'that they (colleges) don't care for you the way that school does'.

Some found the transition from school to college daunting and saw it as a 'big step' as the atmosphere is totally different to school:

> When I first started here I was quite apprehensive because it was like huge but there was a sort of release as well because I just hated school so much that to be treated like a human being here was just really you know so different. I really started enjoying it but the size of it and all the people around was pretty scary at first.
>
> (A-level student)

One BTEC student, however, described his college as 'being a bit dead' while another thought 'it was how I expected it to be'. A group of young people with learning difficulties had welcomed the opportunity of attending an induction day to help them cope with a new institution and thus making them feel comfortable with it:

> I think it was having all the lecturers and tutors coming to you and explaining what was happening, what was going to happen and saying that if there's any troubles come to us and we'll chat about it. And being shown round the college and feeling happy about where you're going to be for two years.

A-level students also appreciated the induction day as they thought it 'broke the ice'. Another continued: 'Yes even if it was like – it seemed a bit silly at the time but it was a good idea. I think it was just the way it was done.' Some tutors were commended for their strategies of helping to overcome a new environment:

> . . . he was when we had GCSEs he was a really, really good teacher. As soon as we got in there we all . . . sitting there and nobody knew each other at all and he just had us going into big groups and chatting to each other and by the end of the day we were all talking but that was good but it really was nerve wracking.

Several of the students revealed that, as is often the case with adults, they support each other with their learning: 'Yes, because if people are away it's like, "Can I borrow your notes?". You don't hear anyone saying, "Oh no, you can't have my notes"'. The A-level group also talked about helping another if they became stressed about exams. All were aware of the learning support facilities in the colleges but some groups did not use them for fear of being stigmatised:

> We had assessments at the beginning of the year on how our skills were and a lot of people needed to go to learning support but no one bothered. They thought it was a joke. Everyone was going, 'I'm not going to Learning Support' because we had a lad last year who wasn't that clever and he went and it did a lot for him but because of that they all thought, 'No, it's just for people who are thick really'. They wouldn't go and it must have been about half our group.

Many found the amount and level of work demanding although this is not the image that their friends in school have:

> College isn't easy. It's hard work most of the time. It's like most of my friends at school they think college is a laugh. It isn't – it's a lot of hard work.
>
> (GNVQ student)

The students' identity with a college is largely confined to their teaching groups/mode of study rather than the college as a whole. The college community and territory for them is limited as there was little evidence that, for example, A-level students mixed socially with GNVQ or any other student groups:

> I think our courses are really far apart and like if you're doing A-levels on a course you probably won't ever really speak to the people

who are doing other courses . . . unless you knew them before you
went you won't ever really get to know others as there's so many
more people here.

Others talked about the anonymity of a college:

> You walk around the whole college and you wouldn't know –
> you don't know the teachers or nothing – usually when you walk
> round in school to get to your lesson – everyone is there teachers,
> everybody just stands there talking. Here you don't feel like part of
> . . . it's so big and there's so many other things going on.

The college principal was perceived as a distant figure. Frequently the
only time that students met the principal was at an induction day.

Many students complained about the financial hardships of being
a student and several admitted to taking on part-time jobs although
they recognised that this affected their studying. Students at one college
pointed out that they had to pay registration fees and pay for trips or
equipment and materials essential for their courses and for some this
caused financial difficulties. The lack of finance was a problem for several
young people in the Scottish study and their plight illustrates the government's contradictions in its lifelong learning and social inclusion policies.
One young male described why he had to leave a Skillseekers course (a
programme initiated by New Labour for young people lacking skills and
qualifications):

> The Skillseekers thing was really difficult to live on (£40 a week plus
> fares). I think I would like to go back at some point, but the money
> would need to change before I did.

Some young people have left parents to live on their own and, for this
group, financing study is hard. As one participant remarked:

> I know someone who doesn't live with her parents and she has to
> work quite a bit to come to college. She works and she's doing A-
> levels and it is very stressing to her because I've noticed the change
> from when she went to school till now. She always says that going to
> college is very hard because people don't realise.

Financial problems were cited as a key reason by fellow students as
to why some people left a GNVQ course.

One A-level student disliked the way that college expected A-level students to aspire to university as their learning goal and felt that as a result her needs were not being met:

Doing A-levels you're sort of geared very much – everyone's hassling you to go to university but I don't want to go to university and I felt really left out because everyone else is going to these meetings and there's none for people like me who just want to work. They completely ignore us. It's like you're a second class citizen.

On the whole, participants were satisfied with the standard and quality of teaching. One group (GNVQ Advanced Health and Social Care) admitted that they had had problems with one tutor so collectively they took action by writing to the Head of School to complain about the standard of teaching. A new teacher was appointed and they were able to catch up with the work they had missed. The same group felt that the pace of a GNVQ course is fast and demanding but they did feel that they had learnt to organise their time for studying better by the end of the year. Another tutor's teaching style was criticised as they felt she 'pushed' them into working which they had not expected at an FE college although one person felt such an approach made them work. Those over the age of 18 also complained about reports on their work achievements being mailed to their parents. They felt that at that age the reports should be given direct to them. The GNVQ group perceived themselves as hard-working students while others were not viewed as serious students:

. . . because I think a lot of people up in the bigger blocks, they're not there to actually do the work, they're just here to socialise. They'll come in and they won't do anything all day. They'll just sit in the community lounge or they'll go over to the pub and just sit there all day and come back for the end of the day and then go home just because that's what their parents want them to do.

Participants in both studies were committed to completing their courses, largely to equip themselves with better opportunities on the labour market:

If you have no qualifications then they are going to think, well if somebody else comes along and they have got qualifications they are going to take somebody on who has qualifications. So that is why going to college is pretty important, and to finish your course.

In discussing the idea of community and FE the group felt that: 'Within the college you get your own little communities, that's the way it is'. Certain groups occupied particular spaces and territory around a college. Some found particular groups, mostly male, intimidating and no longer entered their spaces such as the Students' Union. Territory was staked out according to gender and race:

> A certain group of people separated themselves off in the Students' Union . . . Basically it's white people on one side and Asian people on the other side. That's the only way to put it and it's horrible I hate it . . . I feel really intimidated in there . . . but it's intimidating when you've got big gangs of people hanging around outside . . . because it's kind of their area . . . if you are having a game of pool they just stand there looking . . . sort of saying 'get off because I want a game'.

Instead they preferred to spend time in the community lounge as 'it's mainly mature students' and 'no one bothers you there'. Participants with learning difficulties on a bridging course initially found another area of a college, the canteen, off-putting until they gained confidence collectively. For this group of learners non-teaching staff play a vital role in helping them cope with the institution:

> . . . it's big (canteen), it's quite noisy. When I first came here I was really scared and I didn't want to go in there but now I go with my friends and I found that the staff are really friendly and they help you.

Reception staff were also described as being 'really nice and polite' and helpful. One participant with learning difficulties elaborated: 'They are friendly and comforting. When somebody is upset they'll stay with them until another member of staff comes and helps'.

Several participants offered ideas for improving college life. On the whole they were satisfied with the learning resources provided such as the library and IT rooms. What many wanted was a brighter environment such as pictures on the walls and bright colours, as well as in one college a common room for relaxing and talking to friends: 'They need to jazz up the rooms because this room has breeze blocks. It's very cold'.

Participants were asked whether or not their parents took an active involvement in their education. Most replied negatively: 'They don't really care'; and 'I just think I can do what I like with my life and they never check it out – they don't really care'. In contrast one BTEC student stated:

My parents give me a lot of support because they always want to know what I'm doing at college and stuff and I think it's really good. They give me loads of support.

Learning in FE was viewed as an enjoyable experience by the young people in both two studies as it had turned negative experiences towards learning received in school into positive ones. An FE environment enabled them to develop the self and their identity by treating them in a respectful and adult manner – something they felt they did not experience in school – and this has been identified as a key element in the development of learning in mainstream post-school studies (Hodkinson *et al.*, 1996; Harkin *et al.*, 2001). College had further developed their learning career by increasing their confidence in their learning abilities and enabling them to see the value of learning. Several stated that they wanted to continue with their education at a higher level. For example, GNVQ students, like the A-level students, were hoping to go to university and had career plans in mind for after they leave university such as becoming a social worker, nurse or a psychiatric nurse. Others, taking the BTEC Diploma in Health Science, had aspirations to study to become a nurse. However, they felt that they were at a disadvantage in applying to universities as A-levels continue to be seen as the gold standard:

If you take A-levels it is easier to get into university. BTEC doesn't seem to – you can show it to people – but it doesn't seem to be as good as A-levels. It's getting more recognised but they'll still say A-levels or the equivalent but they still probably just look at A-levels.

The bridging to FE group (moderate learning difficulties) were mostly hoping to continue in FE on a further course or opt for Training for Work which would involve one day at college. This choice was largely due to parental pressure as Ainley and Bailey (1997) also found:

She (his mother) said you're not going to be sitting around the house all day. I'm going to kick you out of the front door and find myself a job.

Another added: 'That's the exact words my mum said if I don't get on this third year. She'll wake me up and beat me out the door.'

FE for many young students offers a bridge and a space for transition and change between the world of school and employment, further study or higher education and between adolescence and adulthood. It is a period for establishing a self-identity/ties in the public world. As Bloomer and Hodkinson (1997: 79) elaborate: 'For those entering FE from school, it is a period of maturation, of unfolding and developing personal identity, transformation and change'.

The adult learners' world in FE

FE has now become a key educational sector offering a range of programmes at all levels for adults wanting to participate in learning, following government lifelong learning policies locating colleges as the main provider (see other chapters). In some colleges adults are now the dominant student group. Why adults choose to return to learn is often the result of a number of complex interacting factors (West, 1996; Merrill, 1999; Gallacher et al., 2000) as the following quote illustrates:

> With me it was a friend I'd met at the school and she'd just started on the course (Access to nursing) in September and she was telling me all about it and my little boy started full-time now. I had nothing else to do and I thought 'well yes I'll start at college' and then I came along to see what there was available and it's convenient to me because I live just round the corner.

Both studies revealed that very few adults consciously plan out a learning career, something they have in common with the 'non-linear' patterns of their younger FE counterparts (Hodkinson et al., 1996). More commonly, something happens in their life, a 'turning point moment' (Glaser and Strauss, 1971) or a critical incident, such as divorce or unemployment, that makes them consider returning to learn. In these situations the influence of a friend, ('word of mouth') or a significant other, or a leaflet through the door are often also critical factors (Bond and Merrill, 1999). Education is perceived as a possibility and even a solution to personal problems and issues. Significant others were influential in the case of several Access students:

> Well, I was in hospital last year and I got talking to a male nurse and he was on the Access a few years ago and he's done really well and I just phoned up for an application form. I came for the interview and that . . . It was the only college that was doing the Access to Nursing anyway.

For many women returning to learn offers a chance for self-development following time spent in the home childrearing; FE provides an opportunity to move out of the private world and into the public one. For others the prospect of improving employment opportunities or careers is an important underlying reason:

> I don't want to be left on my own not doing anything. I don't know about anybody else but I watched my mum dedicate her life to us and now that we're all grown up she's just got nothing. She's looking around and thinking, 'Oh what can I do now?' I've always wanted to be a hairdresser so I'm doing this.
>
> (NVQ student)

Another female student added to this: 'It's getting your identity back as well though, isn't it?'. For some women returning to learn was about re-training in a new field of employment that would give them greater flexibility to organise working around a domestic life. Negative experiences of school make many adults hesitant to return as FE is viewed as being the same as school. Many were unaware, until they talked to friends or careers officers, of the existence of the Access route as a means for entering university.

Adults returning to learn frequently have doubts about their ability to study (West, 1996, Gallacher *et al.*, 2000), yet want to learn to make up for the education they missed when they were young, either because of the inequalities in the education system and/or having to leave school early because of cultural factors such as class and gender:

> I lost my husband five years ago and my children were a bit younger then. Now my youngest is 15 and the others are all in their 20s . . . so now I've got a little bit more freedom but I'd lost my confidence so much. I never had a good education and I felt perhaps . . . I went on the Foundation course thinking I'll go but I'll start at the bottom and I'll see how I do I thought I haven't got much confidence.

As the research by Thomas (2001) has emphasised, FE courses designed to address the low aspirations and motivation of traditional non-participants aim 'to change attitudes and cultures (towards learning), rather than to acknowledge difference' (p. 131). In this respect, FE's traditional adult education function of providing leisure courses for adults still has a role to play:

> . . . a mixture of both leisure/pleasure in so far as I'm interested in computers but in my position at an archery club it helps me to help

them with various parts of the office work that goes with it in my job
– I'm a retired headteacher.

(Desktop publishing course)

Several of the men interviewed in the Scottish study were in their 40s
and 50s, unemployed, some of them long term. A realisation that the
labour market had changed led them to return in order to learn how to
gain new skills and qualifications:

I wanted to learn this (computing) so that I could get it on my CV.
A lot of the jobs I went for – the application forms for Sainsbury's
and B & Q when I've applied for jobs – they all have a wee bit on
them 'Do you have any computer or keyboarding skills? So that's
why I've done this course.

The men, however, were also realistic about what the courses could do
for them as they knew the courses were low level. Several, although they
attended a computing course, were largely resigned to the fact that
they may never obtain paid employment again. Men were pessimistic (or
more realistic?) in relation to employment, while women were optimistic
about using learning to gain better employment after years of domesticity
as they were determined to enhance their career, gain economic independence and find a space for themselves. Many adults in both studies
wanted to re-enter education but at the same time were not confident
about their learning abilities.

Suffering from a lack of confidence in their abilities to study in FE (a
common factor in this sphere which is now being addressed by the DfES,
2002d, in a major adult education drive to expand learning) also extends
to other areas of becoming a student such as asking for information, filling
in an application form, arriving on the first day of term, and course work.
Advice by colleges would have been welcomed in relation to completing
application forms:

I just came in and asked about the Access to nursing course and I was
handed an application form which I had to fill out. I mean nobody
explained to me how to fill it out. I know that sounds very stupid but
they didn't actually show me how and I wasn't aware about the letter
that you had to write in explaining why you wanted to be a nurse and
it was like an essay because they required 200 plus words and to sit
down and be able to write those kind of words when you've been out
of school for quite a few years, it's a bit difficult to do. So it would

be handy if there was somebody there that could give you a bit more advice as opposed to just handing you an application form and saying, 'Well there you go, fill it out and bring it back'.

Outreach centres were better at welcoming and encouraging nervous, potential students:

> The girl at the time who was organising reception – she was really nice – down to earth and I said I don't know if I can do it and she says don't be silly – you are putting yourself down. She just sat and spoke to me. Come and try it. Then I would think, should I or should I not and then they had an open night and I came.

Initial contact and the manner in which a potential student is received can be a deciding factor as to whether or not someone actually makes it through the doors. Making it through the doors of an FE college on the first day of term is a big and daunting step for many:

> It's nerve-wracking walking through those doors for the first time. I walked through the door and thought, 'What the hell am I doing here?' You know, 'Why am I here?' I was petrified – like when we first started the course I was absolutely petrified and right through for the first six weeks. I couldn't settle down at first and then I started to settle down.
>
> (Access student)

One person stated that there were 'hoards and hoards of people' and suggested that it would have been helpful if the college had had people acting as guides to help them find the right rooms. Adult learners are conscious of the age differences in FE, making them feel out of place:

> I was nervous coming in the first time because they had all these trendy youngsters in a lot of up-to-date stuff on and everything and you're thinking, 'Oh gosh, I feel so old'.

Induction days/sessions are a common way of familiarising learners with an institution. There were mixed feelings about the usefulness of induction days. For some they were very good while others described them as silly, childish games. Most adjusted quickly to life in FE and looked forward to going, not only for educational reasons, as one woman described it:

I mean to me to come in here – it's my release. I come in here
especially on a Monday morning . . . I've got the kids off to school,
my husband is off to work and I come in and think 'Oh bliss'.

Many participants in the Scottish study did not have the confidence to
cross the boundary into an FE college. A college campus was viewed as
being too large, too formal, alien and was assumed to be 'not for them'
in contrast to the informality and friendliness of an outreach centre:

> It's a lot more informal for a start. You can come in any time, any
> day, even though it's different modules on different days. If some-
> body has a wee part-time job and they can't manage the morning,
> they can come in the afternoon. You couldn't do that up the road (the
> main campus). They probably have set programmes for set days and
> that would be you.

Others have doubts about participation at an FE college which are
associated with age:

> If I had somebody my age that I knew was going to college at
> the same time I would go with them tomorrow. There's a barrier
> there that I just don't want to go in. Just walking in the first day and
> people sitting there. I'm funny that way. I can walk into this place
> (community learning centre) and talk to everybody, even people that
> I don't know. It's because I'm too set in my ways. If I walked into
> college – I don't know anybody. I would say to myself 'I feel like a
> stupid wee school lassie with no friends'. My daughter says it's not
> like that, 'you'll meet someone'.

Community provision provides a non-threatening learning environment for people who lack confidence in their learning ability. The
availability of community-based FE provision enabled many respondents
to make the transition into learning as smaller-scale, more informal
learning is a more welcoming environment. All were positive about their
learning experiences in outreach centres and it was clear that without
such provision they would not have taken the first step back into learning.
However, there is evidence from the Scottish research that such centres
can become too cosy and tutors overprotective so that learners do not
want to leave and progress to other institutions. Only a minority moved
on to courses at the main campus, but in comparing the two one learner
stated:

I like the way it's informal, not like the main campus. It's an official place. It's like going into a big office, a big building. When I first went I would go to the wrong place and they would say, 'You can't come here and you can't go there' . . . because you get a wee plastic card and I do two or three hours a month and they tick it, copy it and sometimes I forget to take my card and they come after you hounding you.

(Male, new entrant)

Like the younger students the college principal was regarded as a remote person – someone who had minimal contact with students:

We had this meeting with the principal. 'I am Dr X', and the first and only time we've ever seen him. He told us the mature students hang out in the community lounge and the younger students in the refectory and that was it then'.

(Access student)

Adults liked the availability of taster courses but were not always rational in their reasons for choosing particular options:

You sit there and think 'Wow, that sounds good but if nobody else is going to do it then you wouldn't do it either'. Because you didn't want to be on your own so really you went – you chose what the majority were going to do.

Many of the Access students were already launched on a learning career as they had attended a college previously either to take a pre-access course or GCSEs or A-levels. They were hoping that the Access course would take them on to the next stage in their learning career into higher education.

Participants were asked a range of questions about their learning experiences, support and attitudes towards tutors and the resources provided. Adjusting to being a student and studying as an adult is not always easy, such as learning an academic language. If tutors are not clear and supportive in their teaching adult learners will soon drop out. A group of Access students pointed out some of the issues they faced:

In the first couple of weeks you're really eager and you want to do really well. I think it's when the October break came – it was hard to come back afterwards. After that it was hard as the work started coming in then. There were so many of us to start with. Thirty of us started. Now there's twelve that actually continued throughout. The first day that little room was packed and there weren't enough chairs and I think it frightened a lot of people especially if you've never done any further education whatsoever. They'd say like go away and write an assignment and you know a lot of people didn't know how to write an essay. They didn't know what a bibliography was. I'd never heard of a bibliography and I think more help needs to be given.

Another pointed out the need for co-ordination across college departments in relation to the curriculum:

We'd had our first lot of assignments handed in and then we did, 'How to write an assignment', which seemed totally wrong. They should redesign the English programme so that when you first come you're learning how to write an assignment, how to write an essay, how to do a bibliography, how to reference things.

Difficulties and problems were also experienced by those taking a franchised degree but the students believed the responsibility for the problems resided with the university not the college as the latter 'just have to work within the constraints set'. Occasionally students experienced the problems of poor college organisation:

The first day the lecturers didn't turn up – we didn't have any lecturers. They didn't realise so we were sitting there and there were no papers and we were like what are we supposed to be doing? The lecturers hadn't been informed that our course was starting so we attended the actual lessons but there was nobody there.

(Access student)

A group on the first year of a degree programme felt that their college needs to be more aware that adults generally arrive with fewer computer skills than younger students and they, therefore, need appropriate support. They felt that they were at a learning disadvantage:

We haven't grown up with computers and we find computers very difficult. In fact that's one of the drawbacks of this course . . . It makes it more difficult for the mature student. We've got to learn. You see the younger ones come in and they don't even have to learn

IT, they've got a computer at home, they know how to programme it, they know everything on it. We come in and we have to learn all that first.

For those who have been out of the education system for a while adjusting to the demands of academic work can be hard, partly because adult learners often have a continuing self-doubt about their learning ability to study at a particular level (Merrill, 1999):

> I know one thing I find is that my course is very stressful for me anyway. Perhaps it isn't for everybody but one or two have said it's stressful and I'm trying to think why it is but it's probably necessary to prepare us for the degree course. They pile on the essays. It starts off very quietly for the first couple of weeks and you think, 'Oh I'm going to be able to cope OK' and then suddenly it's an essay every three weeks and I think to myself I could do with more time to do my essays. I know on higher education that's how it is because I know people on the 2+2 degree. It's not only one essay it's like three different subjects so you've got three essays and one's got to be in on Tuesday, one Friday and one next Monday. I find it very difficult but I'm not the cleverest of persons but I still like it but I do find it stressful. I won't say there hasn't been quite a few times I've been leaving this course and my children have said, 'Oh yes mum go'.

The following quote from a woman also illustrates the pattern of an uncertain adult learner:

> I must have had reservations when I first started – talking with all these big words. I didn't understand a thing that was being said. I had a dictionary by me all the time. I started in 1995 but I left two months after because I just thought I didn't have it in me to do it and that was it so I left. Then, of course I felt a failure so I came back the following year and I was determined to stick at it for a year and finish the course which I did. When we actually started the lessons and the big words kept cropping up, but the second time round – the first time I was too frightened to say anything, to say that I couldn't understand it – but the second time round I did. I said, 'I can't understand this, you know', and I found the tutor a great help.

Learners on an NVQ course found it demanding, especially understanding theory but the assessment structure minimises stress as they are able to resit an examination if they fail it which they feel 'takes the pressure off' in a way which is 'confidence building'. Support from tutors is regarded as important, but for many adult learners having a network of support from peers is even more significant:

> I've found through both courses last year and this course that my main allies were my own fellow students. I find that your own fellow students are the people that really get you through because say when I have a day when I'm down and I say I'm leaving and they say no, no you're not and they kind of talk you out of it or they phone you up at home and they say, 'How are you this morning? – you're not leaving are you?'. And you get that you see, so you feel you can't leave. I think things would have to be very bad for me to leave.
>
> (Female, degree student)

Being part of a group or a 'gang', as one NVQ group described it, and helping each other with studying is important. The NVQ group also talked about the existence of two adult communities in their class – an 'us and them' – between the younger mature students who are in their early 20s and themselves who are in their 30s and 40s.

Participants discussed their relationship with tutors and the support they received. Some were aware of the impact that marketisation had had on colleges and how this might affect the way tutors relate to students:

> I think there must be a real conscious decision with teachers nowadays about bums on seats in further education . . . so it tends to make people polite when maybe they don't really want to be.

One group of Access students remarked that some tutors are stressed and this is reflected in their behaviour towards them:

> A: The tutor was unapproachable – very stressed.
>
> B: So if you went sometimes the tutor was really rude and when you're an adult – one adult to another – you don't expect that . . . Sometimes I think you've been spoken to like as if you were still at school.

However, relationships were generally considered to be good – they were often contrasted with their experience of teachers in school, as in college the barriers and boundaries between tutor and learner are less prevalent:

The tutors all come out with us. We have our evenings out and they all come out with us and they're on the same level as us. I always feel that anyway, even when they are in the classroom with us. They don't talk down to us. They talk on the same level as us so I don't feel dominated or anything. I don't feel thick.

In terms of the 'classroom environment' participants discovered that, unlike school, tutors in FE are approachable and 'don't talk down to you'. It was often felt that staff took a personal interest in the general well-being of students and were aware of and sympathetic to the personal problems and issues experienced by adult students. Such relationships are often key to students developing a stronger learner identity:

If you go in and do what you are supposed to be doing they will give you as much help as you possibly need, which I found really helpful. I didn't – you know – when you are at school you sort of feel embarrassed to ask your teacher or you're scared to ask your teacher if you don't understand something whereas here if I don't understand something then I'll say so and they will take their time to actually explain it to us so that you do understand.

(Access student)

Others had a different experience:

I think at times some tutors may feel you don't need support, you're a grown woman, you can get on with it but it doesn't mean that we can just go along and do this essay and that essay without thinking . . . I need somebody to check it over, to check I'm doing the right sort of thing. I still need reassurance. I think sometimes we could get left in the dark because they think, 'Oh you can get on with it'.

(BTEC student)

There was a general feeling that, unlike school, tutors 'have time for them'. A tutor's teaching approach can be a critical factor in maintaining marginal learners, particularly those at outreach centres, involved in learning. Tutors have to counteract the legacy of experiences at school:

My tutor was absolutely fabulous – the way they teach you. You don't feel silly. There are no comments like, 'I've told you that before, you should know it by now'. No comments like that are ever made.

It's very positive, everything is very positive and very encouraging.
It is her (the tutor) way and her attitude that rubs off.

(Learner at an outreach centre)

In terms of facilities some adults complained about a shabby
environment, poor refectories and problems with parking. Many wanted
a separate common room from younger students as they feel they 'are
loud and obnoxious'. They also resented the noise they make in libraries
and learning centres.

Despite FE being centre stage in the government's lifelong learning
policy finance continues to be a deterring factor for those on low
incomes:

I had a nursery place. You got your expenses as in your bus fare but
even with that it was too much. I couldn't afford that off my benefit
and try to buy clothes and run the house. I just felt that it was too
much.

Their experiences highlight the contradictions – offering nominal
access without sufficient resources and support (Crequer, 2002) – in New
Labour's lifelong learning policies:

I went the first day. I thoroughly enjoyed it and I came home and my
fiancé wasn't working at the time and he said, 'There's absolutely no
way we can afford this'. I've been to the Welfare Rights officer and
I've been down to the Social Security and there's no way. Because
we are two single people living together we basically have to pay full
rent. It was just a nightmare. We were going to end up worse off
. . . and I spent the whole night crying my eyes out. I really did and
I was very, very disappointed.

The benefits of learning for participants were wide ranging. The social
side for some was just as important as gaining qualifications and the
gateways that this opens up for future learning or employment:

Well, making friends – basically the socialising is brilliant. I'm
going to miss the support you get from each other because you're so
very like minded and your goals are the same.

Like other studies (West, 1996; Merrill, 1999; Ainley and Bailey,
1997), the adult learners expressed the view that they were changed

persons by the end of the course, sometimes in multiple ways – by feeling more self-confident, knowledgeable and stronger:

> Maybe it's because I'm female but I get some people who think I'm stupid . . . 'Why have you got to go and do that at your age?' 'You don't need it.' 'You're too old for that kind of thing.' I get all that, but my own parents think it's great that I'm doing it because they can see that as well as learning it's helping me get my confidence. I don't think a couple of years ago I could have come here and talk to you like I am now. I would have been too shy so it helps you that way and there are a few people who are a bit jealous of me. They know I'm not well off and a lot of people say to me, 'How can you afford to not go to work?', 'You've got a family.' And I say, 'Well, I'm just careful with my money, and of course I don't have to pay for the course, it's free, so that's good.' And they say, 'Is it?' A lot of people are surprised and don't know these courses are free.

For some women, breaking away from being labelled as a mother or wife to seeing themselves as a person with their own identity led to conflict at home with partners and in some cases divorce (the 'Educating Rita' syndrome).

Participants at both the outreach centres and main college campuses can become, in Goffman's (1961) terminology, institutionalised – they are reluctant to leave:

> It's enjoyable mental baggage. You know what you get from college – all your assessments out, once you've done your assessments you feel so good that you've completed them. It's like a weight lifted off your shoulders and you get a level 3 for it. Now since I've finished the course although I'm so happy I'm upset as well because I don't want to leave.

By the end of their first programme of study in FE several had become hooked into a learning career:

> We're not sitting there saying gosh we've done it – it's like what can we do next. Once you go and get a taste for it then you want to go back again and again and we've had a taste of this now and it's like we want to do some more. I want to achieve more. I want to get better. Now you're thinking about going to university – you're just driven by it and you want the best.

Another woman who started on a cookery course to get her and her son out of the house explains:

> It's like once you start and you get some modules, and you know you can do the HNC and you think well I'll keep going because if I don't I will be back to where I was before. And I don't want that. I suppose I want better – I don't mean that in a bad way – but I want different things now. Different jobs anyway.

Summarising the complexities of the student experience

Talking to younger and older students on different modes and levels of study in FE reveals some similarities, such as frequently comparing FE with school, but also differences. FE colleges consist of a number of communities based on age and mode/level of study. Younger students do not mix with the post-21 age group even in mixed classes. Yet these two communities can be broken down further, as A-level and NVQ students, for example, do not associate with each other. This pattern of distance is repeated among adult students. Perceptions and attitudes about what an FE college does is limited and localised to a small social and geographical space.

Students chose FE because it is local and flexible. However, despite the improvements in recent years to reception areas and student support and guidance, stepping through the door remains a big hurdle for many adult students for structural, dispositional and institutional reasons. For a minority, the uncertain, marginal adult learners, it is one journey they cannot make. FE colleges need to continue and expand their community provision for such adults. This group of adult learners did not see themselves as FE students and felt no identity with the main campus even though they were registered as FE students and entitled to use the facilities on campus.

Reasons for participation, particularly with adults, are complex and the decision to return to learn at a particular moment in their lives illustrates the interaction between structure and agency in people's lives. Learning careers can be identified in both younger and adult students although these may not have been consciously planned at the beginning and may be discontinuous as some, mostly adults, may participate on one course or even drop out and return a year or so later. Many, rather than planning a return to learn, to use Matza's (1964) term 'drift' into education. Similarly with younger students some drift in because it is perceived as being better than the alternatives of either unemployment or a low paid job. Once in a situation of learning, the benefits of learning, both present and future, become apparent: such as self-esteem, self-development, enjoyment of learning, and prospects of a better job. FE colleges have been successful in widening participation and launching people into learning careers (Smithers and Robinson, 2000). Some however, still remain outside FE, either by choice or because their socio-economic position and/or their own disposition (often related to structural issues) does not allow them to transcend the boundary between participant and non-participant. Although some of these reasons are external to FE, such as the contradictions in government policy, FE could listen more closely to the voice of the learner (and non-participants) to improve the quality and experience of being a student in FE.

Chapter 6

Colleges and their communities

Community: a contested concept

Community is a word frequently used in both academic discourse and everyday language, yet it is also a nebulous, problematical and contested concept. Hillery (1955), a sociologist, in his attempt to define community discovered ninety-four definitions. Bauman, in his recent book *Community: Seeking Safety in an Insecure World* reminds us that:

> Words have meanings: some words, however, also have a 'feel'. The word 'community' is one of them. It feels good: whatever the word 'community' may mean, it is good 'to have a community', 'to be in community'.
>
> (2001, p. 1)

Community, as Bauman points out, gives us a feeling of security, a sense of belonging and an ideal place to be:

> To start with, community is a 'warm' place, a cosy and comfortable place . . . Out there, in the street, all sorts of dangers lie in ambush; we have to be alert when we go out, watch whom we are talking to and who talks to us, be on the look-out every minute. In here, in the community, we can relax – we are safe, there are no dangers looming in dark corners . . . What that word evokes is everything we miss and what we lack to be secure, confident and trusting.
>
> (2001, pp. 1–3)

At the same time community is an elusive place/space – 'a paradise lost' (Bauman, 2001). For Bauman 'community stands for the kind of world which is not, regrettably, available to us – but which we would

dearly wish to inhabit and which we hope to repossess' (2001, p. 3).
Earlier Raymond Williams had similarly observed that:

> Community can be the warmly persuasive word to describe an
> existing set of relationships. What is most important is that unlike
> all other terms of social organisation (state, nation, society, etc.)
> it seems never to be used unfavourably, and never to be given any
> positive or opposing or distinguishing term.
>
> (1988, p. xx)

Williams also commented that community 'always has been'. In
talking about community there is the tendency to romanticise the past in
the belief that postmodernity and the rise of the individualised society
have signalled the decline of community. Communities continue to shape
our identities which are shared with others through social relationships
and networks. Crow and Allen suggest that:

> Community stands as a convenient shorthand term for the broad
> realm of local social arrangements beyond the private sphere of home
> and family but more familiar to us than the impersonal institutions of
> the wider society.
>
> (1994, p. 1)

This is what Bulmer describes as the 'intermediary structures' (1989,
p. 253). Communities, therefore, exist in a space between what C. Wright
Mills (1970) calls the micro level of 'personal troubles' and the macro
level of 'public issues'. Community is a dialectical process – a space
where people act collectively through agency to overcome the constraints
of structure. Giddens' (1987) structuration theory and Bourdieu's (1993)
notion of habitus are useful concepts for understanding these processes.

Community suggests a sense of belonging, shared membership and
identity and solidarity between human beings. Yet at the same time of
wanting security through community we are also striving within the
postmodern world for individual autonomy. This reflects a fundamental
tension in modern society: the individual and social nature of human
life. Community also suggests a locality – a geographical territory. However, with the rise of what Castells (1996) calls the information society
it is possible to belong to a virtual community without meeting face-
to-face.

Sociologically the term community derives from the classical work of
Tönnies (1887/1955) in which he distinguished between two concepts

of community: Gemeinschaft and Gesellschaft. Tönnies' dichotomy contrasts the community of the premodern world with the instrumental relationships of the state in the modern capitalist world. In Gemeinschaft relationships are close-knit, centred on the family and kinship, where life is lived in a community which is stable and conflict free as values are shared. Gesellschaft, on the other hand, is characteristic of large-scale modern societies in which relationships are impersonal, contractual and rational. The public and private life is separated with a focus in society on individual liberalism. Etzioni's study, *The Spirit of Community: Rights, Responsibilities and the Communitarian Agenda* (1993), strives to recapture the close-knit and moral values of Gemeinschaft through the concept of communitarianism. His perception of communitarianism values the role of the family and other local institutions, such as educational ones, in the community as they produce values of self-help and self-reliance without reliance on the state and which in turn secure integration and cohesion. Later models of communitarianism reject the individualism and authoritarian features of Etzioni's ideal. Tam's (1998) perspective focuses more on a new social and political structure of community. Values are agreed through discussion, equal participation and inclusion. Community acts as an arena for the engagement of active citizenship in civil society.

There is no one single factor which characterises community but several. Social relationships and geographical factors are important elements in defining community since social groups share a common sense of identity and belonging by living in the same locality. The sense of identity may be based on social class, ethnicity, values, socio-economic position, housing, etc. Shared values, social interaction and social relationships create a local social system:

> A social system is a human collective (though immediately linked with its physical environment) made up of people having distinctive parts to play, but who operate together as an integral whole. Such a collective must be identifiable – culturally, socially and economically – and have boundaries that make this possible. Such a collective must also be sustainable, in that its members' life together continues long enough for them to recognise themselves and be recognised as an enduring entity.
>
> (Clark, 1996, p. 28)

Clark summarises the different sociological approaches to community in the following way:

- community as a human collective
- community as territory
- community as shared activities
- community as close-knit relationships
- community as sentiment.

Earlier MacIver and Page (1949/1961) related the importance of community not only to locality but also to providing a means for social coherence. For them, 'A community then is an area of social living marked by some degree of social coherence. The bases of community are locality and community sentiment' (1949/1961, p. 8). Community in the modern state does not imply homogeneity:

> In practice individuals identify themselves as members of different networks and communities of interest, some of them place-centred and others not. The places of community themselves vary from the immediately local, the neighbourhood, to the citywide, that is, people's attachment to place and its investment with meaning exists alongside networks of social relations.
>
> (Hill, 2000, p. 56)

As lives become more fragmented with individuals participating in a range of social contexts and organisations locally, nationally and globally community no longer merely resides in place. Communities of interest and communities of identity also become significant where common interests and values can be shared without being rooted to a particular space or territory. Community is both physical and social. Social interaction and networks are constructed through communities of interest.

Numerous sociological studies have been undertaken throughout the UK looking at a range of communities, many of which are now classic studies, such as Willmott and Young's work on working class communities in East London. Willmott (1986), like Clark, identified a number of meanings of community. First, territorial community representing a shared geographical area. Second, interest community whereby people are linked by common factors such as occupation, ethnicity, or class. Often there is a strong relationship between the two types of community. His third meaning of community he entitles community of attachment, as this centres on collective action. Suttles (1972) argues for the role of human agency in constructing communities within favourable local social structures. Communities within this framework are perceived as natural. Following on from this notion Cohen (1985) argues for the symbolic construction of community whereby community plays a symbolic role:

> The reality of community lies in its members' perception of the vitality of its culture. People construct community symbolically, making it a resource and a repository of meaning and a referent of their identity.
>
> (1985, p. 118)

More recently Colls' (1995) study of working-class communities in north-east England notes the decline of such communities as a result of economic competition. He identifies three levels of community: the local, associational and regional. The local community is constructed by those who live there through, for example, loyalties, symbols and memories. Associational community for Colls refers to trade unions and the labour movement, while the last level, regional, ' . . . interprets itself only in contradiction to what is national' (Colls, 1995, p. 16).

Crow and Allen's (1994) study provides a useful review of research and literature on community and community studies. In reviewing the field they outline aspects of communities. First, they refer to communities as 'active creations' located and developed within specific contexts of history and policy. Second, communities are situated at the intermediate level of society, and it is at this level where people live out the socio-economic, and political realities of society. Change is impacted through class, gender and race. Last, communities are problematic and contradictory.

In moving to focus on FE, education and communities, the definition of community by Wright (1989) is helpful as FE institutions consist of numerous internal communities occupying the same space (see Chapter 4) while also interacting with a diverse range of external communities. As Wright observes: 'People live in different worlds even though they share the same locality: there is no single community' (1989, pp. 284, 285). Perceiving each FE college as consisting of several communities introduces another way of viewing communities through the concept of boundary. People identify with a particular community as a result of the commonalities they share separating them off from other people beyond the boundary of their community (Cohen, 1987). It is a situation of insiders/outsiders; a process of difference and exclusion. Within an FE college community boundaries are often marked out by territory and space; for example, in the refectory or the Students' Union (see Chapter 5). Paul Gilroy (1987) also relates community to boundaries in relation to the black experience in British society in which his analysis of community is no longer a cosy, comforting word:

Community is as much about difference as it is about similarity and identity. It is a relational idea which suggests, for British blacks at least, the idea of antagonism, domination and subordination between one community and another. The word directs analysis to the boundary between these groups.

(Gilroy, 1987, p. 235)

Community can, therefore, be contradictory: both 'cosy' and inclusive and repressive and exclusionary. Our research revealed that such a pattern exists among FE students as they identified themselves as belonging to a particular student community, excluding them from others. In searching for the ideal good community its oppressive and excluding side are often forgotten. In many ways it is a utopian search but there is scope through democratic active citizenship to strive for a more just and equal community.

At a policy level community has been an important aspect of urban politics. Under the modernising policies of New Labour government it has assumed a new meaning with a focus on partnerships between local people and local organisations to tackle poverty, work towards regeneration of communities and a new moral order. The government's recent National Strategy for Neighbourhood Renewal argues for democratic renewal and active citizenship:

Communities need to be consulted and listened to and the most effective interventions are those in which communities are actively involved in their design and delivery and where possible in the driving seat . . . this applies as much to communities of interest . . . as it does to geographical communities . . . it is impossible to turn around a deprived area without the help of local residents . . . building capacity will mean helping local community leaders in different places to learn from each other.

(*A New Commitment to Neighbourhood Renewal: National Strategy Action Plan*, 2001)

In this new form of democracy representatives of local people are included on local forums to discuss and identify regeneration strategies for communities rather than being imposed from above and outside their local communities. Similarly, Ranson (1994) has called for community forums enabling community groups, parents and employers to meet to discuss and take part in decision-making about educational provision and other local services. For Ranson such a process is important for the development of active citizenship and a democratic society. Some of these partnerships involve FE through initiatives such as the Active Community Fund (ACF). Parallel developments are also happening in the education sphere at regional level through the Learning and Skills Council Partnerships, not only with FE but also with adult and community organisations and universities, widening participation in learning by consulting and listening to learners.

Linking community with education

The concept of community was originally largely associated with initial schooling and the development of community education and community schools, initiated by Morris in Cambridgeshire in the 1930s. Morris' vision of community education – or the 'village college' – was confined to rural areas, engendering an image and belief of what a rural community life should be. For Morris education has an important role to play in re-building and sustaining a rural community through a process of rural and communal regeneration. It was in many ways radical for its time in arguing for the 'village college' to become the focus of village life in not only an educational sense but also in terms of cultural, recreational and social activities at a time when state education was limited and the Church still dominated society. Education, for Morris, should be lifelong, open, inclusive and integrative. His ideas on community education spread in post-war Britain to other rural areas and also urban areas and by the 1970s community colleges/schools were popular particularly in deprived urban areas. Like the concept community, community education was interpreted and applied in different ways, ranging from liberal to radical or even reactionary. Most approaches were integrative, offering a model for recurrent or lifelong learning. As Mee and Wiltshire describe:

> Their claim is that education is a continuous and lifelong process, and that it should not be artificially divided into separate sectors or stages. Instead, it should be conceived as a totality and administered through institutions which provide for the whole range of educa-tional needs from childhood through adolescence to adulthood and old age. Adult education therefore ceases to exist as a separate entity with separate institutions; it is replaced by community education which is addressed to all age groups and all sectors in the population.
> (1978, pp. 14–15)

The Educational Priority Areas (EPA) project in the late 1960s and 1970s in Liverpool involving Midwinter and Lovett is often cited as an important example of good practice in community education. Community development approaches were utilised to re-establish at grassroots level democratic processes in communities. From this perspective community development approaches of partnership, participation and self-help were harnessed to education in linking parents, schools and community in a triangular relationship. The curriculum and education focused on the reality of living in disaffected communities. Further education colleges have not adopted such a holistic approach to community education although in some colleges there are pockets of community development type work and links with disadvantaged community groups. Bilston Community College, established after 1992 through the merger of an FE college and sixth-form college, was perhaps one exception although it has not survived. Bilston did, however, appoint a Community Directorate to promote the college's community objectives across the whole institution.

Outside of the FE system examples of community education could be found in the 1950s, 1960s and 1970s in the tradition of working-class adult education through such organisations as the Workers Educational Association (WEA). It offered critical learning perspectives to the political economy and social inequalities experienced by working-class people in society. Working-class adult education was about engaging with the problems faced by working-class people in their communities. The values and philosophy of the 1973 Russell Report on adult education contrasts greatly with the perspective implied in the 1992 Further and Higher Education Act. The Russell Report viewed education as a social process which encouraged active citizenship and self-development:

The value of Adult Education is not solely to be measured by direct increases in earning power or productivity capacity or by any other materialisitc yardstick, but by the quality of life it inspires in the individual and generates for the community at large. It is an agent of changing and improving our society: but for each individual the means of change may differ and each must develop in his own way, at his own level and through his own talents.

(Russell, 1973, p. xi)

A community approach to education breaks down traditional relationships both inside and outside an educational institution:

... 'community' represents the changing world outside the institutional cocoon of the professional worker, and 'community education' is about evolving more open, participatory and democratic relationships between educators and their constituencies ... Community education should be about partnership and solidarity rather than paternalism or manipulation ... it implies sustained educational engagement with the social reality of people's lives in the community.

(Martin, 1987, p. 17)

For Martin community is a slippery and ambiguous concept, yet at the same time potentially positive in that it enables the boundaries between educational institutions and their local community to be blurred. He argues that community education should be a grassroots movement whereby learning is based on experience, involves political education, community action and, importantly, that the outcome should be transformative. In presenting a seminar in connection with the FEDA communities project Martin stated:

I want to argue that when we think about 'community' in its relation to education, we should be thinking about not only the quality of internal institutional life, but also our relations with the world outside and, in particular, our commitment to opening up education to new constituencies by connecting our work to the experience of ordinary people 'out there' in communities.

(Martin, 1999, p. 10)

Community is a social construct. Community education, according to Martin (1996) is an ideological construct characterised by competing and conflicting ideologies:

In its relation to education, 'community' should be viewed as an ideological construct which is both historically and contextually specific. 'Community education' therefore only makes sense if it is located historically and situated in relation to state policy in a systematic and discriminating way.

(Martin, 1996, p. 109)

Historically the main ideological constructions of community in relation to education can be summarised in the following way:

Ideology	Purpose	Strategy	Construction of 'community'
consensus	sponsorship	universalism	the 'whole' community
pluralism	co-option/ incorporation	state reformism/ selective intervention	'disadvantaged' dissonant
conflict	independent control	autonomy/ resistance	dissident/ dissenting communities
'free' market	competition	commodification/ marketisation	competing communities of interest

(Martin, 1999, p. 16)

A community approach to the curriculum encourages a democratic style of learning and teaching. It breaks down the 'us' and 'them' situation produced by traditional methods, replacing them with more egalitarian and participatory relationships between students and tutors. Lecturers/ tutors have to focus beyond the confinement of the educational institution and look at the educational needs of people in the local community. This moves education away from the provision-led model. Historically adult education, and in particular radical adult education, has a tradition of relating the theory and practice of community and education through, for example, working-class education and women's education. Good practice has been developed, for example, through the adult education residential movement such as Ruskin and Northern College which includes FE level, and outside residential adult education through Jane Thompson's work with women and Tom Lovett's work with traditionally non-participant groups.

Lovett (1975) in *Adult Education, Community Development and the Working Class* argues for a community development approach for working with non-traditional student groups. For Lovett the task of the educator is to offer locally based learning and a process of learning which illustrates the relevance of adult education to the daily lives of ordinary people. Once trust and confidence has been built through community development work educational intervention can begin. The roles of the adult educator are multiple. First, that of network agent to establish contact and relationships with groups of local people and identifying the type of action, support and provision required. Second, to act as resources agent by identifying existing local educational resources and collaborating with these agencies and organisations. Third, to be an educational guide through making the access of support and educational guidance in existing institutions available to learners. Last, to assume the role of teacher.

Community-based education as advocated by Lovett, Jackson, Mayo, Thompson and Martin employs a curriculum which originates from the lived experiences of individuals and groups in communities and one which critically engages and intervenes in the dialectics of community. Education is focused around specific social and political realities whereby educators engage with groups of people collectively to pursue education and social action through active citizenship. Jackson describes his approach in the following way:

> By referring to 'communities' . . . we meant specified groups of actual people, not society as a whole and certainly not a market. In short, we used the term to indicate the 'place' and 'moment' of engagement with specific groups of people around their interests.
> (Jackson, 1995, p. 194)

It is positioned at the radical or popular education end of community education, for as Steele (1997) reminds us, adult education is 'politics by other means'. Such an approach can also be applied to younger people in FE.

Community and its meaning for FE

FE colleges have the potential, like Morris' 'village colleges' to become focal points in local communities in ways which engage with the realities and needs of local people rather than being merely service providers. Colleges, for example, have resources that could be shared with local organisations and community groups – something which community groups asked for in the FEDA project. Such groups viewed an FE college as being part of its local community and, therefore, they felt that they had the right to access and feel ownership of its resources and facilities. Hall maintains that, 'Further education colleges have, in the main, responded pragmatically to local demand' (1994, p. 11). In the post-1992 era colleges may be more likely to respond pragmatically to those groups such as employers who have the most voice and the most money, rather than powerless local voluntary and community groups. Further education colleges with their now broader student population, particularly in the post-18 age group, have the potential to become lifelong learning institutions, and by adopting community education approaches to emerge as the new community colleges. Green and Lucas (1999d) argue strongly for the realignment of FE in a way that resembles community colleges in the United States. Following the merger in some areas after 1992 of LEA community education services and colleges, a small number of institutions called themselves community colleges, particularly those with a large adult education provision. Changing a name, however, does not ensure that a community education/ development approach permeates the curriculum, ethos, relationships and philosophy of an institution. It is problematic, as a community approach does not sit easily with the ethos and practice of marketisation in colleges. Some aspects of college life have witnessed a decline in local representation and ownership since the loss of LEA control. FE college boards of governors, for example, are now dominated by a particular kind of community – that of local employers. Some communities are, therefore, more visible and more vocal than others. Wymer (1996) is critical of the growth of marketised strategies as these have undermined the community mission:

> . . . unless the point of departure . . . is the experiences of people in their communities, there is no chance of creating access to further education and training for the millions currently denied it . . . The refusal to base education and training programmes on where people are, rather than where vocationalists judge they should be, is the crucial weakness of the curriculum in the United Kingdom, including a great deal of further education provision.
>
> (Wymer, 1996, pp. 49–50)

Three years after the 1992 Act Jackson was equally pessimistic about the ability of FE colleges to engage with and relate to the social needs of their local communities:

> A further education sector with wide responsibility for post-16 education, and therefore for adult education, appears to disregard the role of education in society at large, beyond the world of work in the economy. Consequently, whilst the division between academic and vocational was removed, an unnecessary demarcation between vocational and non-vocational education was introduced with serious consequences for achieving the sector's own objectives.
>
> (Jackson, 1995, p. 190)

The market approach whereby 'clients' choose courses from a list of modules to buy will not attract those groups who lack, in Bourdieu's term, cultural and social capital – that is those who lack power trapped, in what Freire calls, their 'culture of silence'. Brook (1993) argues for a 'community further education' as a strategy for reaching non-traditional students and a means for moving away from the individualising of students:

> In Britain, if further education is going to make any impact on whole sections of the population – especially traditional non-users – it will do so only when it sees and deals with them not as isolated individuals but members of groups, of communities.
>
> (1993, p. 21)

Ranson (1999) in a seminar paper presented as part of the FEDA project argued that FE should address itself to rethinking its ideals, values and philosophy as part of its change process. To achieve this he believes that 'many colleges will have fundamental relearning to do' (1999, p. 50):

> Social institutions must be living human creations, continually reviewing and remaking themselves to adapt to and actively shape the changing world in which we live. And so the FE college must continually review and refashion itself, if it is to further the ideals that inspired it; of creating a more equal and fairer society of opportunity for all to develop their powers and capacities. My argument will be that at the centre of the new learning is the making and remaking of civil society.
>
> (p. 39)

In such a scenario FE has a major role to play as learning organisations in developing and supporting a learning society. Ranson (1999) has high hopes in relation to the potential of FE for creating agency and change in the lives of people living in disadvantaged communities through learning for active citizenship:

> Despite the scale of such corrosive disadvantage, colleges can and are, succeeding in motivating young people and adults to realise their potential. What we learn from them is that if they are to alter the way students think of themselves and what they are capable of, to transform hopelessness into purpose and kindle capacity, it requires a sharing of vision, an energy and cohesiveness of purpose

amongst lecturers, students and community traditions. Working together, colleges with their communities, will generate the sense of purpose that can dissolve the boundaries that emphasise place above horizons and generate the agency necessary for the recreation of civil society.

(Ibid., p. 54)

In a different form of partnership colleges are being drawn (as cited above) into New Labour's policy agenda of community regeneration, involving local people identifying solutions to the problems confronting their communities. Colleges, for example, are included as possible bidding partners with community groups in the Adult and Community Learning Fund:

We want to support activities that will take learning into new sectors of the community not reached by traditional educational organisations, providing opportunities that are relevant to the people involved and delivering them in ways that will interest and attract the people who are hardest to reach.

(DfEE, 1998e, p. 3)

In practice, the percentage of ACLF projects involving colleges is small. Yet ACLF funding provides a space for colleges to offer community-based learning and address the social inclusion agenda outside of the 'mainstream' curriculum. Some colleges with a commitment to community and adult learning have succeeded in finding other creative ways through the funding mechanism and its insistence on qualifications and vocational education. Unwin (2000) cites the example of South Trafford College and its partnership with the local WEA. In an article entitled 'Community and identity' in the journal *Adults Learning* (1997), Chris Jude, the Director of Lifelong Learning at Lewisham College, London, describes that it was a necessity for the college to offer an alternative curriculum to that prescribed by the FEFC in order to reach out to deprived groups. This meant drawing on the traditions of adult education teaching, particularly that of radical adult education and the notion of basing the curriculum on people's experiences.

Residential adult education colleges in the UK are learning institutions, firmly rooted in communities teaching FE and HE level work. Historically they have espoused a radical adult education tradition committed to education for social purpose and social and political action. Strong links were forged with the labour movement and community activists. Following the 1992 Act residential adult education colleges were eligible for FEFC funding. This type of funding resulted in modifications and limitations on the curriculum. Ruskin College, for example, in order to receive funding from the FEFC had to comply with Schedule 2, forcing the institution to shorten its diploma courses from the two years needed by their learners, who generally have few qualifications, to one year. Other residential institutions also had to go through similar struggles. Northern College's aim is to provide second chance learning opportunities for adults who have few qualifications but are active in their local community and who feel the need for education. The purpose of the curriculum is to enable community activists to be more effective in their community organisations. Over the years they have worked with tenants' groups, women's organisations and black organisations. Some of their recent work has focused on the regeneration of communities such as the 'coalfields learning programme' in former mining areas. The college works in partnership with a range of organisations, such as local authorities, trade unions, local FE colleges and universities, WEA, voluntary organisations and employers. A key aspect of Lovett's work in Northern Ireland was the establishment of the Ulster People's College. The mission of the college is innovative in the context of Northern Ireland. Adult students from across the sectarian divide are brought together to study and explore the factors that have divided them through a community studies curriculum.

Post-compulsory communities: FE and HE

In response to government policy advocating widening participation over the past ten years or so and, more recently its policy of aspiring to a 50 per cent participation rate in HE for adults aged 18 to 30, FE colleges, particularly the larger ones, are now delivering a higher percentage of HE work through a wide range of partnership arrangements with higher education institutions. Abrahson *et al.* (1996) talked about the blurring of boundaries between FE and HE. Colleges are increasingly offering sub-degree work in response to Dearing as well as undergraduate, and in some cases, postgraduate programmes. FE colleges as places to learn at HE level are favoured by many non-traditional adult students as they are local and perceived as less daunting and intimidating than universities. In rural areas isolated from a local HEI, such as Cornwall and Suffolk, FE colleges offer the only possibility for adults rooted in their communities to study at HE level. However, an HE experience in FE is different to that in HE. Scholarly activity, for example, which is regarded by HEFCE as an important aspect of HE is largely absent from FE as a recent study for HEFCE by NIACE and the University of Warwick indicates (2002). This absence reflects a lack of funding and resources together with high teaching loads for FE staff.

Government policy is pushing for closer relationships and partnerships between FE and HE in relation to the widening participation agenda. Consortium arrangements are increasingly common where colleges are directly funded by HEFCE yet there is still a feeling by many colleges involved that it is not an equal partnership. Some colleges are mixed economy, being both directly and indirectly funded for their HE work, while others are totally indirectly funded. Each model of partnership results in a different form of relationship with the HE community. Despite the partnership arrangements there are signs of increasing competition between some HEI institutions, particularly the new universities, and the larger FE colleges for HE students. More research is needed to map and understand the FE/HE landscape in terms of collaborative arrangements and its implications for the experiences of adult learners and the communities in which they live in relation to social and educational regeneration.

Looking at economic communities

The impact of globalisation, the decline of manufacturing industries and the emergence of new technologies requiring new skills have created a new economic role for FE. Kypri and Clark (1997) maintain that the economic health of local communities is now more dependent upon the success of local development than in the past. Economic communities consisting of local industries and businesses are essential to colleges in a market driven economy, yet the term community is infrequently discussed in relation to such groups and organisations. Colleges do, however, have a central role to play in not only the social regeneration but also in the economic regeneration of communities. In a paper presented at the FEDA communities project seminar Owen outlined three ways in which colleges can contribute to the economic regeneration of their communities:

- through their mainstream activities, including their contributions to government funded training, business development and student guidance
- through contributing to the process of economic regeneration, including strategic planning

- through their economic impact as major organisations in their own right

(1999, p. 27)

Owen (1999) argues that colleges should play more of a major role in strategic planning and economic regeneration 'rather than part of a second tier of consultees' (p. 35). According to Owen this would not only enhance a college's finances but also ensure that they are serving their local communities.

FE colleges are themselves an economic community 'with a diverse series of links into the local and regional economic development processes' (Kypri and Clark, 1997, p. 1). Their study, 'Furthering local economies' (funded by FEDA), is one of a few studies that debate the economic role of FE in the community. The study highlighted that 514 colleges in England and Wales spend approximately £3.2 bn on the development of skilled people and businesses each year, acts as a major employer with over 200,000 full-time equivalent staff while also being a developer of land and a consumer of products and services. With government policy moves towards sub-regional and regional regeneration colleges in partnership with other agencies and organisations such as LLSCs, Connexions, New Deal, Education Action Zones and Single Regeneration Budget (SRB) initiatives, FE has a central role to play. The latter initiatives introduced a new element to government strategy as partnerships of local agencies have to bid competitively for funding. A more recent development, Regional Development Agencies (RDAs), together with regional chambers, offers both a new mechanism and opportunities for FE colleges to participate in the economic regeneration of communities. Colleges are centrally engaged, for example, in the New Deal for the Unemployed.

Another key source for regional economic regeneration utilised by colleges is the EU through its Structural Funds, ESF and Community Funds. EU funding addresses measures to both prevent and tackle unemployment, influenced by the 1992 Delors White Paper on *Growth, Competitiveness and Employment*. In a report for the FEDA communities project entitled, *Perceptions of Local/Regional Partners*, Parkinson and Carter (1999) emphasised that: 'In responding to these agendas, the FE sector is having to demonstrate to a wide range of interests its potential and ability to play a key role in economic development and regional activities' (p. 5).

In this report Parkinson and Carter (1999) identify several strands of the role of FE in furthering a local economies model. First, that of 'service provider' – their key role – the transmission of skills, knowledge, learning and the application of new knowledge. FE has increasingly become a major provider of training and post-compulsory education. Training and development programmes for local organisations and businesses also represent an important source of income for colleges.

Parkinson and Carter argue that in this area colleges are 'already playing a critical role in helping business associations, building competitive industrial clusters, and developing new centres of excellence' (1999, p. 6). Second, as a 'stakeholder' FE is embedded in the local economy as a major employer and landowner. According to Parkinson and Carter (1999) over 50 per cent of colleges are among the top ten employers in the local economy. Third, colleges act as a 'strategic partner' through partnerships with other groups and organisations such as Labour Market Information Groups, Economic Strategy working committees. At present colleges are struggling to establish this role and have yet to reach their potential as they are perceived as contractors rather than strategic policy players. Most of the partner relationships formed by FE are with local authorities and local government offices such as Chambers of Commerce, universities, TECs.

As part of our FEDA project Parkinson and Carter undertook research 'to explore the economic development dimension of the relationships between FE and regional partners' (1999, p. 10). The study was confined to the West Midlands region and involved obtaining the perspectives of employers in local councils, TECs and the government office for the West Midlands and the extent of their involvement with FE colleges. One county council reported that its relationship with local FE colleges had been *ad hoc* since incorporation:

The local authority recognises that its view of FE until recently – as peripheral and driven by business opportunity rather than strategy – has been narrow. There are now opportunities for increased engagement which will renew original efforts to involve the colleges and provide greater continuity.

(Parkinson and Carter, 1999, p. 11)

Other local authorities also viewed colleges as service providers rather than strategic partners in the local economy. This feeling was also shared by the Chambers of Commerce and other sub-regional partnership groups. With some of the sub-regional groups the strategic role was perceived as belonging to local universities rather than FE. A cultural change is required to shift these traditional attitudes. Relationships are different in one borough council where there is only one large FE college. Here the college was viewed as a strategic partner with considerable resources to offer. While the relationship is a robust and stable one it is also undermined by feelings of suspicion between organisations and ownership issues.

FE, according to Parkinson and Carter (1999) continues to hold an underdeveloped understanding of its economic/social impact on localities. At the same time regeneration work demands different types of skills to the education ones traditionally associated with FE in its work with communities. This also has implications for staffing. Unless these issues are addressed FE will continue to play a marginal role in partnerships and strategies for economic regeneration, viewed as a minor partner by other agencies. However, Parkinson and Carter (1999) argue in their study that it is possible for colleges to achieve a more major role in local economic regeneration as:

> FE has a long and robust history of delivering vocational skills education and training to local business and residential communities. It operates with a strong sense of its own area and with a developed sense of local need . . . FE, therefore, affects whole communities and localities and is a critical tool of social regeneration. Colleges are hungry for recognition and resources and are therefore highly motivated to address new economic imperatives and social needs.
>
> (p. 29)

Conclusion

A commitment to community, community development and community education requires FE to adopt a particular philosophy and practice. Education from this perspective is not just about gaining qualifications but importantly engages the learner and communities in a process of empowerment, as Freire advocated, through social and political education and action. Learning is located in the experiences of the learner and communities, what is called in the radical adult education tradition 'really useful knowledge' (Johnston, 1988). A community college, therefore, needs to go beyond what Brook sees as: 'one which practises commitment to the community, or at least is making a sustained effort in that direction in its deeds and not just its words' (1993, p. 25). Yet this approach does not sit easily alongside the current drive towards marketisation and individualisation in FE, whereby educational institutions act more like a private enterprise rather than a public good. As a result, students become clients buying courses in the marketplace. Commodification, now enshrined in the FE system, is characteristic of the postmodern world. Allman and Wallis (1995) reflect:

> Increasingly it seems that the only element of the social or broad scale communality that remains is the social world of commodities. This is a social world in which our relation to 'things' increasingly becomes more important than human social relations for the continuous reconstitution of 'the self', paraphernalia of the 'commodified self'.
>
> (p. 26)

In periods of social, economic and political change educational institutions are fundamental for providing arenas for understanding and critically reflecting upon these changes. As Ranson (1994) highlights:

> In periods of social transition learning becomes central to our future well-being. Only if learning is placed at the centre of our experience will individuals continue to develop their capacities, institutions be enabled to respond openly and imaginatively to change, and the differences within and between communities become a source for effective understanding.
>
> (p. ix)

Spaces for community education and action, active citizenship and social purpose are harder to find, yet there is beginning to be a re-emergence of radical/popular adult education within the UK which attempts to claim back the collectivities of community. FE colleges rooted in the heart of diverse communities can learn from the current approaches of radical adult education in order to enable learners to think critically and act upon the social, economic and power inequalities within their local areas. Many FE colleges need to move out of the confines of a purely economistic policy towards an education system which embraces a wider social philosophy and practice. As Mayo (1995) reminds us:

> And education and training, including adult education, should also be the focus of attention precisely because, as Freire argued, education can also be the means by which men and women discover how to participate in the transformation of the world.
>
> (p. 16)

Government reports (DfEE, 1998a, *The Learning Age*; Kennedy Report, 1997), espoused high hopes for the new FE to play a central role in the lifelong learning agenda of local communities. *The Learning Age* (1998) advocated that colleges should become 'beacons of learning' in their local communities, while Kennedy believed that they could tackle inequalities through widening participation. To achieve this, Kennedy argued the need for mechanisms to be put in place to ensure the involvement of further education in providing for local community needs:

> If further education is to fulfil its potential in terms of social cohesion and economic prosperity, all stakeholders need to ensure wide involvement on the part of employers and members of the community . . . Formal arrangements are necessary to ensure that it can respond more effectively to the needs of the wider community. This cannot be left to chance. Both government and the Council have roles to play in the changes needed to promote the systematic development of community involvement in planning.
>
> (Kennedy, 1997, p. 42)

A few years on there is evidence that some cultural transition has taken place within FE since incorporation. Colleges have changed much more than people's perceptions of them. This change is continuing with internal and external communities still being worked out. 'It is important that the less powerful voices in the community are not forgotten in the emerging further education as it competes to establish an influential role within the post-compulsory sector' (Merrill, 2000, p. 50). In reflecting upon the changing philosophy of FE and its relationship to its communities one college principal stated:

> The future possible scenario is a beguiling one, with colleges clearly located in the heart of the community, looked on with admiration or respect as powerful agents for beneficial change. They would be open and welcoming to every individual or group, all year, all day. They would provide ways in, progression through and ways out. They would be models of cost-effectiveness, efficiency and transparent accountability, and they would lead in matters of public concern, from equal opportunities to a new motorway proposal, from environmental awareness to local government reorganisation. We would all salute that flag but we are, of course, still miles away from that vision . . . The means of getting from here to there, from obscurity to recognition, lie in the hands of college managers . . . We

are responsible for an immense asset of almost limitless potential.
We have no acceptable reason for failure.

(Austin, 1994, p. 138)

In the nearly ten years since Austin's statement on the philosophy
and culture of FE how much closer is it in fulfilling its potential as a
key institution of lifelong learning, equity and social inclusion in local
communities?

Chapter 7

Learning, teaching and the curriculum

Introduction

The first point to make about the three concepts which form the subject matter of this chapter is that – in terms of recent policy developments – only learning seems to matter anymore. As mentioned in earlier chapters, debate about the curriculum seems to have been replaced by skill-talk of various kinds, lifelong learning is now preferred to lifelong education, and teaching is described in terms of the management and support of learning. Much of this of course – as the perusal of any history of educational ideas would reveal – is not to be taken too seriously on the grounds that political rhetoric, professional sloganising and the natural cycles and changes of terminology and priorities seem to be an inevitable and natural feature of educational developments. However, changing educational discourse and language is often itself an external reflection of fundamental internal changes in educational systems, so it is always necessary to try to distinguish between deep and surface meanings in examining trends and issues.

Learning and teaching

It was considered useful to examine the two concepts together since most contemporary accounts consist of a conflation of the two by defining the latter in terms of the former. The standards for teachers in PCET established by FENTO, for example, are concerned – not principally with teaching *per se* – but with the 'management and support of learning' (FENTO, 1999) as are the criteria for admission to the ILT for HE teachers (ILT, 2001). Indeed, almost all contemporary accounts of teaching indicate a move away from the teacher's role and towards the learner's role or – in terms of the ideological dichotomies adapted from Meighan (1981, p. 161) listed below – from the left to the right-hand side column.

teacher-centred	v	child-centred
closed teaching	v	open teaching
meaning making	v	meaning receiving
authoritarian	v	democratic
traditional	v	progressive
transmission	v	interpretation
dependent study	v	independent study

A useful question to ask about all this is whether any of it makes sense in terms of either philosophical or epistemological conceptions of learning and teaching or in the context of current practices in the FE sector.

Hirst (1974) offers a formal definition of teaching as a broad label for 'those activities of a person A, the intention of which is to bring about in another person B, the intentional learning of X' (p. 109). Now, although it may appear that – in contemporary models of active, experiential, autonomous, student-centred or computer-assisted learning (CAL) – the A element of this triad has been displaced by B and X, this view could be misleading and too simplistic. It is more accurate to say that the *activities* of A (i.e. the roles and priorities of teachers) have been substantially changed so as to place more emphasis on the activities of learners and to foster self-directed learning and achievement. Thus, even if the mainstream activities of teachers are now seen largely as the management and support of learning, they are still *teaching* activities carried out by the many thousands of people employed as lecturers and trainers in the FE sector.

Scheffler's (1973) analysis of three important and influential models of teaching provides a useful background to the debate in this sphere. The 'impression' model (pp. 68–70), associated with Locke's philosophy, pictures the mind of the learner as a *tabula rasa* upon which is to be imprinted the knowledge and experience deemed desirable by the cultural traditions and needs of society. The teacher's task, on this account, is to exercise the mental powers of the student engaged in receiving and processing this information. Whereas the impression model supposes the teacher to be conveying ideas to be stored by learners, the 'insight' model (which Scheffler associates with Plato and St Augustine (pp. 71–5) denies that knowledge is acquired in this mechanistic fashion. The mind is not a passive storage room of ideas but needs to be prompted into extracting order and meaning from the experiences it has to make sense of. The idea of inert knowledge is thus replaced by a dynamic picture of active, experiential learning. Finally, what Scheffler calls the 'rule' model of teaching (attributed to the influence of Kant, pp. 76–9) stresses the fact that knowledge, experience and insight need to be interpreted and understood against a background of organising concepts, principles and reasons. The interaction between learners and teachers is thus mediated by general principles of rationality and public criteria to which all parties are bound and which determine and guide the development of knowledge and understanding.

Like their earlier counterparts in the progressive tradition (Hyland, 1979), current models of experiential learning and learner-centredness in the PCET sector all derive their meaning to some extent from a contrast with and reaction to the impression model which is associated with traditional didactic teaching. Gibbs (1988), for instance, described the replacement of teaching strategies based on 'conventional didactic knowledge-centred methods' with an 'experience-based programme' of learning based on an 'experiential learning cycle' which makes use of 'learning logs', 'problem groups' and 'learning reviews' (pp. 102–3) to demonstrate the values of a learning-by-doing methodology. In a similar vein, the Further Education Unit (FEU) vision of the modern 'flexible' FE college as a provider of 'learner services' involved fundamental changes to college organisation and structures to incorporate such new services as 'initial assessment, accreditation of prior learning/achievement (APL/A), action planning, individual learning programmes, top-up facilities, roll-on/roll-off, assessment on demand, records of achievement, credit accumulation, work-based learning and work-based assessment' (p. 2).

In order to supplement this futuristic and essentially utopian vision for FE colleges in recent years, the role of information and communications technology (ICT) has been accorded a central place. In the post-incorporation years, ICT has been seen as a way of managing the FEFC's demands for efficiency gains: teaching more students with fewer staff. Most colleges now have a section – often under the umbrella of open or flexible provision – in which on-line and e-learning is being developed to cope with changing requirements. At the the national level also ICT has been proposed as a panacea for all our current problems and a way of achieving the key aims of lifelong learning in terms of upskilling the workforce and enhancing social inclusion (DfEE, 1998a).

In addition to being one of the three principal key skills which now underpin everything from GCSEs to degrees, ICT is seen as a 'key aid in both delivering learning to adults and in engaging adults in learning' (DfEE, 2000a, p. 20). Since April 2001, an ICT infrastructure – the National Learning Network – has linked all FE and HE institutions through the JANET network to provide a resource base and a means of sharing knowledge across the sector. In addition, the flagship Ufl learn direct initiative (Hyland, 1999) is founded squarely on the use of ICT to encourage individuals and businesses to engage in the new lifelong learning culture. The economic response to globalisation rests almost exclusively on the use of ICT (Barnett, 2002), as indeed does the project of widening participation by involving non-traditional educational students in learning of all kinds (Kennedy, 1997).

Guile and Hayton (1999) have linked the ICT revolution with all major aspects of lifelong learning and FE policy, but argue that the links with 'learner centredness' call for more critical inspection than they currently receive. Observing that there 'can be little doubt that concern with economic, equity or political issues and the imperative to provide access to resources are inescapable elements of public policy for ILT in any sector of education', they go on to note the connections with 'cost-cutting' in FE and the perception on many FE teachers that 'providing students with access to on-line and multi-media resources is primarily a way of reducing staff costs rather than enhancing the quality of teaching and learning' (pp. 122–3).

Recent developments in the field, however, have indicated that ICT is not always a cheap option and that – rather than dispensing with the need for teaching – on-line learning actually increases the need to develop new ways of managing and supporting learning. The over-ambitious claims about the promise and potential of e-learning are now being criticised as 'myths', and there is a growing realisation that ICT learning is neither a cheap alternative nor a solution to the problems of post-school education and training (Twining, 2001c). Moreover, the tendency of ICT to individualise learning and marginalise its important social context has come to be seen as counter-productive, particularly in relation to youngsters in FE who achieved little in their school years (Guile and Young, 2002). Summing up many of these key issues arising from the introduction of ICT and on-line learning, Mayes (2002) argues that the new technology calls for much radical re-thinking about the teacher's role and the context of learning. Attention to the 'design of learning technology' (p. 165), therefore, requires careful thought about how the learning cycle at various stages can best be supported.

There is a growing awareness within lifelong learning discourse that, as Ranson (1998) puts it, there 'is no solitary learning: we can only create our worlds together' (p. 20). For students entering colleges – or adults returning to learning after a number of years out of the system – the 'communities of practice' in which FE learning is situated are seen as crucial to successful achievement and progression (Bloomer and

Hodkinson, 1997). In this respect, it is important for FE teachers to reflect upon – what Harkin *et al.*, (2001) – describe as their 'communication style', and they offer advice on staff development which can 'lead to more enjoyable and more fruitful and fulfilling patterns of working together' (p. 137).

Although we would want to offer broad support for the renewed emphasis in FE on learning processes – and the centrality of individual learners' needs, interests, motivations and requirements – it has to be said that the sort of support necessary to the success of such approaches (particularly in the case of work-based learning and studentship models mentioned later) may require *more* rather than less planning and involvement on the part of teachers. In other words, it is not the replacement of teaching by learning that is required but the transformation of the teachers' role in the PCET sector in the light of the important social context of learning mentioned above. As Dearden (1976) notes – in connecting discovery learning and 'learning how to learn' with the central educational principle of student autonomy – making:

> learning how to learn an objective does not dispense with the need for teaching. At the very most, it shifts the content of what is taught from particularities to the skills, principles and methods of general application which constitutes having learned how to learn.
>
> (p. 74)

Since this notion of learner empowerment is integral – not just to current conceptions of staff and student learning in the FE sector (Armitage *et al.*, 1999) – but also to discourses of lifelong learning (Edwards *et al.*, 2002), the implications for pedagogic relations and the organisation of learning support mechanisms become central to all policy implementation.

Young (1998) brings out the central issues in this sphere in discussing the development of 'learner-centredness' as a response to both the modularisation of the curriculum and the rise of outcomes-based models (such as G/NVQs) in FE colleges. As he notes, 'modularization focuses on students as *managers of their own learning* who need feedback to provide a basis for improving their own learning strategies, and as *decision-makers* and *choosers* of learning programmes' (p. 86, original italics). However, a number of serious problems may arise if such notions are accepted without qualification and due consideration. The ability to make learning decisions, as Young notes, is 'itself something which has to be learned, something recognized in the fashionable idea of learning to learn'; thus a 'learner-centred approach, even if it begins by separating outcomes from processes, has to be complemented by a focus on how learners are supported by teachers' (ibid., p. 86). There are, therefore, certain 'limitations of approaches that over-emphasize the active role of learners', and Young concludes by arguing that:

> In suggesting that students or trainees will learn by themselves if certain barriers, such as college attendance at particular times, are removed, the proponents of learner-centredness may be searching for a modern version of the old apprenticeship idea of 'learning by doing'. Whereas, at least in the apprenticeship model, there was some institutional support for the apprentice to learn from experience, in the new model learning is entirely up to the individual . . . It is difficult to see how learner-centred approaches can, on their own, get beyond encouraging students to learn by trial and error. This would not seem to be the basis for raising levels of achievement or preparing young people for a world of work in which more and more jobs are likely to require conceptual knowledge and skills that cannot be learned on the job alone.
>
> (p. 87)

The important caveats in relation to new active learning approaches offered by Young are paralleled in the literature on andragogy. The basic concept has Greek origins though, in modern times was resurrected first by Lindeman and then reconstructed by Knowles (Davenport, 1993) to distinguish between principles of learning and teaching for adults and children. Defining andragogy as the 'art and science of helping adults to learn', Knowles (1970) identified key features of adult learning – such as 'self-directedness', 'experiential techniques' and 'problem-solving' (pp. 43–4) – which were designed to 'progressively decrease the learner's dependency on the educator' (Mezirow, 1983, p. 136). The central error in all this – later acknowledged by Knowles (1979) – is assuming that self-direction is a natural trait of adults and that the learning habits and critical capacities which underpin such learning will develop without the guidance and support of teachers. Brookfield (1986) expresses the main criticisms well in his observation that:

> to act as a resource person to adults who are unaware of belief systems, bodies of knowledge, or behavioural possibilities other than those that they have uncritically assimilated since childhood is to condemn such adults to remaining within existing paradigms of thought and action. It is misconceived to talk of the self-directedness

of learners who are unaware of alternative ways of thinking, perceiving or behaving.

(p. 124)

If this is true for adults, it is even more significant for younger learners
in FE colleges, many of whom have left school with few qualifications,
poor study habits and a lack of confidence in their own abilities. Thus,
whereas models of 'open' and 'flexible' learning – involving IT packages
and distance materials (Frankel and Reeves, 1996) – are often rhetorically
emphasised in FE mission statements, the reality is that most FE students
experience fairly traditional methods of teaching with the 'proportion
of college provision delivered through open learning typically between
2 and 3 percent of enrolments' (FEFC, 1996, p. 19). Certainly, in the
transition from school to FE, younger students expected the college ethos
to be less authoritarian than that of school. As one of the participants
(then a Training Officer at an African Caribbean Women's Centre) in our
FEDA project commented:

> At college you have lecturers and they guide you – your develop-
> ment. It is left to you, the individual, how you develop. Basically
> you are an adult so you decide. The lecturers are there to help and
> support you.
>
> (Merrill, 2000, p. 17)

In similar vein, an A-level FE student remarked that at 'the old school
you did not work because you were doing it for the teachers . . . Here they
just say, "If you do not work then that is your problem"' (ibid.). The FE
students in Ainley and Bailey's (1997) research made similar comments
about how FE tutors treated them more like 'adults' and 'human beings'
(p. 80).

However, with the emergence of a new funding system rewarding
retention and achievement of students, the problem is placed squarely
at the door of college tutors and managers. Since staying-on rates across
the country have been 'normalised' (Ainley and Green, 1996) in recent
years by a range of factors – from a lack of jobs for young people to
parent and peer group pressure – the FE sector is now taking increased
numbers of students with few qualifications and a lack of achievement
from their school years. Hence, the increased emphasis on learning
support mechanisms in colleges (Harris and Hyland, 1995) to ensure
student retention and satisfactory completion of programmes. Thus, in
addition to specialised support in basic skills such as literacy, numeracy

and ICT, current practice tends to be couched in terms of 'individual learning programmes, primary learning goals and personal training plans' (Dimbleby and Cooke, 2000, p. 73). All such FE learning developments, however, need to be qualified by reference to the plurality and wide diversity of the student experience in colleges. As Ainley and Bailey (1997) express this point, 'FE may be polytechnic but it is not comprehensive' (p. 78), and the experience of students at foundation, intermediate and advanced levels of learning are vastly different. Motivations for entering or returning to FE vary widely (Merrill, 2000, p. 26) as do learning needs and capacities, and – if the messages of Tomlinson (1996) and Kennedy (1997) about the need to change institutional practices to enhance inclusion are attended to – then colleges still have much to do in terms of providing effective support mechanisms which reflect learning diversity. These issues will be taken up later in the discussion of work-based learning and models of studentship in the PCET sector.

Curriculum

As mentioned earlier, the FE sector is essentially polytechnic and its curriculum reflects this being 'based on a range of models reflecting different academic and vocational cultures and the traditions and qualifications that go with them' (Dimbleby and Cooke, 2000, p. 77). Although, unlike the schooling system, there is no post-school national curriculum, a combination of educational market forces, funding mechanisms and qualification requirements has produced a more or less standardised pattern of provision across the sector. The policy developments referred to in the first two chapters have coalesced in recent years to bring about a divided curriculum and qualifications system based on a 'triple-track' model (illustrated in Figure 7.1).

Young and Spours (1998, pp. 87–91) provide a useful summary of the 'stages of development of a national 14–19 system' in terms of distinct, though overlapping and interrelated, phases 1979–1991, characterised by *ad hoc* expansion of programmes and new pre-vocational developments (such as TVEI, CPVE, YTS) linked to the 'new vocationalism'. Curbs placed on internal course assessment for A-levels and establishment of the NCVQ in 1986 to replace traditional qualifications such as BTEC, and RSA with competence-based NVQs. Further development of NVQs during 1991 to 1995 and the introduction of GNVQs in 1992/3 were meant to offer a broad vocational foundation for either work or further study. The triple-track system was firmly embedded during this phase,

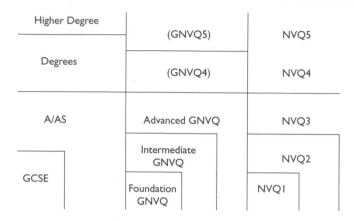

Figure 7.1 The triple-track qualifications framework
Source: based on Hyland (1999, p. 90)

though there was much lobbying (Finegold, *et al.* 1990, NCE, 1993) for the creation of a more unified curriculum.

Between 1996 and 1998 and after the Dearing (1996) review of qualifications, there was emphasis on developing linkages between the different tracks through overarching certificates, modularisation and underpinning key skills.

Educational policy and practice in relation to the 14–19 curriculum has tended to be qualification-led (particularly in the case of G/NVQs), often to the neglect of processes and methodology. Hodgson and Spours (1997) neatly summarise the key themes in this sphere in their observation that:

> Fundamentally, the debate about the English 14–19 qualifications system is a debate about whether it evolves in a more unified direction or whether it remains a distinctive track-based system, emphasizing the division between academic and vocational learning and certification.
>
> (p. 18)

The 1996 Dearing review of qualifications contained ambivalent recommendations for reform in that they not only served to consolidate the three-track system of academic, general vocational and work-based vocational awards but also (paradoxically) allowed for 'students to change pathways' (Dearing, 1996, p. 10) and created National Awards which combined elements of the different tracks to 'encourage studies in depth, with complementary studies to give breadth' (ibid., p. 21).

In response to Dearing, three policy perspectives on 14–19 qualifications reform began to emerge (Hodgson and Spours, 1997, pp. 11–13): (1) Trackers: those who believe in three distinctive qualification tracks (e.g. Raffe, 1993; Smithers, 1993; Prais, 1995) based on alleged different abilities of students, resulting in different goals and purposes for academic as against vocational learning. (2) Frameworkers: those who support the retention of pathways (FEU, 1995; HMC, 1995; Dearing, 1996) but allow for overarching frameworks (such as national awards, credit systems or underpinning key skills) to create greater flexibility and inclusive access to the curriculum. Supporters of GNVQs (Higgins and Merson, 1995; Halsall and Cockett, 1996) see these broad-based vocational awards as a means of enhancing the frameworking goals. (3) Unifiers: those who argue for a completely unified system (NCE, 1993; Hyland, 1994; Hodgson and Spours, 1997) which would involve a core PCET curriculum (especially for the 14–19 age group) and the replacement of existing qualifications by a single overarching structure.

Proponents of all three positions agree on the need for 14–19 reform to raise general levels of achievement, trackers and unifiers both admire the general educational foundation of Continental VET systems, and frameworkers and unifiers both favour the unitisation and modularisation of education and training. As Hodgson and Spours (1997) observe, the 'arguments for a unified qualifications system have become stronger' in the last few years, and there has emerged a large 'degree of consensus between the frameworkers and the unifiers because there is a mutual acceptance that the unified system is the long-term aim' (p. 13). However, as Young (1999) argues, although the New Labour government has developed a more proactive agenda on qualifications linked to the key themes of lifelong learning and social inclusion, it is still the case that the 'basic structure of the qualification system has changed little' (p. 178) in recent times.

There are three principal aspects of current PCET policy which point towards the need for a more unified system – social inclusion, vocational programmes and lifelong learning.

1 *Social inclusion.* The importance of this aspect of current policy was described in Chapter 2, and it is the links with widening participation in F/HE and removing barriers to progression that have implications for curriculum and qualifications reform. The main function of the qualifications system in the past has been in screening and selecting students for either progression to HE or for particular forms of

employment. The arguments of those identified as 'trackers' are essentially supported by an attachment to a stratified education system – within which A-levels represented both a gold standard and means of controlling entry to HE and high status work – based on the tripartite legacy of the 1944 Education Act. In a review of forty years of debate about post-16 qualifications, Pound (1998) concluded that 'A-levels provide an insurmountable barrier to the quest for breadth in the post-compulsory curriculum as a whole'. With the transition from an elite to a mass system of higher education – with the ultimate objective that 'by 2010, 50% of young people should have the opportunity of benefiting from HE by the time they are 30' (DfEE, 2000c, p. 3) – there is now even less justification for the maintenance of a system whose whole *raison d'etre* is the identification of an elite group of students suitable for entry to university. Moreover, the growth of access and non-traditional, second chance routes to HE has demonstrated that mature students on such programmes do as well and, in many cases, better than traditional candidates (Hartley *et al.*, 1997).

2   *Vocational programmes.* Vocational learning (as the discussion below elaborates) is now central to all current policy drivers and the role of FE in achieving 'vocational excellence for all' (DfEE, 2001a, para. 28) is centre stage. Our VET systems have consistently underachieved and compared unfavourably with continental models, whether these are 'schooling' or 'work-based' models of vocational preparation (Skilbeck, *et al.*, 1994). Green (1997b) describes two major strategies for ensuring that VET is underpinned by the general educational foundation necessary for adult and working life. The 'general technical and vocational education' paradigm – which characterises VET in France, Germany, Japan and Sweden – is 'based on the precept that vocational learning rests on a common foundation of general education, or *cultural generale* as it is termed in France' (p. 92). This approach assumes that all forms of study – whether academic or vocational – require a common foundation and a basic minimum cultural entitlement. The 'core skills paradigm', on the other hand – operating in the United States and Britain – assumes no such general foundation or entitlement but bases VET on strictly utilitarian considerations and workplace skills. As Green comments, on this latter model, 'general education is only necessary to the extent that it underpins competent performance in expected work tasks' (ibid., p. 93). The inadequacy of this approach – especially in the light of the current ambitious targets for vocational learning in

F/HE – is now being acknowledged (DfES, 2001) and recommendations for reform suggested along the lines of a more unified system of provision and qualifications.

3 *Lifelong learning.* There is a sense in which only some form of unified curriculum and assessment framework would be capable of achieving the objectives of lifelong learning in helping to create a 'frame-work of opportunities for people to learn and to lift barriers that prevent them from taking up those opportunities' (DfEE, 1998a, p. 13). A learning culture requires curricula and qualifications which acknowledge the value of *all* learning achievements and which positively encourages progression and continuity at all levels. In this respect, the current obsession with performance indicators and learning targets might easily prove counter-productive. Coffield (2000) has warned of the dangers of sliding into the performative society, where the maximisation of performance becomes the highest good, and where 'the transformative power of education is reduced to the increasingly rigorous measurements of inputs and outputs' (p. 28). Learning targets, therefore, may be useful in raising aspirations, motivating individuals and groups and demonstrating accountable, but learning must also be accorded an *intrinsic* value if we are to avoid becoming what Ainley calls a 'certified society' (1999, p. 3) rather than a genuine learning society.

Current curriculum and qualifications reform has tended to foreground the 14–19 stage as a lever of change to raise standards, enhance progression and upgrade vocational studies. The key policy documents in this field – *Qualifying for Success* (DfEE, 1998d) – heralded reform in four key areas:

- A-levels split into two three-unit blocks at AS (Year 11) and A2 (Year 12) with the aim of encouraging students to do four or five AS units in the first year then three A2s in the second.
- Key skills to underpin all 14+ learning, communication, application of number and IT as mandatory with optional ones of improving own learning and performance, problem solving and working with others.
- Upgrading vocational studies through the reform of N/GNVQs, mainly bringing vocational qualifications into line with academic ones by strengthening external assessment.
- A unitised qualifications system at 14+ to harmonise and rationalise the national framework with an overarching advanced certificate to bridge the vocational/academic divide

Introduced under the Curriculum 2000 label in September 2000, the new system has met with mixed success. Although there were some 'real gains' noted in the first year, with students and teachers endorsing the 'greater breadth of study and . . . increased choice and flexibility', there were also problems connected with 'excess of content' connected with AS levels and problems with the implementation of key skills (QCA, 2001a, pp. 1–2). Proposed reforms include the slimming down of AS levels, changing of exam sequences and allowing greater flexibility in the teaching of key skills. However, the new framework – supported by the encouraging take-up of the new Vocational A-Levels (formerly advanced GNVQs) and the introduction of Advanced Vocational Education Certificates (VCE) single awards equivalent to single A-levels (Educa, 2000) – is now firmly in place and provides the foundation for all future developments, including the introduction of Vocational GCSEs to replace Foundation and Intermediate GNVQs in Autumn 2002 (Educa, 2001b).

The most recent curriculum reforms have sought to reinforce standards and consolidate the vocational studies route for 14–19 year olds. The Green Paper – *14–19: Extending Opportunities, Raising Standards* (DfES, 2002a) – is designed to solve a number of key problems linked to the task of raising standards for 14–16 underachievers, maintaining A-level excellence and strengthening the work based route. To this end the following proposals are put forward (ibid., p. 1) intended to:

- raise achievement for all at age 19, with GCSEs as a progress check
- increase challenge at A-level by incorporating more demanding 'Distinction' questions into both vocational and academic subjects
- increase flexibility to ensure that individuals can learn at a pace which is right for them
- free up the curriculum with young people post-14 able to pursue individually focused programmes (Maths, English, ICT and Science will remain compulsory)
- build parity of status between vocational and academic GCSEs and A-levels
- introduce a Matriculation Diploma that recognises achievement at 19 across a range of disciplines
- provide individually tailored support through Connexions which will focus on giving help and support for those who need it most.

The proposed reforms have attracted positive and negative criticisms, with some commentators describing them as an 'historic chance to raise the status of vocational skills and create a broader, less restrictive curriculum' (Hargreaves, 2002, p.

19), whereas others have expressed concern about the relegation of modern foreign languages to an entitlement rather than a compulsory subject, in addition to the cross-institutional problems associated with 'flexible' 14–19 provisions (Twining, 2002a).

What is certain is that the success or failure of the new 14–19 curriculum will turn on how far the core ingredient of vocational studies – and the crucial work-based learning element – is organised and supported by FE colleges and their community partners.

Vocational studies and work-based vocational learning

The vocational aspect of lifelong learning in the context of the FE mission was mentioned in the first two chapters. Recent emphases in New Labour PCET policy have tended to highlight the failure of past policies to solve the persistent problems of VET: under-investment by employers and the state, mismatch between vocational programmes and employers' skill requirements and, most entrenched and worrying of all, the subordinate and under-valued status of vocational learning compared with its academic/general educational counterpart. The recent proposals for 14–19 reform were specifically addressed to bringing about a 'vocational renaissance that captures the imagination of young people and challenges prejudice' (DfES, 2002b, p. 1) in education and training in this sphere.

The inferior and essentially classed nature of vocational learning (with liberal study for upper classes and vocational studies for others) has been a feature of the hierarchical values placed on knowledge and education of different kinds since the Ancient Greeks (Schofield, 1972), and entered the English system around the sixteenth century when, as Kenneth Richmond (1945) explains, the ideals of the 'common' school for all were transformed by political events:

> The conviction that there are two distinct brands of education, one for the rulers and another for the commoners, dates from the sixteenth century. The divergence was not at first clearly marked; under the Stuarts, for example, the rich were less cut off from intermingling with other classes in the schools than they are today; but the eighteenth century confirmed it as a hard-and-fast rule.
>
> (p. 53)

These distinctions were reinforced in the nineteenth century with the 'gentleman ideal' (Wilkinson, 1970) and public school tradition informing the establishment of a stratified system of schooling which – in the triple-track system mentioned earlier – survives to this day and frustrates attempts to reform VET. In this respect it is interesting that – in the then Secretary of State's response to the report of the National Skills Task Force in 2001 – the 'relative weakness of our vocational education and training system' was dated 'back to the establishment of the Samuelson Royal Commission in 1884' (DfEE, 2001a, p8).

Esland (1990) has noted that – although VET issues have remained high on the political agenda since the 1970's oil crisis and recession – the state's response has typically been one of 'crisis management . . . giving rise to schemes and initiatives designed to limit the social damage which followed de-industrialisation' (p. v). More recently in introducing the flagship UfI blueprint, Hillman (1997) remarked that 'deficiencies in British education and training have been a cause for concern for policy-makers for the last 150 years' and that – response to the main problems – there had been a 'flurry of reforms in the last ten years . . . an array of short-term and narrowly focused initiatives' (pp. 29–30). Amongst this 'flurry of reforms' were the schemes associated with the new vocationalism of the 1980s – TVEI, YTS, Training Credits, TECs and the NCVQ experiment. Only time will tell if the post-1997 reforms in this sphere – UfI, New Deal Welfare to Work, Curriculum 2000, reconstructed Modern Apprenticeships, and so on – will prove any more successful.

Certainly the emphasis on upgrading vocational studies – particularly as far as PCET policy and the FE sector is concerned – has never been so high on the political agenda. In setting out the policy blueprint and mission for FE in the twenty-first century, the then Secretary of State, David Blunkett, observed that:

> Not only have we had to contend with an elitist academic culture which has failed to value technical study and attainment, we have also had unnecessary conflicts between different models of technical education and vocational training. And our system of vocational qualifications has remained immensely complicated. We must build on the reforms I have recently set in hand, to put in place a balanced system, which is transparent to all concerned, gives due weight to every element of the system and encourages high standards and progression.
>
> (DfEE, 2000a, para. 36)

More recently, the former Secretary of State, Estelle Morris, has (DfES, 2001b) observed that 'vocational education has been persistently undervalued' and outlined plans to 'break down the traditional prejudice against vocational education as a route to success' (paras. 4.2, 4.4). In addition to the vocational GCSE and A-level reforms already noted, there are plans to enhance basic skills and to establish a £38 million programme of work placements for 14–16 year olds following vocational routes (ibid., para. 4.7).

In addition to a new emphasis on the 14–19 curriculum and qualifications structure, current policies demonstrate a determination to challenge the key problems of vocational studies, and the chief vehicle in this respect is work-based or work-related learning. Work-based learning holds a central place in the building of the 'new vocational ladder of opportunity' (DfEE, 2000a, para. 33) and figures prominently in 14–19 reforms and in the new Foundation degrees and reconstructed Modern Apprenticeships currently coming on stream. Since FE colleges – working with schools, employers, HE institutions and other agencies – will be expected to play a central co-ordinating role in the new work-related or work-based activity, it is important to clarify its main features.

Work-based learning (WBL) – described by Boud and Symes (2000) as 'an idea whose time has come' and an acknowledgement that 'work . . . is imbued with learning opportunities' (pp. 14–15) – has emerged as one of the key features of VET reforms as systems respond to the demands of global competitiveness and the knowledge economy. Ideas are derived from a number of sources connected with the learning organisation, the attempt to integrate theory and practice, and the need to respond to the challenges of knowledge creation in the light of new ICT and global economic developments. As Marsick and Watkins (2002) observe, the 'rapidly changing world in which we have been living is giving birth to a host of new ways of understanding work, jobs, organisations, technology and change' (p. 34). On first inspection, few of these policy drivers have much to do with curricular or pedagogic matters and – from the point of view of FE staff and students – it will be important to distinguish between educational and economic issues if work-based learning is to be successfully managed and supported.

In the wide-ranging study by Levy et al. (1989, p. 4) WBL was understood to mean 'linking learning to the work role' which was identified in terms of three interrelated components:

1 Structuring learning in the workplace.
2 Providing appropriate on-job training/learning opportunities.
3 Identifying and providing relevant off-job learning opportunities.

Further perspectives are provided in the study by Seagraves *et al.* (1996) in their distinctions between:

*   learning *for* work (general VET programmes)
*   learning *at* work (in-house education and training)
*   learning *through* work (the application of job-related knowledge and skills to work processes).

As Brennan and Little (1996) suggest in their comprehensive study of WBL schemes in HE, 'learning *for* work may well include elements of learning *at* work and learning *through* work' (p. 5), and this is certainly the case in Modern Apprenticeships, traineeships, G/NVQs and, more than likely, the planned vocational GCSEs for 14–16 year olds.

Barnett (2002) also reminds us that – although 'work and learning are not synonymous' – the 'two concepts overlap' since:

> Work can and should offer learning opportunities; much learning is demanding, calling on the learner to yield to certain standards, and contains the character of work . . . the challenge here is that of bringing about the greatest overlap between work and learning.
>
> (p. 19)

This optimistic vision – especially as far as FE students are concerned – needs to be tempered by the realities of the modern workplace which, as the *Learning Society* research findings indicated, often provide few opportunities for positive learning to take place. Although some of the larger British firms do encourage workplace learning, according to Ashton *et al.* (2000), 'something like two thirds of the work force do not work in such organisations' and 'there has been little or no increase in the autonomy enjoyed by the average British worker' (pp. 222–3). Similar findings apply in particular to small firms which account for around 35 per cent of total employment (Hyland and Matlay, 1997). This gap between rhetoric and reality in relation to learning and work – along with the myths about post-Fordism and the global economy discussed in Chapter 2 – will need to be taken into account by all those managing and supporting learning in the FE sector. In terms of organisational and support structures, the increasing centrality of forms of apprenticeship – a traditional paradigm of vocational studies generally and WBL in particular – to all current PCET policy initiatives is worth noting and, in this respect, the recent reconstruction of modern apprenticeships merits special attention.

Reconstructed modern apprenticeships

The centrality of the concept of apprenticeship in VET systems may be explained in terms of traditional forms of society in which the vital vocational functions of passing on skills, knowledge and practices were essential to survival and reproduction. Both the formal and informal educational practices of the earliest societies would have required systems in which young people could learn to hunt, fish, fight, prepare food and clothing, and care for children (see, for instance, Benjamin's 'Saber-tooth curriculum' [1939/1975] made up of the skills of fish-grabbing, horse-clubbing and saber-tooth tiger-scaring). Such practices would have eventually been formalised as tribes developed religious, puberty and organisational/leadership mores, norms and rituals (Wilds and Lottich, 1970).

Gospel (1998) has assembled a substantial body of research on apprenticeships and offers a clear account of what might be described as the 'traditional' model which he defines as:

> a method of employment and on-the-job training which involves a set of reciprocal rights and duties between an employer and a trainee . . . the employer agrees to teach a range of skills, usually of a broad occupational nature; in return, the apprentice agrees to work for an extended period at a training wage which is low compared to the qualified workers' rate.
>
> (p. 437)

Emerging from the medieval craft and guilds systems, the first apprenticeships reflected the fact that almost all education at this time consisted in 'on the job' training based on fixed periods of indenture which, as a general rule, was for seven years between the ages of 14 and 21. The institution was codified during the Elizabethan period through the 1563 Statute of Artificers which imposed the traditional seven-year identure on some 30 crafts and which – along with the 1601 Poor Law Act – allowed pauper children to become apprentices (Coffey, 1992).

The decline and dilution of apprenticed trades and occupations began in the late nineteenth and early twentieth century as a result of the onset of mass production and the increasing tendency of employers to split traditional skilled jobs such as metalworking into constituent parts. As Adams (1996) observes, from the 1920s onwards the apprenticeship system was subjected to fierce criticism on the grounds that it:

involved unnecessary time-serving [satirised as time-wasting], that it did not train to consistent standards, was not well suited to modern technological occupations, perpetuated outdated and irrelevant demarcations betweeen trades and was predominantly restricted to young male workers.

(p. 6.)

As a result of the widespread de-industrialisation of much of Britain throughout the 1980s there was a sharp decline in apprenticeships – from 107,400 in 1978 to 34,500 in 1990 (Gospel, 1995, p. 37). Along with employers' perennial complaints about the failure of schooling to match industrial needs, the decline in apprenticeships fuelled an increasing concern over the erosion of the national craft and technician skills base.

The Modern Apprenticeship (MA) programme – announced in 1993 with a three-year budget of £1.25 billion – was established as a prototype in 1994 and launched nationally in 1995. Principal aims of the programme included the provision of employer-based learning for 16–25 year olds to NVQ level 3, the improvement of the supply of intermediate skills (especially in craft, technician and supervisory occupations) to remedy shortages, and the incorporation of 'job-specific, key skills and broad occupational knowledge' to ensure that the 'Modern Apprenticeship offers both a relevant and flexible structure to the training needs of industry' (Skills and Enterprise Network, 1997, p. 1). By October 1997 there were 144,576 MAs in the scheme, 56 per cent male and 44 per cent female (Gospel, 1998, p. 22), and by the beginning of 1999 almost 225,000 youngsters had completed MA schemes, 126,000 were undertaking training in 80 industrial sectors, and plans were announced to increase numbers by a further 10,000 (DfEE, 1999b, p. 3).

In purely quantitative terms, there is a degree of support for the official government 'success story' (Skills and Enterprise Network, 1997, p. 1) evaluation of the MA schemes. By spring 2000, 325,000 16–25 year olds had joined the programme covering 82 industrial sectors (Unwin and Wellington, 2001, p. 13) and there are currently around 213,000 youngsters undertaking MA training (Educa, 2001c, p. 15). Moreover, the new models have incorporated new occupational sectors – such as local government and the armed forces – enhanced the basic minimum achievement from level 2 to 3, helped to break down some of the prejudice against VET investment to bring Britain closer in line with Continental systems (Green, 1997a) and, of considerable importance, encouraged many more young women to undertake apprenticeships, going some way towards breaking down the traditional white male stereotype of former years. The number of young people leaving the work-based route with level 3 qualifications doubled between 1995 and 2000, and in some regions 'over 90% of those completing their MAs were still in employment after their training – around half of them with the same company that they had trained with' (LSC, 2001c, p. 1).

On the demerit side, a number of problems and shortcomings have emerged. A 1998 report by the Centre for Economic Performance noted that – although the take-up of MAs trebled between 1994 and 1997 – they were 'still the post-school choice of only 10% of young people compared to two-thirds in Germany' (Hart, 1998, p. 27). Similar unfavourable comparisons were cited in the DfEE (2001a) response to the National Skills Task Force Final Report in the observation that 'around 4 in 10 of those in jobs in the UK hold the equivalent of A-level qualifications, but in Germany the figure is double' and 'among young adults in Japan and Korea more than double' (p. 11). In addition, the relatively low level of completion rates for MAs (i.e. those leaving with level 3 qualifications) continues to be a cause for concern. Typically, completion rates average out below 40 per cent in most sectors, ranging from 56 per cent in Construction and 52 per cent in Engineering manufacture to 16 per cent in Retailing and Hotel and Catering (Unwin and Wellington, 2001, p. 14).

Moreover, Adams stressed the weaknesses of the original MA links with the 'pseudo-minimalist approach of NVQS as opposed to the 'broad-based skills acquired by apprentices in traditional occupations' (p. 47), particularly in view of the key lifelong learning objective of fostering flexible and multi-skilled workers required by post-Fordist economies. The Ernst & Young evaluation of MAs also reported the problem of having to 'convince employers of the benefit of NVQs' (1995, p. 11). Perhaps more worrying than all these issues has been the lack of adequate support, guidance and co-ordinating of learning on work-based schemes. A Training Standards Council Report on MAs noted that 'trainee support services, as a whole, were poorly co-ordinated' (Sherlock, 1999, p. 10), and Unwin and Wellington's (2001) data revealed similar unsystematic, piecemeal and ad hoc monitoring and supervisory procedures on the workplace elements of MA programmes.

The reconstruction of MAs in 2001 – incorporating the establishment of Foundation Modern Apprenticeships (FMAs to replace level 2 National Traineeships), Advanced Modern Apprenticeships (AMAs to level 3), in addition to Foundation Degrees and Graduate Apprenticeships (DfEE, 2001a, p. 11) – can be seen as a direct response to the principal problems highlighted in the original MA programme. Taking the lead on these developments, the LSC announced plans to increase the number of entrants by 255 – from 140,000 to 175,000 – over the next three years, in addition to improving completion rates and strengthening the content of MAs through technical certificates and diplomas incorporating a wider range of vocational knowledge and skills (LSC, 2001b). Improvements in the light of previously identified weaknesses are also evident in the reconstructed MA provisions for:

> a national framework for apprenticeship which defines basic standards and strengthens the relationship between the employer and the apprentice . . . [and] an entitlement to a Modern Apprenticeship place for all 16 and 17 year olds with five or more GCSE passes at grades A to G from September 2004.
>
> (DfES, 2001d, p. 1)

FE institutions will have a principal role to play in delivering, managing and supporting learning on the MAs and other WBL programmes in the years ahead and, in this respect, it will be vital to ensure that appropriate monitoring and supervisory procedures are firmly embedded in the new partnerships in the PCET sector.

Studentship and learning careers in FE

The expansion of FE over recent years has been accompanied by the development and reinforcement of guidance, counselling and learning support mechanisms at all levels. Kennedy (1997) called for a 'national entitlement to information, advice and guidance' for all post-16 learners, in addition to emphasising the need for impartial and 'specialised careers education and guidance' to 'help learners plan their long-tern career pathway' (pp. 89, 91). The official government response to Kennedy acknowledged past weaknesses and promised to 'ensure that all learners have easy access to information' so as to 'promote young people's entitlement to post-16 learning' (DfEE, 1998b, p. 19).

As a direct result of the expansion of FE in recent years, there is now a correspondingly expanded group of students – adult returners as well as 16–19 year olds – who have few formal qualifications and who possess below-average literacy and numeracy skills (hence the continuing emphasis in government policy on basic skills work; DfEE, 1998a; DfEE, 2001a). As a way of dealing with this new cohort of students, FE institutions have invested much time and effort in developing appropriate support mechanisms. There is a sense in which the FE sector – in its traditional role of providing 'second chance' routes for those who have been failed by the school system – already had a history of learning support involving the diagnosis of problems, the monitoring of progress and the counselling of students. Further impetus to such developments was provided by the post-incorporation funding formula, referred to in Chapter 1, which allocated finances to students – not just on enrolment – but on programme completion and the achievement of qualifications.

In spite of the new mechanisms of support in the sector, however, student drop-out (or non-completion) of programmes remained unacceptably high throughout the 1990s. A report by the Audit Commission in 1993 indicated that around 150,000 young people aged between 16 to 19 were leaving sixth-form and FE colleges without achieving the qualifications they were registered for (Audit Commission/HMI, 1993). More recently, FEFC figures revealed that – although student numbers in FE grew by 16 per cent between 1994 and 1996 – drop-out rates also increased to 18 per cent for full-time students and 16 per cent for part-timers (Thomson, 1997). A report on achievement and retention rates published by the Audit Office in March 2001 noted that – although student achievement of qualifications had gone up on average from 65 per cent in 1994–95 to 73 per cent in 1998–99 – there were still colleges with achievement rates below 50 per cent and that 'greater improvements must be made if the government is to achieve national learning targets set for 2002' (FEFC, 2001, p. 1).

Problems and difficulties concerned with achieving impartial and genuinely neutral student guidance – particularly on admissions to programmes – were inevitably caused by the competition brought about by incorporation and by the 'overriding commitment to a market ideology' (Cantor *et al.*, 1995, p. 13) which dominated the FE field. In the new marketised and 'McDonaldised' (Hyland, 1999) PCET sector learners have, until relatively recently, been encouraged – by means of glossy college brochures, training credits and smart cards for purchasing education and training courses (Avis *et al.*, 1996) – to think of themselves as self-interested consumers shopping for educational commodities (mainly employability credits through G/NVQs) in the FE supermarket (Reeves, 1995).

Bolstered by the post-1993 funding mechanisms, this system resulted in a squalid scramble for students and, in this atmosphere, the idea of impartial guidance services was distorted in a desperate bid to boost numbers at any cost. As Nicholls (1995) observed at the time, whereas in former years the LEA had a duty of service to ensure that all students had access to the best possible advice, post-incorporation competition and funding regulations had often caused individual needs to be overlooked.

He went on to ask the emotive question of whether 'the development of free market competition was being paid for by the life chances of young people' (p. 20). As mentioned earlier, following the Kennedy report official government statements on the FE sector have sought to emphasise collaboration and partnership between providers as against competition and market forces. The recently launched 'Connexions' service (DfEE, 2001b) will be the principal vehicle for the new 'joined-up' approach to learning support and guidance. In the recent Grant Letter for 2002–3 sent by the Secretary of State to the LSC Chairman (DfES, 2001c) the LLSCs are instructed to:

> Work with the developing *Connexions* partnerships, especially in joint planning and information sharing, to ensure that young people are on appropriate and relevant learning opportunities; thereby increasing the proportion of 16–18 year olds participating in structured learning in 2002 by at least 2 percentage points compared to 2000, and reducing significantly the number of 16–18 year olds not in education training or work.
>
> (p. 3)

The new approach to learning support and guidance will have a crucial role to play in the planned government initiatives in the FE sector over the next few years. New programmes involving work-based learning as a central element were mentioned above and, in this respect, foundation degrees and restructured modern apprenticeships will be the chief vehicles in the creation of the planned vocational ladder of opportunity. Foundation degrees (HEFCE, 2000) were launched in 2001/2 – offered by '21 consortia, involving 35 higher education institutions, 70 further education colleges, and a range of employers, national training organisations and other organisations' (p. 1) – are 'vocationally-oriented qualifications' delivered in two years and intended to be routes into employment or to further HE study. Work-based learning will form a significant ingredient in this new tertiary route, and will also be central to new modern apprenticeships – in both foundation (level 3) and graduate (level 4) modes – and in all these initiatives 'further education colleges will play a central part' (DfEE, 2000a, para. 42).

FE institutions will also be at the centre of the re-engineered 14–19 system in which raising achievement and standards in vocational learning is a principal objective. Underachieving pupils – those who in the past might have left school with few or no qualifications and little in the way of aspirations and motivation for learning – in the 14–16 range are a particular focus, and there will be an emphasis on the basics as well 'work-related vocational programmes . . . followed by a Modern Apprenticeship or full-time vocational study at college and a foundation degree for those who have the potential' (DfES, 2001b, p. 3). Again, in the grant letter to the LSC the objectives of this phase are highlighted in the form of an intention to:

> Support the development of a more coherent and well-balanced 14–19 phase of learning . . . This will help to launch the new GCSEs in vocational subjects in 2002 and create up to 40,000 part-time vocational placements for 14–16 year olds who undertake at least part of their study in school, FE college or with a private training provider.
>
> (DfES, 2001c, p. 3)

Given that some form of work-based or work-related learning will be central to all these developments – vocational GCSEs, vocational A-levels, foundation and graduate apprenticeships and foundation degrees – designed to build 'our new vocational ladder of opportunity' (DfEE, 2000a, para. 33) – it is vital that these adequate partnerships and support mechanisms are firmly in place. Such a ladder of opportunity can only be constructed on the basis of *equitable* partnerships between all the various agencies and stakeholders of the sort suggested in the 'local learning strategies' outlined in the LSC corporate plan (LSC, 2001a, p. 15). In the past, FE institutions have often been regarded as cheap providers of HE for non-traditional students, with little acknowledgement given of the specialist knowledge and expertise – particularly that related to work and vocationalism – of FE staff. For the new partnership initiatives to succeed, the FE role will need to be strengthened considerably. A useful model in this respect is the University of Huddersfield Consortium for PCET involving over thirty FE and HE providers across the North of England and founded on the principles of 'equality, reciprocity, openness and shared resources and responsibilities' (University of Huddersfield, 2001, pp. 2–3).

The success of the new work-based learning initiatives will also turn significantly on the notion of collaboration and the sharing of resources and knowledge across and between agencies. It has to be said that earlier schemes of this sort have not been able to meet fully the objectives set for them. The Training Credits scheme investigated by Hodkinson (1996), for instance, betrayed an attachment to a model of choice, decision-making and learning progression which was far removed from the lives of the young people for whom the system was designed. Mechanisms underpinning the then post-16 training market were characterised by what Hodkinson called 'technical rationality' by which the 'decision-making process is seen as a production line along which the young person progresses, completing the decision stage by stage' (p. 124).

Research on the choice and decision-making processes actually employed by young people in real-life contexts, however, indicates how far these were at odds with the technical-rational model. In real-life situations – as against those imagined or hypothesised by the DfES, Employment Service or careers advisers – judgements about work and learning were influenced by a whole range of diverse factors, such as local contacts, work experience, family and peer influences, and the general milieux of people and cultures which impact upon and shape the lives of young people. Such a combination of factors and influences leads naturally to decisions which are – neither technically rational nor irrational – but, in Hodkinson's terms, 'pragmatically rational' in the sense that choices and judgements are 'embedded in the complex struggles and negotiations' (ibid., p. 133) of the post-school VET scene.

Moreover, as Bloomer and Hodkinson's (1997) study of young people in FE demonstrated, guidance processes at this stage must crucially acknowledge how 'needs, wants and intentions . . . change over time. For some, what appeared a perfect match in May was inappropriate in October' (p. 84). To take account of such diversity and complexity, post-school guidance and counselling needs a conceptual foundation which relates to what Bloomer (1997) calls a young person's 'learning career' which often follows – not the neat and tidy linear pathway assumed by rationalist technical planners – but one which is able to respond creatively and pragmatically to the myriad of factors and pressures facing post-16 learners. To accommodate such real-world forms of agency and choice, Bloomer suggests a concept of 'studentship' which, in general terms, refers to the 'variety of ways in which students can exert influence over the curriculum in the creation and confirmation of their own personal learning careers' (p. 140). Such a conception allows – in ways similar to Young's (1999) notion of curriculum 'connectivity' designed to forge links between all forms of learning and knowledge – that the views of young people about all aspects of life, learning and work must be taken into account by VET tutors and counsellors.

Such studies of students within mainstream FE have been paralleled by those concerned with part-time and day-release learners in the sector. Unwin and Wellington's (2001) investigation of the experiences of modern apprenticeships, for instance, revealed young people taking responsibility for their own learning careers against the background of the diversity of pressures impacting upon their lives after leaving school. The study indicated that most of the modern apprentices interviewed were:

> not rejecting academic study, nor were they embracing a narrowly-defined job-related training course. On the contrary, they were seeking a means of continuing their education in such a way as to give equal prominence to their academic and practical abilities.
>
> (p. 51)

It is also worth remembering that – as all research on post-school participation reveals – all learning at this stage tends to be determined by factors linked to early experiences. Although family, social and economic characteristics are important, the age at which people leave school is still the crucial variable. For those who leave at 16, 28 per cent participate in further learning, compared with 53 per cent for those leaving at 17 and 18, and 61 per cent for those who stay in the system until the age of 21 (Hillage et al., 2000, p. 55).

Moreover, work on lifelong learning 'trajectories' done for the Learning Society project (Rees et al., 2000) has demonstrated the power of certain factors in determining, fairly precisely, individual learning identities and biographies. As Rees and his co-workers expressed the main findings of their study of young people and adults living in the South Wales coal-mining regions:

> those characteristics which are set very early in an individual's life, such as age, gender and family background, predict later life-long learning trajectories with 75% accuracy. Adding the variables representing initial schooling increases the accuracy of prediction to 86%. And this rises to 89% and 90% respectively, as the variables associated with adult life and with respondents' present circumstances are included.
>
> (p. 182)

Similarly, when the focus turns to individuals' own accounts of their experiences of education and training – the factors which shaped their 'learner identities' – they tend to emphasise the

> specificities of their learning histories, the particular family circumstances or labour market shifts to which they have had to react and so on. Certainly, there are no *simple* patterns in these individual accounts, even among those who follow the same trajectory.
>
> (Ibid., p. 183, original italics)

This last point – concerning the fact that often people with broadly similar social and economic backgrounds experience different experiences of learning – is of the first importance and reinforces the points made earlier about the need for flexible, practical and tailor-made guidance and counselling provision for all post-school learners. The vital role of the Personal Adviser in helping youngsters steer their way through the complexities of post-school VET was illustrated vividly by the New Deal for Young People (NDYP) schemes (Hyland and Musson, 2001), and these experiences are now being incorporated into the new joined-up *Connexions* service for the sector.

The new service currently rolling out across the country is designed to be a 'more integrated learning and support' service for learners, bringing together 'partners from learning health, youth justice, employment and voluntary agencies in the same areas as LLSCs' (DfEE, 2001b, p. 1). Although its full implementation has yet to be monitored, there still seems to be a rather technicist ethos to the new strategy which displays an attachment to 'economic' as opposed to 'social' capital and is, moreover, unduly influenced by the 'over-simplified version of the theory of human capital' (Coffield, 2000, p. 11) which bedevils so much of lifelong learning policy and practice. The *Connexions* 'smart card' – influenced directly by Training Credits and similar measures favoured by the last Tory administration – provides a good example of the main weaknesses in this sphere.

The new card (DfEE, 2001c) aims to 'encourage more young people to choose learning as a positive option' and 'assist young people to attain qualifications'; to this end the smart card will function as 'an electronic key to personal information . . . be used to facilitate enrolment on education and training courses . . . validate payment of Education Maintenance Allowances [and] act as a learning reward card' by triggering 'discounts on transport, books and learning materials' (p. 1). Much of this is practical common sense which could conceivably remove many barriers for post-16 learners. However, there is more than an echo here of the 'technical-rational' approach which was criticised earlier with its suggestion that the only real problems in this area are *quantitative* – those concerned with access and finance.

Nevertheless all the evidence about guiding and supporting learning at this level indicates that all the potential problem areas – particularly in this central sphere of work-based learning which underpins so many current PCET developments – are linked to *qualitative* issues concerned with providing the right sort of management, advice and monitoring of learning across different forms of setting. Unwin and Wellington's

(2001) comments about the haphazard nature of key skills delivery on modern apprenticeship schemes apply equally to learning support in general. Their data showed:

> quite vividly that systematic, well-planned mentoring, and structured, ongoing assessment are not occurring as they should on the modern apprenticeship. Mentoring is dependent upon personal, sometimes chance or fortuitous relationships and meetings . . . Assessment is equally *ad hoc*, depending on the willingness of an employee to interact with an apprentice, or on the energy and enthusiasm of a young person to 'bother' or 'hassle' a fellow worker.
>
> (p. 109)

As the NDYP experience demonstrated, such unstructured and unsystematic supervision and monitoring of learning can easily result in failure and drop-out. Similar research findings have been produced to explain student failure and drop-out in FE generally in terms of factors which colleges are in control of, such as the quality of teaching and the structure of learning programmes (Twining, 2002a, p. 3). General research on the ways in which people acquire knowledge, skills and values in new settings – particularly in workplaces in which learners are often seeking admission to communities of practice and culture – has confirmed the importance of 'social' as opposed to solitary learning. The development of vocational knowledge in particular seems to require attention, not just to cognitive activity, but to the 'social and cultural context in which cognitive activity occurs' (Billett, 1996, p. 150).

What Lave and Wenger (2002) call 'legitimate peripheral participation' relates to the ways in which newcomers – apprentices of various kinds represent the paradigm cases here – come to gain that knowledge and culture which allows them to transform from outsiders to insiders in communities of practice. All learners on post-school programmes may be regarded as newcomers and apprentices in this sense, and the points about the social practice of learning need to be noted by all tutors and counsellors in the sector.

The points about the values of social as against individual learning referred to above in the context of learning careers were also mentioned in connection with the social theory of lifelong learning explored in Chapter 2. As a way of drawing all strands of our discussion together it is now time to return to this wider moral and social dimension in the attempt to construct a 'philosophy of further education' for the sector in the twenty-first century.

Chapter 8

A philosophy for further education in the new learning and skills sector

Introduction

The changing face of the FE sector in the age of the LSC and New Labour's lifelong learning agenda was examined in the first two chapters, and subsequent chapters have traced the impact of current policy trends on staff, students, learning, teaching, the curriculum and the wider community. The principal aim of this final chapter is to determine how far these trends add up to a coherent philosophy for FE institutions and the LSS and, more significantly, to discover (or uncover) the overarching values which may (or ought to) guide and inform developments in this sphere.

It is remarkable that – in spite of the radical and dramatic changes which have transformed education and training in general and the LSS in particular in recent times – there has been very little discussion of the overarching values framework in which all this development has taken place. Indeed, debate in this area has tended towards moral vacuity as an all-pervading technicism and 'McDonaldisation' (Hyland, 1999) of the PCET sector has marginalised ethical debate, thus leaving largely unexamined ideological conceptions of learning as a commodity to be competed for by self-interested consumers in search of employability skills (Avis *et al.*, 1996). However, although a predominantly economistic model of education and training (now tempered by the 'third way' values of New Labour) came to dominate the FE system, we were also asked to believe that such an ethos was in some sense 'value-neutral' (Halliday, 1996) and that educational judgements consisted in simply determining the most cost-efficient means of achieving universally agreed ends concerned with enhancing economic competitiveness both for individuals and for society. Within particular institutions this 'morally impoverished' (Fish, 1993, p. 10) conception of learning and the educational task has been serviced well by the 'new managerialism with its vocabulary of efficiency and effectiveness, choice and markets' (Standish, 1997, p. 440).

Our own research indicated that – although FE colleges were rapidly transforming themselves into multi-purpose institutions – the economic imperative was still dominant and there was a real danger that outreach community provision was declining. The acknowledgement that the first four years of the New Labour administration had failed to achieve the social inclusion goals of lifelong learning is now evident in the spate of recent reforms in the sector: the re-organisation of 14–19 education, the reconstruction of Modern Apprenticeships, fresh initiatives in basic skills provision, and the review of HE student finance in line with efforts to increase participation in the sector. Most of these initiatives – though underpinned by third way values linked to social inclusion – are still unduly technicist and require a more explicit values foundation if they are to achieve their objectives for the LSS. The following components of a 'philosophy for further education' are intended as a small step on what is necessarily a very long journey.

The nature and purposes of education and training

There are many ways of characterising and underpinning educational systems in terms of value frameworks and ideological/philosophical principles. In traditional philosophical fashion, we might start with fundamentals by asking what sort of society we envisage our education system supporting and nourishing. Harkin et al. (2001) express this point:

> Education systems reflect the nature of the society in which they exist . . . a fundamental link between the nature of society and the nature of its education provision is demonstrable. It is important, therefore, to ask what sort of society would constitute a 'good' society? For in answering this question we cast light on what we would take to be a 'good' education.
>
> (p. 139)

In the writings of the early Greek philosophers, discussions of education are inseparable from discourse about the 'good life' and – in seeking to answer the crucial philosophical question concerning 'what are the ingredients of the good life in pursuit of which we undertake to educate people' (Warnock, 1977, p. 129) – a more recent philosopher, Mary

Warnock, provides a modern answer to the questions first posed by Plato and Aristotle. Her answer is constructed under the three principal headings of 'Virtue, Work and Imagination', a list of categories which may, perhaps, provide a refreshing antidote to the sterile instrumentalism of current debate about the aims of post-school education and training.

Virtue

In answering the famous Socratic question – 'Can virtue be taught?' – in the affirmative, Warnock enters the caveat that 'morality, or virtuousness, can and should be taught, and can be learned, but not in special lessons' (ibid., p. 143). This view connects with the general consensus that the moral aspects of education and training should be conveyed – as a sort of underpinning theme or dimension rather like key skills – through the standard curriculum subjects at school or through normal learning provision in post-school institutions.

It was mentioned in early chapters that a social theory of lifelong learning requires specific values elements linked to social justice, community and citizenship. In terms of VET, this results in provision which 'acknowledges social and personal aims, values and needs, and locates education and training goals in relation to the kind of society we wish to see develop' (Skilbeck *et al.*, 1994, p. 46). Such a conception goes beyond the fostering of economic capital since economic activity and working lives cannot exist in a vacuum which artificially excludes developments and consequences at the societal, global and ecological level. As Hart (1996) argues, the narrow technical, industrial model of work concerned exclusively with productivity and growth:

> generates an interpretation of the current crisis which screens out the most important and troubling aspects of this crisis: the increase in precarious, unstable work relations, the growing North/South division, the feminization of poverty in conjunction with a new sexist division of labour, and the continued destruction of the environment.
> (p. 109)

An ethical policy would adopt an appropriately critical stance in relation to such issues, and examine a range of alternatives to the post-Fordist and global economic 'myths' which currently dominate debate in this area. Orthodox global and free market views are increasingly being challenged by economists such as Ormerod (1994) who proposes an alternative conception in which:

economic success can be achieved, and achieved more successfully, within a broader and more beneficial framework than that driven by the pure, individual rationality of the economics textbooks . . . The power of markets needs to be harnessed to the wider benefit of society.

(pp. 204–5)

Indeed, the 'pure, individual rationality' of economists would soon lead us to the Hobbesian state of chaos and anarchy – where the life of humankind is 'solitary, poor, nasty, brutish and short' (Hobbes, 1651/ 1965, p. 65) – if it were not tempered by non-economistic, community values of various kinds. A market of purely egotistic individuals would not, without the existence of other values and motivations, reproduce itself since this would require 'that purely self-interested individuals enter into relationships with each other in order to produce, nurture and care for other self-interested individuals like themselves' (Poole, 1990, p. 49). The operation of markets, therefore, is entirely dependent upon the inculcation of values of a non-market, other-regarding kind, namely, those values such as trust, loyalty, respect for persons and general benevolence which educational institutions are typically asked to transmit to future generations.

There have been positive signs in recent years that this traditional values dimension of provision is accorded its rightful place in the curriculum. In the Dearing (1996) review of qualifications for 16–19 year olds, for instance, we are informed that:

Education means preparing young people for life in the widest sense. As adults they will assume responsibility for the quality of our society and civilisation. Spiritual and moral values must therefore be an essential element in education.

(p. 4)

If we choose to interpret this in a non-rhetorical way – taking seriously the idea that the 'spiritual and moral dimensions should be taken into account and consciously included in the curriculum and programmes of young people' (ibid., p. 37) – this would entail doing rather more than paying lip-service to the values dimension which has characterised past initiatives (notably the 'citizenship' movement designed to challenge increasing crime rates and civil disorder in the early 1990s; NCC, 1990; Hyland, 1992).

Citizenship, and the wide range of civic virtues and values associated with it, is once more at the centre of education reform (QCA, 2000). It is to be accorded a statutory place in the national curriculum from the 2002/3 academic year, and a citizenship theme – along with key skills – is to be incorporated into the new overarching certificates which are part of the recent re-organisation of 14–19 education (DfES, 2002a). It is important that such values components are taken seriously and do not – as in past schemes – come to be regarded as irrelevant frills. The best way to ensure that values are central to education and training is to integrate them fully into learning programmes at all levels, ideally through the learning careers models of support which will be crucial to the success of the WBL components of 14–19 curriculum reform in the years ahead.

Work

Jarrett (1991) has argued that perhaps the 'single most important goal for a teacher to work towards has to do with the basic attitude towards work' (p. 206), and similar sentiments inspire Warnock's philosophy of education in which 'work is, and always must be an important ingredient in the good life' such that a 'life without work would always be less good than a life which contained it' (1977, p. 144). Aspects of vocational studies were examined in the previous chapter and specific recommendations for the WBL elements which are central to current reforms are proposed in the next section. Clearly work is central to the education of most youngsters and must be foregrounded in any 'philosophy of FE'. The problem is that most accounts of issues surrounding work are organisational, technicist and uncritical – concerned with economic rather than social capital – and fail to offer any account of the wider aspects of work linked with personal relationships and different conceptions of the role of work in contemporary society.

What Avis et al. (1996) have called the 'vocationalization of everyday life' (p. 165) has been concerned principally with re-orienting the curriculum at all levels towards industrial needs and has not been accompanied by any critical perspectives which might help students to understand the changing nature of work in post-Fordist economies. What is missing from most vocational programmes is any discussion of the nature and scope of work and, specifically, an account of the differences picked out by Arendt (1958) between work as creative endeavour and the more mundane forms of paid work associated with labour and toil. However, although VET programmes should include a consideration of White's (1997) distinction between 'autonomous' work, which is freely chosen and whose 'end product constitutes one of your most important goals in life', and 'heteronomous work whose end product has not been chosen as a major goal' (p. 234), it is also important to avoid intellectually elitist conceptions of work and vocational studies.

Although there is, as White suggests, a real distinction to be made between constrained and unconstrained work, this does not necessarily imply any hierarchy of work activities. Wringe (1991) is surely right in arguing that part of the 'morality of work' lies in the recognition that 'work does not have to be sublime or spectacular . . . to be worthwhile' (p. 38). Craft skills and the work of artisans are highlighted in Ainley's (1993) study and, in a similar vein, Corson (1991) calls for a consideration of work as 'craft . . . having value for its own sake' (p. 171). On this account, motorcycle maintenance – as Pirsig (1974) illustrates graphically – can be as creative, craftlike and valuable as evolutionary biology, fashion design or metaphysics. Simple pride in achievement is worth stressing here, if only to combat the de-skilling tendencies and belittling of underpinning practical and intuitive knowledge characteristic of recent trends in VET.

The pragmatic, aesthetic and moral features of work find their fullest expression, perhaps, in poetry and literature rather than in vocational texts (Hyland, 1999). Seamus Heaney's poems provide vivid illustrations in this respect, and the sheer joy of useful, careful and productive work is nowhere better described than in Primo Levi's *The Wrench* (1988) in which the central character, Faussone, relates stories about his work as a rigger on construction sites all over Europe. Similarly in *The Ragged Trousered Philanthropists*, Tressell (1914/1993) describes the work of painters and decorators in the early years of the twentieth century who – in spite of constant hardship and fear of dismissal – struggled to give meaning to their work by doing the best possible job in all areas. One of the leading workmen, for instance, forced with his colleagues constantly to rush jobs in the interests of quick profits:

> could not scamp the work to the extent that he was ordered to; and so, almost by stealth, he was in the habit of doing it – not properly but as well as he dared. He even went to the length of occasionally buying a few sheets of glasspaper with his own money.
>
> (p. 162)

Programmes that emphasise only the economistic features of working life provide a narrow and limited conception in which the only value of human work is the exchange or use value identified in Marxist economics. As Rikowski's (1999) post-Marxist analysis of contemporary education and training puts it, as the:

capitalisation of humanity deepens and strengthens we become a
life-form which increasingly incorporates the contradictions of capital
. . . we progressively come to live, drink, sleep and exist through
the contradictions of ourselves as capitalised life- form . . . it is the
human element that is marginalised.

(pp. 50–1; original italics)

The glaring one-sidedness and moral vacuity of this conception of
work – its cavalier dismissal of the 'traditional work ethic which stressed
the integration of work and personal development' (Carlson, 1982,
p. 135) – cannot be disguised by the rhetoric of the enterprise culture and
post-Fordist narratives about the knowledge society and the need for
flexible, multi-skilled workers.

Esland (1996) warns us of the dangers of such a narrow, technically
rational conception of VET in his assertion that it is a:

> system which renders both human labour and its skills as commodi-
> ties to be utilised or discarded as circumstances – and profits –
> determine. There is at the heart of technical rationality an ethical
> indifference towards the non-economic values of employment and
> the social costs of an oppressive employment environment.

(p. 24)

This 'ethical indifference' is – not only responsible for the complete
failure of most vocational programmes to capture the moral and aesthetic
features of work mentioned above – but also flies in the face of all the
findings of the human-relations school of industrial psychology (Peters,
1987) which stress the importance of creating a committed and self-
motivated workforce by colonising the meanings attached to productive
work activity.

It is not just unethical, however, but also counter-intuitive to neglect
the personal development and communicative-collaborative aspects
of work. Zuboff (1988) has suggested that the most successful and
genuinely flexible industrial organisations have been those which have
interpreted the new conditions as calling for 'relations of equality' in
the working environment which can 'encourage a synthesis of members'
interests' so that the 'flow of value-adding knowledge helps legitimate
the organisation as a learning community' (p. 394). This idea of the learning community – whether it is in the public or private sector, education
or industry – is dependent upon 'collective intelligence' (Brown and
Lauder, 1995, p. 28) and action generated by consensual understanding.

It is an architectonic concept which informs the ideas on community, critical pedagogy and group/collective learning in the workplace which are elaborated more fully below and – on a national level – is perhaps best illustrated in the 'social partnership' (Green, 1997a) models of educational provision characteristic of continental Europe.

Imagination

For Warnock (1977) imagination represents a 'human capacity shared by everyone who can perceive and think, who can notice things and can experience emotions'. It is that 'image-making capacity . . . by means of which we characterise and feel things to be familiar, unfamiliar, beautiful, desirable, strange, horrible, and so on' (pp. 131–2). This aspect of general educational development is self-evidently of the first importance yet – outside the remit of specialist art or literature courses – it receives little attention at either school or post-school levels. Indeed, even in specialised courses, imagination and creativity are often stifled in the pursuit of behaviourist learning outcomes or instrumentalist employability ends.

Now recognised as a national curriculum theme in which 'creativity' is given greater emphasis, those features of imagination that consist of creative criticism and the consideration of alternative perspectives are now incorporated in the plans for overarching certificates and diplomas for 14–19 year olds (DfES, 2002a). In terms of content it will be important for such certificates and diplomas to acknowledge the need for what Young (1999) calls curriculum 'connectivity' which seeks to integrate and make sense of all the different aspects of learning. This links to the process of learning in the form of the learning career models discussed in the previous chapter which, as Bloomer (1997) puts it, places:

> studentship, learning and personal development in a dynamic, mutually constitutive relationship . . . it also links, dynamically, the formation of personal identity and dispositions to the transformation of social, moral, economic and other conditions . . . It thus has the potential to yield not simply the knowledge *that* young people 'act upon' learning opportunities in the way they do through their studentship but to generate an understanding of *why* they do.
>
> (p. 154, original italics)

On another level such strategies translate into what Rikowski (1999) has described as a 'critical pedagogy' which both allows and enables students to consider possibilities and alternatives for improving work, life and society in line with democratic and ethical principles. Similarly, Tarrant (2001) has criticised the 'predominantly utilitarian ethic of PCET', arguing that an 'education which is exclusively vocational . . . ignores the wider role of persons in society' thus frustrating the goal of fostering a 'democracy based on the critical citizen' (p. 376). In this respect, Harkin *et al.* (2001) point to the importance of acknowledging and fostering the 'communicative nature of language in all areas of democratic life' (p. 141), especially in the sphere of teaching and learning in which language plays such a crucial role. It is only through such approaches that the imaginative capacities of learners can be developed in the interests of shaping the just community and socially inclusive society.

Work-based learning, apprenticeships and social capital

In the previous chapter reference was made to work-based learning (WBL) in the context of developments within FE colleges in the areas of learning, teaching and the curriculum. Since developments in the WBL sphere (and the related expansion of apprenticeships) are central to current policy initiatives in terms of the re-organisation of 14–19 education and training and the re-alignment of the sector under the LSC, it will be important to ensure that the lessons and precepts learned from past experience are underpinned by social capital values in a coherent philosophy for FE.

As mentioned in earlier chapters, the current plans for reconstructing 14–19 provision are informed by the ambitious goal of 'vocational excellence for all' (DfEE, 2001a, p. 9) realised through a vocational ladder of opportunity provided by centres of vocational excellence in FE and through the new vocational GCSEs and A-levels, foundation degrees and reconstructed modern apprenticeships (DfES, 2001c). To this end the DfES seeks to bring about a 'vocational renaissance that captures the imagination of young people and challenges prejudice' (DfES, 2002a, p. 1). The 'prejudice' referred to here concerns the undervaluing of vocational learning, the privileging of academic pursuits and the inequalities of provision which result from this. If such prejudice is to be overcome, policies in this area will need rather more emphasis on social values and capital than the current overly economistic interpretations of social inclusion and lifelong learning allow for.

The tendency noted in earlier chapters to stress the economic aims of lifelong learning over the socially inclusive ones is still all too prevalent in the current reform plans. The rationale for 14–19 re-organisation, for example, is said to be:

> both social (reducing the likelihood of exclusion in later life, through raising young people's qualification levels and employability) and economic (meeting certain skills shortages; savings through preventing social exclusion.)
>
> (p. 2)

In spite of other references in the policy document to citizenship and personal development, it is difficult to avoid the judgement that social and economic objectives are here being conflated to such an extent that vital social values – those concerned with 'trust and benevolence' which are the 'working principles of society' (Trusted, 1987, p. 114) without which no community can survive for long – are completely submerged under economic pressures.

It is important that robust, normative conceptions of social capital are utilised in the planning and organisation of learning and teaching in the sector, and that reforms in the system are not frustrated by the narrowly technicist strategies of the past. The notions of such capital relevant here are those which are:

> constituted through the social relationships that people have with each other, through the collective knowledge of a group, and the moral, cognitive and social supervision that the group exercises over its members . . . Social capital in this sense has a strongly moral dimension . . . often described in terms of the norms of trust prevalent within a society.
>
> (Winch, 2000, p. 5)

A similar interpretation is found in Schuller and Field's (1998) idea of 'kinds of context and culture which promote communication and mutual learning' (p. 234), which indicates how closely the conceptions of learning, knowledge and social structures are interrelated. In the light of the important values dimension under discussion it is worth noting and stressing the significant parallels and symmetries between what is required for both successful learning in the light of current reform objectives and the key characteristics of WBL and apprenticeships which hold centre stage in current reform programmes. Moreover, it is interesting to note that this all relates directly to the wider social inclusion and citizenship elements of current policy and practice, all of which are ultimately underpinned by social justice and democratic values.

Within learning theory generally there is solid empirical support for the notion that – as Harkin *et al.* (2001) put it, 'effective learning is facilitated by social interaction' (p. 52). Psychological work on intellectual development by Bruner (1966) and on language formation by Vygotsky (1978) has demonstrated that learning 'has its basis in the relationships which exist between people' (Harkin *et al.*, 2001, p. 53). Studies of the ways in which people acquire knowledge, skills and values – especially in workplaces in which learners are typically seeking admission to communities of practice and culture – has also confirmed the importance of social as opposed to individualistic learning. The development of vocational knowledge and skill in particular seems to require attention – not just to the cognitive/intellectual capacities which dominate traditional models – but to the 'social and cultural context in which cognitive activity occurs' (Billett, 1996, p. 150).

Wenger (2002) outlines clearly the foundational principles of learning linked to groups and communities in the observation that:

> Since the beginning of history, human beings have formed communities that share cultural practices reflecting their collective learning: from a tribe around a cave fire, to a medieval guild, to a group of nurses in a ward, to a street gang, to a group of engineers interested in brake design. Participating in these 'communities of practice' is essential to our learning.
>
> (p. 163)

What Lave and Wenger (2002) call 'legitimate peripheral participation' refers to the ways in which newcomers – and, interestingly, apprentices of various kinds are cited as paradigm examples here – come to acquire that knowledge and culture that helps them to move from being outsiders to insiders. We are reminded that 'newcomers participate in a community of practitioners as well as in productive activity' and that it is important to view 'learning as part of a social practice' (pp. 121–2). They go on to argue that:

> The social relations of apprentices within a community change through their direct involvement in activities; in the process, the apprentices' understanding and knowledgeable skills develop . . . newcomers' legitimate peripherality provides them with more than an 'observational' lookout post: it crucially involves *participation* as a way of learning – of both absorbing and being absorbed – in the 'culture of practice'.
>
> (p. 113; original italics)

Moreover, as Guile and Young (2002) have suggested, the concept of apprenticeship development has radical implications for the content as well as for learning contexts and processes. Drawing on the psychological work of Engestrom (1996), Guile and Young (2002) point to the limitations of the traditional model of apprenticeship – based upon a 'transmission model' – which are outlined and supplemented by strategies which concentrate on the 'processes of work-based learning and the skill development that take place within the institution of apprenticeship' (ibid., pp. 149–50). Continuities between formal and informal learning (crucial for the fostering of learning careers and studentship on modern apprenticeship programmes) need to be recognised and exploited so that the 'concept of apprenticeship might serve as a basis for an alternative learning paradigm for formal education and training' (ibid., p. 159). Hager (2000) makes similar proposals in arguing for a conception of workplace knowledge which moves away from academic, disciplinary forms towards a model of 'work-based learning in terms of people learning to make judgements' (p. 60) in all spheres of occupational work.

Thus, not only do the new emphases on WBL lend themselves to the fostering of important social capital in line with current social inclusion and citizenship objectives, such strategies – in the form of apprenticeships and forms of workplace learning – are shot through with collective learning values which are themselves supportive of the goals of economic capital and competitiveness. This neat integration of the social and the economic is illustrated vividly in research undertaken by the Centre for Research and Learning in Regional Australia (Kilpatrick *et al.*, 1999). Concerned with small farming businesses which are combined in collectives – learning organisations called *Executive Link* – to facilitate non-formal training and business development, not only were the training objectives of the collective boards more easily achieved through group activity, such shared planning and development also achieved important social capital aims in fostering trust and identification with the local community. As the researchers conclude:

> The learning processes that occur in the Executive Link community are oiled by the social capital of the community. Executive Link has been set up as a learning community, and a deliberate effort has been made to build networks, commitment and shared values. These elements of social capital have built through the development of shared language, shared experiences, trust, self-development and fostering an identification with the community.
>
> (pp. 142–3)

Such notions and principles can be usefully employed in the new models of learning and partnership that will shape the development of the LSS over the coming years.

Education, individuals and community

Langford (1985) has attacked the long-standing obsession 'with the difference which being educated makes to an individual' (p. 3) and recommended instead a greater concern with the social dimension of education and training. For him, to 'become educated is to become a member of society and so to have learnt what it is to be and live as a member of that society' (ibid., p. 181). Individualism was, of course, the dominant feature of the technicist and monocultural conception of the educational task driven by notions of market forces and nation-state economic competitiveness which, as mentioned earlier, prevailed throughout much of the 1980s and 1990s. Even the short-lived revival of citizenship tended to be couched in individualistic terms in the form of expressions about consumer rights and responsibilities to the state and the economy (NCC, 1990). As Kingdom (1992) put it, the citizen within the enterprise culture of rampant economic individualism was little more than a sort of 'calculating machine living a cost-benefit-analysis existence' (p.10).

Although current conceptions of both citizenship and the purpose of VET are underpinned by a broader and more robust social agenda, individualism is still present and it is important to acknowledge and make sense of its perennial and universal appeal to people of all political and moral persuasions. The roots of individualism – along with an explanation of its persuasiveness as a general doctrine – were traced by Bertrand Russell (1946, Chap. XII) to the Greek Stoics and Cynics down through the medieval Christian tradition until the ideas found their fullest expression in the work of Descartes which itself provided a major source and inspiration for the development of political and economic liberalism in the sixteenth and seventeenth centuries. Within the liberal tradition, individualistic notions went hand in hand with the growth of capitalist mercantilism and, in political theory, the basic ideas go back at least as far as Hobbes and Locke encapsulated in the concept of what Macpherson (1964) called 'possessive individualism' which asserts that the 'individual is essentially the proprietor of his own person, and capacities, for which he owes nothing to society' (p. 263). The obvious attractiveness – based on the superficial plausibility and self-evidential nature of their expression – explains their enduring centrality in moral, political, economic and educational systems.

Within educational theory, individualism finds its expression in notions of autonomous, independent and self-directed learning to which, on the surface, nobody would object. However, apart from its neglect of the crucial social context and the values of group learning outlined earlier, the superficial attractiveness of individualism as an educational goal needs to take account of the fact that concepts such as autonomy and independence are meaningless until they are located within a social dimension. As Dearden (1972) has argued, by valuing freedom and autonomous development in education, we do not thereby 'mark the eclipse of such other values as truth and morality' (p. 461). Similarly, Lawson (1998), in qualifying the extremism of 'andragogical practices' which result in misguided attempts to abolish all teaching and guidance in favour of independent student learning, points to the dangers of such 'deontological liberalism'. Eschewing educational content in favour of process, such a philosophy is 'suited to a society which has no vision' and 'produces societies which no longer debate or seek the good' (p. 41).

In his study of autonomy within political and citizenship education, Smith (1997) observes how – especially in developed industrial societies – the concept 'typically works alongside notions of choice and the market, separating individual persons from their world and their fellows, the better to render them subject to control' (p. 128). Linked to the technicist notions of alienated work discussed earlier, such processes result in what Rikowski (1999) calls 'capitalised trans-human life forms' (p. 73) in which notions of autonomy (typically linked to the market and consumer choice) are entirely illusory. Smith (1997) argues that such facile conceptions now threaten 'in the name of freedom, to re-shape the emotional lives and identities of young people especially, alienating them from the aesthetic and reflective modes of being' (p. 128). As an antidote to technicist and consumerist conceptions, he goes on to recommend that:

> Autonomy, then, should not be thought of in terms of an essentially individualistic journey towards an abstract and determinate rationality, but as a process involving other people in which reasons are demanded and given in dialectic. And if autonomy means having a degree of control over our lives, then we have to help each other understand the ways in which power is taken from us and exercised over us.
>
> (p. 134)

In a similar vein, Jonathan (1997) has pointed to the 'illusory freedoms' of market individualism in education, arguing that the 'distribution of education is a matter for public action' on the grounds that such distribution 'reflects and modifies public judgements of worth' (p. 215). Since education is a key determinant of life chances for all citizens, its organisation and distribution must be a matter for public debate against the background of democratic and social values and goals. Arguably, such public/collective – as against private/individualistic – conceptions of education which held sway in the 1980s and 1990s are inseparable from any view which seeks to be incorporated into the broad social theory of learning outlined in Chapter 2. However, although all current policy initiatives seek to address this important social agenda, the underlying principles required to justify the policies are rarely stated with sufficient clarity and openness.

Fairclough (2000) has pointed to the influence of 'communitarian discourse' on New Labour (and, in particular, the Prime Minister's) policy statements suggesting that they combine 'Christian socialism and a conservative critique of the individualistic world view of liberalism' (pp. 37–8). One of the leading theorists in communitarian philosophy is Etzioni (1995) – according to Levitas (1998), a key influence on New Labour thinking and third way values – whose main ideas have been placed in an educational context recently by Arthur (1998). The principal agenda is founded on the belief that:

> Neither human existence nor individual liberty can be sustained for long outside the interdependent and overlapping communities to which we all belong. Nor can any community long survive unless its members dedicate some of their attention, energy and resources to shared projects. The exclusive pursuit of private interest erodes the network of social environments on which we all depend.
>
> (pp. 358–9)

The concept of community – as discussions in earlier chapters pointed out – is, of course, never a value-neutral one and is open to manipulation and interpretation in the light of different interest groups and FE stakeholders. However, amidst the welter of competing goals and values informing FE policy and the work of colleges an overarching concept of community – underpinned by the social inclusion policy agenda and concepts of citizenship – is now being defined in an attempt to remedy the overly individualistic and economistic conceptions which held sway until recent times.

The new agenda – an extension of earlier post-incorporation conceptions of FE institutions as 'serving the community' (Lucas, 1993, p. 138) and being 'genuinely open and accessible to the whole community' (NATFHE, 1992, p. 8) – is still, in line with 'third way' values, concerned with economic matters, but it is what Berry (1993) calls the 'economy of community' rather than that concerned exclusively with the 'private exploitation of the public wealth and health' (p. 138). As Rozema (2001) explains, these different conceptions of human economy lead to radically different perspectives on the nature and purpose of education. On the one hand there is the 'economy of profit' with 'information as the commodity an education provides . . . as a means to profit and power' and which sees the 'student as a consumer' (p. 238). Against this, there is the 'economy of community' which seeks to:

> foster persons who will maintain and preserve the essential characteristics of community [and] will inevitably gravitate towards the practice and personification of proper care: care for one's family, friends, neighbours and countrymen . . . In an education of community, knowledge-as-information will be subservient to knowledge-as-practice . . . What gets taught, and how it gets taught, will be determined and shaped by the idea that an education – like friendship, citizenship or marriage – cannot be bought or sold, only given and received.
>
> (p. 252)

Both these perspectives – an economy of commodity and of community – are present in contemporary lifelong learning policy and, as earlier chapters have indicated, the former commodious conception still exerts more influence on the LSS and the work of FE institutions than communitarian versions. However, within the framework of the new social inclusion agenda, emerging emphases on citizenship and regional learning partnerships there is a foundation upon which to reconstruct the sector making use of a communitarian template that gives more emphasis to the values of social justice, trust and democracy than the instrumentalist perspectives which have dominated post-school education and training over the last few decades.

Conclusion: community and partnership in FE

Reference was made in the Introduction to assertions that 'community and partnership are two of the most powerful terms in the current further education lexicon' (Gravatt and Silver, 2000, p. 116) and that the sector was 'evolving towards a broader community-wide comprehensive college future' (Scott, 1996, p. 52). Can these claims be justified in terms of current practice and future policy plans for the PCET sector? In terms of current LSC policy plans for the sector there can be little doubt that partnerships of various kinds – at least at the level of policy statements – are set to play a key strategic role at all levels of the system. The achievement of all targets for the sector is to be realised through strategic plans designed in the forty-seven LLSCs on the basis of 'three linked strategies' covering skills, participation and learning (LSC, 2001a, p. 15). There is a strong emphasis on 'cross-agency planning' in taking advantage of the:

> opportunity to bring together a number of agencies at local level and agree common goals for the locality which all can share and adopt . . . The currency of our proposed learning targets . . . have a strong correlation with successful implementation of social, employment and community regeneration policies . . . Co-ordinating local planning for skills across key Government-funded agencies should not be a matter merely of consultation, but an active process of sharing priorities which other agencies can support. These priorities can be defined in terms of *local impact measures*.
>
> (pp. 17–18; original italics)

It is not difficult to discern here all the key characteristics of 'third way' policy-making discussed in earlier chapters: public–private collaboration, links between employment skills, training and inclusion, and close auditing of targets in line with the prudent control of public funds. The new *Connexions* service – bringing together 'partners from learning, health, social justice, employment and voluntary agencies' (DfEE, 2001b, p. 1) – is a paradigm example of such centrally negotiated local partnership strategies with greater public accountability and value for money in mind.

Social inclusion objectives are also emphasised separately in line with generally accepted equal opportunities principles. The LLSC plans must 'give high priority to improved access and participation by groups currently under-represented in learning and training' (LSC, 2001a, p. 13), a message reinforced in the Secretary of State's Grant Letter to the LSC in the expressed expectation that 'the Council builds equality of opportunity into all its policies, programmes and actions . . . to ensure that equality becomes a reality' (DfES, 2001c, p. 3). It is a moot question whether partnerships and equality can be achieved by central government diktat or not, but the intention to provide strong frameworks to permit such developments is clearly discernible. Moreover, FE – as in so many other policy areas – will have a central role to play, with the LSC expecting colleges 'to seek closer partnerships with higher education institutions over the next five years' and the FE sector 'negotiating a rapidly changing world in which it would need to reach out to as many partners as possible' (Tysome, 2002a, p. 3). The conflation of social and economic capital in lifelong learning policy and practice was examined in Chapter 2. Current post-school education policy fully reflects this mixture and ambivalence about ultimate aims and values, and it is only to be expected that LSC plans for the future should display similar characteristics. The 'equality of opportunity' in all programmes called for by the present Education Secretary was defined by her immediate predecessor as 'not simply a moral objective – it is an economic imperative' (DfEE, 2000b, p. 3). This is explained by the assertion that:

Economic performance depends increasingly on talent and creativity. And in this new economy, it is education and skills which shape the opportunities and rewards available to individuals.

(p. 3)

This line is maintained in the recent DfES introduction of the Green Paper on 14–19 re-organisation which described the proposals as forming:

a radical agenda that challenges long-held educational traditions . . . Our continued economic success and social cohesion depends on us meeting this challenge.

(DfES, 2002a, p. 1)

All this is, of course, fully in line with what commentators such as Giddens (2000) have proposed as a way of reconciling social democratic principles of 'equality and pluralism' with the forces of globalisation so as to 'achieve a balance between government, the economy and civil society' (pp. 120, 123). Education has a key role to play in this process since it can foster both 'economic efficiency and civic cohesion' (p. 23). Indeed, the concept of social capital discussed above comes into its own at this level of policy principles since the 'cultivation of social capital is integral to the new knowledge economy' and, moreover, is 'not refractory to cooperation and collaboration – cooperation (rather than hierarchy) is positively stimulated by it' (p. 78). Giddens goes on to explain these notions in terms of the fact that:

> Social capital refers to the trust networks that individuals can draw upon for social support, just as financial capital can be drawn upon for investment. Like financial capital, social capital can be expanded – invested and reinvested.
>
> (ibid.)

The key question here though – particularly in light of critical accounts of New Labour education policy which assert that it is still too individualistic rather than collective in its general thrust (Ainley, 1999; Hill, 2000) – is how post-school education can be reformed in ways which enhance the development of this crucial social capital. Trowler (1998) suggests that – although there has been a clear commitment to increasing education funding on the part of New Labour and the commitment to a 'new partnership with all those involved in education' – there has also been 'a lack of recognition of and a determination to tackle the causes of underachievement' (p. 91). Concluding their wide-ranging analysis of recent educational reform, Hodgson and Spours (1999) ask whether PCET policy will be:

> based on individual responsibility, a voluntaristic and enabling state, relying on weak frameworks . . . or will the stress on individual responsibility be supported by strong frameworks from a reforming state which seeks to mobilize and lead public opinion. The early signs are that it is the former that is making the running, but as New Labour progresses through this Parliament, pressures may be building for the latter.
>
> (p. 21–2)

The 'strong frameworking' approaches mentioned in Chapter 2 were illustrated by Hodgson and Spours through reference to a unified post-16 funding system, a unified curriculum and a strengthened national framework for Modern Apprenticeships. Progress in all these areas has been made over the past few years, particularly in relation to Modern Apprenticeships which have been expanded, strengthened and standardised through the work of the LSC and the NTO National Council (NTO, 2001). The harmonisation and increase of funding for FE announced in Colleges for Excellence and Innovation (DfEE, 2000a) has been realised in the '5.9% real terms increase' (DfES, 2001c, p. 2) and – although there is still no unified curriculum – moves to break down traditional divisions and barriers are contained in the recent 14–19 curriculum and qualification reforms.

From a social inclusion standpoint, however, lifelong learning plans to increase adult learning generally and HE participation in particular are still hampered by the constraints placed on economically disadvantaged groups. It is now demonstrably clear that the abolition of student grants and replacement by loans has discouraged working-class students from participation in HE so that:

> committing to a full-time course in higher education is likely to become an increasingly risky investment for low-income students [and] even when students from low-income backgrounds do take this risk, they are more likely to experience financial difficulties whilst studying and that this is likely to affect their performance and chances of completing their courses successfully.
>
> (Callender and Kemp, 2001, p. 4)

In addition, the so-called 'postcode premium' (Thomson, 2002, p. 7) – which rewards universities with 5 per cent funding top-up for each student recruited from postcode areas deemed to be less affluent – has failed to attract the most disadvantaged groups, and new ways of helping and encouraging traditionally non-participant groups are currently being planned alongside reviews of the whole HE student funding system.

Against this background, we also need to place the recent decline in general adult participation in learning noted in a NIACE survey (Tysome, 2002b) and the LSC finding that fewer adults were studying in FE colleges in recent years, both of which indicate that 'little progress' (Crequer, 2002) has been made towards the achievement of lifelong learning aims and the goals of the learning society. Earlier chapters have indicated the centrality of the FE sector in overall lifelong learning plans but – if colleges are to achieve the ambitious goals – a number of strategic and funding reforms need to be implemented to support the work of staff and students in the sector. Perhaps some lessons for the future can be learned from the recently published plans for re-structuring the whole national system of education in Scotland which 'gives people access to education at any stage in life, whatever their means' (Wotjas, 2002, p. 6). Such a general entitlement to learning, along with paid training leave for those in work (Twining, 2002b), would go some way towards remedying some of the key shortcomings in the new LSS.

However, although funding and organisational frameworks may be necessary to progress towards a just and democratic system, they can never be sufficient. What is missing is the important values dimension emphasised earlier in which communitarian networks of trust come to be translated into practical projects. This may involve political leadership which moves beyond the 'third way' towards an FE system founded on serving communities and guided by what Gleeson (1996) has called a 'new educational settlement' which 'combines conceptions of social unity and community with competitiveness and productivity' (p. 16). Given the persistent social class inequalities in Britain – many of which seem to resist all educational attempts to overcome them (Hook and Learner, 2002) – the NIACE position on lifelong learning policy becomes particularly relevant to the future of FE colleges and the communities they serve. Acknowledging the government's 'serious commitment to extending learning to excluded and disadvantaged groups', NIACE (2001) calls for a 'commitment to greater social justice' since:

> For the most disadvantaged groups, inclusion requires particular sensitivity to the broader social and cultural contributions of lifelong learning policy as well as its economic goals.
>
> (p. 5)

Bibliography

A New Commitment to Neighbourhood Renewal: National Strategy Action Plan, SEU, 2001.

Abrahson, M., Bird, J. and Stennett, A. (1996) (eds) *Further and Higher Education Partnerships* (Buckingham, Open University Press/SRHE).

Adams, J. (1996) *Apprenticeship: A Comparative Study of the Traditional and the Modern Apprenticeship* (Warwick University, Department of Continuing Education). Unpublished MA thesis.

Adult Education Committee of the Ministry of Reconstruction (1919) *Final Report* (London, His Majesty's Stationery Office).

Ainley, P. (1993) *Class and Skill* (London, Cassell).

Ainley, P. (1999) *Learning Policy* (Basingstoke, Macmillan).

Ainley P. and Bailey, B. (1997) *The Business of Learning* (London, Cassell).

Ainley, P. and Green, A. (1996) Education without employment; not meeting the national education and training targets, *Journal of Vocational Education and Training*, 48(2), pp. 109–26.

Allen, G. and Martin, I. (1992) *Education and Community: The Politics of Practice* (London, Cassell).

Allman, P. and Wallis, J. (1995) Challenging the postmodern condition, in Mayo, M. and Thompson, J. (eds), *Adult Learning, Critical Intelligence and Social Change* (Leicester, NIACE).

Arendt, H. (1958) *The Human Condition* (Chicago, Chicago University Press).

Armitage, A. *et al.* (1999) *Teaching and Training in Post-Compulsory Education* (Buckingham, Open University Press).

Arthur, J. (1998) Communitarianism: what are the implications for education?, *Educational Studies*, 24(3), pp. 353–68.

Ashton, D., Felstead, A. and Green, F. (2000) Skills in the British workplace, in Coffield, F. (ed.) (2000), op. cit.

Audit Commission/HMI (1993) *Unfinished Business: Full-Time Courses for 16–19 Year Olds*, 1 August.

Austin, M. (1994) Conclusion, in Flint, C. and Austin, M. (eds), *Going Further* (Blagdon, The Staff College).

Avis, J. (1996) The myth of the post-Fordist society, in Avis, J. *et al* op. cit.

Avis, J. (2000) Policing the subject: learning outcomes, managerialism and research in PCET, *British Journal of Educational Studies*, 48(1), pp. 38–57.

Avis, J., Bathmaker, A-M. and Parsons, J. (2001) Reflections from a time-log diary: towards an analysis of the labour process within further education, *Journal of Vocational Education and Training*, 53(1), pp. 61–80.

Avis, J., Bloomer, M., Esland, G., Gleeson, D. and Hodkinson, P. (1996) *Knowledge and Nationhood* (London, Cassell).

Baker, K. (1989) *Further Education – A New Strategy* (Address to the ACFHE Conference).

Bales, K. (2000) *Disposable People: The New Slavery in the Global Economy* (Berkeley, University of California Press).

Ball, S.J. (1999) Labour, learning and the economy: a 'policy sociology' perspective, *Cambridge Journal of Education*, 29(2), pp. 195–206.

Barnett, R. (1998) 'In' or 'For' the Learning Society, *Higher Education Quarterly*, 52(1), pp, 7–21.

Barnett, R. (2002) Learning to work and working to learn, in Reeve, F., Cartwright, M. and Edwards, R. (eds), op. cit.

Barrow, P. (1991) The Education Reform Act and the future of the tertiary college, in Chitty, C. (ed.) *Post-16 Education* (London, Kogan Page).

Barrow, R. (1987) Skill Talk; *Journal of Philosophy of Education*, 21(2), pp. 187–99.

Bates, I. and Riseborough, G. (eds) (1993) *Youth and Inequality* (Buckingham, OUP).

Baty, P. (2000) Quality boss mars new Labour vision, *Times Higher Educational Supplement*.

Bauman, Z. (1998) *Postmodernity and its Discontents* (Cambridge, Polity Press).

Bauman, Z. (2001) *Community: Seeking Safety in an Insecure World* (Cambridge, Polity Press).

Benjamin, H. (1939/1975) The saber-tooth curriculum, in Goldby, M., Greenwald, J. and West, W. (eds), *Curriculum Design* (London, Croom Helm).

Berry, W. (1993) *Sex, Economy and Freedom* (New York, Pantheon Books).

Billett, S. (1996) Constructing vocational knowledge: history, communities and ontogeny, *Journal of Vocational Education and Training*, 48(2), pp. 141–54.

Blair, T. (1999) *Romanes Lecture*, University of Oxford, 2 December.

Blair, T. (2000) Leading the country by the head and heart, *Times Higher Education Supplement*, 25 February.

Bloomer, M. (1997) *Curriculum Making in Post-16 Education* (London, Routledge).

Bloomer, M. and Hodkinson, P. (1997) *Moving into FE: the voice of the learner* (London, Further Education Development Agency).

Bloomer, M. and Hodkinson, P. (2000) Learning careers: continuity and change in young people's dispositions to learning, *British Educational Research Journal,* 26, 5, pp. 528–97.

Blunkett, D. (1998) Opportunities to live and learn, *Times Higher Education Supplement,* 27 February.

Blunkett, D. (2000) *Speech on Higher Education,* University of Greenwich, 15 February.

Bond, M. and Merrill, B. (1999) Advertising, information and recruitment to return to learning in six European countries, *Journal of Access and Credit Studies,* 1, 2, pp. 204–13.

Boud, D. and Symes, C. (2000) Learning for real: work-based education in universities, in Symes, C. and McIntrye, J. (eds), *Working Knowledge* (Buckingham, Open University Press).

Bourdieu, P. (1977) *Outline of a Theory of Practice* (Cambridge, Cambridge University Press).

Bourdieu, P. (1993) *Sociology in Question* (London, Sage).

Brennan, J. and Little, B. (1996) *A Review of Work Based Learning in Higher Education* (London, Department for Education and Employment).

Bristow, A. (1976) *Inside the Colleges of Further Education* (London, HMSO).

Brook, L. (1993) *Serving Communities* (Bristol, The Staff College/Association for Colleges).

Brookfield, S. (1986) *Understanding and Facilitating Adult Learning* (Milton Keynes, Open University Press).

Brown, P. and Lauder, H. (1995) Post-Fordist possibilities: education training and national development, in Bash, L. and Green, A. (eds), *Youth, Education and Work* (London, Kogan Page).

Bruner. J. (1966) *Towards a Theory of Instruction* (Cambridge, MA, Harvard University Press).

Bulmer, M. (1989) The underclass, empowerment and public policy, in Bulmer, M., Lewis, J. and Piachaud, D. (eds), *The Goals of Social Policy* (London, Unwin Hyman).

Callcnder, C. and Kemp, M. (2001) Burdened by debt: changing student finances in the UK, *Higher Education Digest,* No. 29, pp. 2–4.

Cantor, L., Roberts, I.F. and Pratley, B. (1995) *A Guide to Further Education in England and Wales* (London, Cassell).

Carlson, D. (1982) Updating individualism and the work ethics: corporate logic in the classroom, *Curriculum Inquiry,* 12(2), pp. 131–42.

Castells, M. (1996) *The Information Age: Economy, Society and Culture,Vol.1, The Rise of the Network Society* (Oxford, Blackwell).

Clark, D. (1987) The concept of community education, in Allen, G., Bastiani, J., Martin, I. and Richards, K. (eds), *Community Education: An Agenda for Reform* (Milton Keynes, Open University Press).

Clark, D. (1996) *Schools as Learning Communities* (London, Cassell).

Clarke, J., Hall, S., Jefferson, T. and Roberts, B. (1976) Subcultures, cultures and class, in Hall, S. and Jefferson, T. (eds), *Resistance Through Rituals* (London, Hutchinson).

Coffey, D. (1992) *Schools and Work: Developments in Vocational Education* (London, Cassell).

Coffield, F. (ed.) (1999) *Speaking Truth to Power: Research and Policy on Lifelong Learning* (Bristol, Policy Press).

Coffield, F. (2000a) *Differing Visions of the Learning Society: Research Findings* (Bristol, Policy Press).

Coffield, F. (2000b) Lifelong learning as a lever on structural change? *Journal of Education Policy*, 15(2), pp. 237–46.

Cohen, A. (1985) *The Symbolic Construction of Community* (London, Tavistock).

Cohen, A. (1987) *Whalsey: Symbol, Segment and Boundary in a Shetland Island Community* (Manchester, Manchester University Press).

Colls, R. (1995) What is community and how do we get it? A message for the member of Sedgefield, *Northern Review,* Vol. 1 Spring, pp. 9–27.

Corson, D. (ed.) (1991) *Education for Work* (Clevedon, Multilingual Matters).

Crequer, N. (2002) 'Little progress' to learning society, *Times Educational Supplement,* 10 May.

Cripps, S. (2002) *Further Education, Government's Discourse Policy and Practice* (Aldershot, Ashgate).

Crossan, B., Field, J., Gallacher, J. and Merrill, B. (2003) Understanding participation in learning for non-traditional adult learners: learning careers and the construction of learning identities, *British Journal of Sociology of Education* 24 (1).

Crow, G. and Allen, G. (1994) *Community Life* (Hemel Hempstead, Harvester Wheatsheaf).

Davenport, J. (1993) Is there any way out of the andragogy morass?, in Thorpe, M., Edwards, R. and Hanson, A. (eds), *Culture and Processes of Adult Learning* (London, Routledge/Open University).

Dawn, T. (1995) *Fifty Years of Further Education – Celebration or Wake?* (Oxford Brookes University, School of Education).

Dearden, R.F. (1972) Happiness and education, in Dearden, R.F., Hirst, P.H. and Peters, R.S. (eds), *Education and the Development of Reason* (London, Routledge & Kegan Paul).

Dearden, R.F. (1976) *Problems in Primary Education* (London, Routledge & Kegan Paul).

Dearden, R.F. (1984) *Theory and Practice in Education* (London, Routledge & Kegan Paul).

Dearing, Sir Ron (1996) *Review of Qualifications for 16–19 Year Olds* (Hayes, School Curriculum and Assessment Authority).

Dearing, Sir R. (1997) *Higher Education for the Learning Society* (London, The Stationery Office).

Delors, J. (1992) *White Paper: Growth, Competitiveness and Employment,* EU.

Dent, H.C. (1968) *The Education Act 1944* (London, University of London Press).

Denzin, N. K. (1989) *Interpretative Biography* (New York, Sage Publications).

DES (1973) *Adult Education: A Plan for Development* [Russell Report] (London, Her Majesty's Stationery Office).

DES (1985) *The Curriculum 5 to 16* (London, Her Majesty's Stationery Office).

DfEE (1997) *Design of the New Deal for 18–24 Year Olds* (London, Department for Education and Employment).

DfEE (1998a) *The Learning Age: A Renaissance for a New Britain* (London, Department for Education and Employment).

DfEE (1998b) *Further Education for the New Millennium* (London Department for Education and Employment).

DfEE (1998c) *University for Industry: Pathfinder Prospectus* (London, Department for Education and Employment).

DfEE (1998d) *Qualifying for Success* (London, Department for Education and Employment).

DfEE (1998e) *Adult and Community Learning Fund: Prospectus*)(udbury, Department for Education and Employment Publications).

DfEE (1999a) *DfEE News* (London, Department for Education and Employment) 17/99.

DfEE (1999b) *Learning to Succeed: a new framework for post-16 learning* (London, Department for Education and Employment).

DfEE (2000a) *Colleges for Excellence and Innovation* (London, Department for Education and Employment).

DfEE (2000b) *Opportunity for All: Skills for the New Economy* (London, Department for Education and Employment).

DfEE (2000c) *Foundation Degrees, Consultation Paper* (London, Department for Education and Employment).

DfEE (2001a) *Opportunity and Skills in the Knowledge-Driven Economy* (London, Department for Education and Employment).

DfEE (2001b) *Connexions Service* (London, Department for Education and Employment).

DfEE (2001c) *Connexions Card* (London, Department for Education and Employment).

DfES (2001a) *First 16 New Specialist Colleges Announced by Morris* (London, Department for Education and Skills) 2001/0318.

DfES (2001b) *Schools – Achieving Success* (London, Department for Education and Skills).

DfES (2001c) *Grant Letter 2002–3* (London, Department for Education and Skills).

DfES (2001d) *Morris, Brown and Hewitt Announce New Plans for Modern Apprenticeships* (London, Department for Education and Skills).

DfES (2002a) *Choice and Excellence: A Vision for Post-14 Education* (London, Department for Education and Skills).

DfES (2002b) *Advisory Group on Citizenship for 16–19 Year Olds in Education and Training* (London, Department for Education and Skills).

DfES (2002c) *New Transformation Programme to Raise Standards in Further Education and Training* (London, Department for Education and Skills).

DfES (2002d) *Thousands More 'Get on' as Adult Learners' Week Kicks Off* (London, Department for Education and Skills).

Dimbleby, R. and Cooke, C. (2000) Curriculum and learning, in Smithers, A. and Robinson, P. (eds), op. cit.

Dore, R. (1997) Reflections on the Diploma Disease – Twenty Years On, *Assessment in Education* 4(1), pp. 198–205.

DTI (1995) *Competitiveness – Forging Ahead* (London, Department of Trade and Industry).

ED (1993) *Development of Transferable Skills in Learners* (Sheffield, Employment Department).

Educa (1999) Disadvantage, *Educa*, No.195, pp. 3–4.

Educa (2000) Vocational A levels; *Educa*, No. 205, September.

Educa (2001a) The new department, *Educa*, No. 214, p. 5.

Educa (2001b) Vocational GCSEs; *Educa*, No. 211, March.

Educa (2001c) Modern Apprenticeships; *Educa*, No. 211, December, pp. 13–15.

Education and Employment Committee (1998) *Sixth Report of the House of Commons Education and Employment Committee* (London, The Stationery Office).

Edwards, R. (1997) *Changing Places? Flexibility, Lifelong Learning and a Learning Society* (London, Routledge).

Edwards, R., Miller, N., Small, N. and Tait, A. (eds) (2002) *Supporting Lifelong Learning, Volume 3: Making Policy Work* (London, Routledge-Falmer/Open University).

Engestrom, Y. (1996) *Innovative Learning in Work Teams* (Helsinki, Centre for Activity Theory and Developmental Work Research).

Ernst & Young (1995) *The Evaluation of Modern Apprenticeships Prototypes* (University of Sheffield, Centre for the Study of Post-16 Developments).

Esland, G. (1996) Knowledge and nationhood: the new right, education and the global market, in Avis, J., *et al.*, op. cit.

Esland, G. (ed.) (1990) *Education, Training and Employment* (Wokingham, Addison-Wesley/Open University Press).

Esland, G., Flude, M. and Sieminski, S. (1999) Introduction, in Flude, M. and Sieminski, S. (eds), *Education, Training and the Future of Work II: Developments in Vocational Education and Training* (London, Routledge/Open University Press).

Etzioni, A. (1993) *The Spirit of Community: Rights, Responsibilities and the Communitarian Agenda* (New York, Crown).

Etzioni, A. (1995) *The Spirit of Community* (Glasgow, Harper Collins).

Evans, B. (1992) *The Politics of the Training Market* (London, Routledge).

Evans, K. (1975) *The Development and Structure of the English Education System* (London, Hodder and Stoughton).

Evans, K., Hodkinson, P. and Unwin, L. (2002) *Working to Learn* (London, Kogan Page).

Fairclough, N. (2000) *New Labour, New Language?* (London, Routledge).

Farley, M. (1983) Trends and structural changes in English vocational education, in Watson, K. (ed.), *Youth, Education and Employment: International Perspectives* (London, Croom Helm).

FEDA (1998) *Evidence to the Sixth Report of the House of Commons Education and Employment Committee* (London, The Stationery Office).

FEFC (1996) *College Responsiveness, National Survey Report from the Inspectorate* (Coventry, Further Education Funding Council).

FEFC (2001) *National Audit Report Gives Pointers For Further Success* (Coventry, Further Education Funding Council).

FENTO (1999) *Standards for Teaching and Supporting Learning in Further Education in England and Wales* (London, Department for Education and Employment).

FEU (1992) *Flexible Colleges* (London, Further Education Unit).

FEU (1995) *A Framework for Credit* (London, Further Education Unit).

Field, J. and Leicester, M. (eds) (2000) *Lifelong Learning: Education Across the Lifespan* (London, Routledge-Falmer).

Field, J. (2000a) Learning in the Isles, in Field, J. and Leicester, M. (eds), op. cit.

Field, J. (2000b) *Lifelong Learning and the New Educational Order* (Stoke-on-Trent, Trentham).

Finegold, D., *et al.* (1990) *A British Baccalaureate* (London, Institute for Public Policy Research).

Fish, D. (1993) Uncertainty in a certain world: values competency-based training and the reflective practitioner, *Journal of the National Association for Values in Education and Training,* VIII, pp. 7–12.

Flint, C. (1998) Don't educate Jude, *Times Higher Education Supplement,* 20 October, 1998.

Florian, L. (1997) 'Inclusive Learning': The reform initiative of the Tomlinson Committee, *British Journal of Special Education,* 24, 1, pp. 7–11.

Frankel, A. and Reeves, F. (1996) *The Further Education Curriculum* (Wolverhampton, Bilston Community College Publications).

Fryer, R.H. (1997) *Learning for the Twenty-First Century* (London, National Advisory Group for Continuing Education and Lifelong Learning).

Furlong, A. (1992) *Growing Up in a Classless Society? School to Work Transitions* (Edinburgh, Edinburgh University Press).

Gallacher, J., Crossan, B., Field, J., Leahy, J. and Merrill, B. (2000) *Education for all? Further Education, Social Inclusion and Widening Access* (Glasgow, Centre for Research in Lifelong Learning, Glasgow Caledonian University).

Gardner, P. and Johnson, S. (1996) Thinking critically about critical thinking, *Journal of Philosophy of Education*, 30(3), pp. 441–56.

Gibbs, G. (1988) *Learning By Doing* (London, Further Education Unit).

Giddens, A. (1987) *Social Theory and Modern Sociology* (Cambridge, Polity Press).

Giddens, A. (1998) *The Third Way: The Renewal of Social Democracy* (London, Polity).

Giddens, A. (2000) *The Third Way and Its Critics* (London, Polity).

Gilroy, P. (1987) *There ain't no Black in the Union Jack: The Cultural Politics of Race and Nation* (London, Hutchinson).

Glaser, B. and Strauss, A. (1971) *Status Passage* (Chicago, Aldine).

Gleeson, D. (1996) Continuity and change in post-compulsory education and training, in Halsall, R. and Cockett, M. (eds), op. cit.

Goffman, E. (1961) *Asylums* (Harmondsworth, Penguin).

Gospel, H. (1995) The decline of apprenticeship training in Britain, *Industrial Relations Journal*, 26(1), pp. 32–44.

Gospel, H. (1998) The revival of apprenticeship training in Britain, *British Journal of Industrial Relations*, 36(3), pp. 435–57.

Gravatt, J. and Silver, R. (2000) Partnerships with the community, in Smithers, A. and Robinson, P. (eds), op. cit.

Gray, J. (1998) *False Dawn: The Delusions of Global Capitalism* (New York, The New Press).

Green, A. (1990) *Education and State Formation* (London, Macmillan).

Green, A. (1997a) *Education, Globalization and the Nation State* (London, Macmillan).

Green, A. (1997b) Core skills, general education and unification in post-16 education, in Hodgson, A. and Spours, K. (eds), op. cit.

Green, A. and Lucas, N. (eds) (1999a) *FE and Lifelong Learning: Realigning the Sector for the Twenty-First Century* (University of London: Institute of Education).

Green, A. and Lucas, N. (1999b) Repositioning further education: a sector for the twenty-first century, in Green, A. and Lucas, N. (eds) (1999a), op. cit.

Green, A. and Lucas, N. (1999c) From obscurity to crisis: the further education sector in context, in Green, A. and Lucas, N. (eds), *FE and Lifelong Learning: Realigning the Sector for the Twenty-first Century* (London, Institute of Education, University of London).

Griffiths, M. (1987) The teaching of skills and the skills of teaching, *Journal of Philosophy of Education*, 21(2), pp. 203–14.

Guile, D. and Hayton, A. (1999) Information and learning technology: implications for teaching and learning in further education, in Green, A. and Lucas, N. (eds) op. cit.

Guile, D. and Young, M. (2002) Beyond the institution of apprenticeship, in Harrison, R., Reeve, F., Hanson, A. and Clarke, J. (eds), op. cit.

Hager, P. (2000) Knowledge that Works, in Symes, C. and McIntyre, J. (eds), op. cit.

Hall, V. (1994) *Further Education in the United Kingdom* (London, Collins Educational).

Bibliography 191

Halliday, J. (1996) Values and further education, *British Journal of Educational Studies*, 44(1), pp. 66–81.

Halpin, D. (1999) Sociologising the third way: the contribution of Anthony Giddens and the significance of his analysis for education, *Forum*, 41(2), pp. 53–57.

Halsall, R. (1996) Core skills – the continuing debate, in Halsall, R. and Cockett, M. (eds), *Education and Training 14–19: Chaos or Coherence?* (London, David Fulton).

Halsall, R. and Cockett, M. (eds) (1996) *Education and Training 14–19: Chaos or Coherence?* (London, David Fulton).

Hargreaves, D. (2002) We must not botch the job, *Times Educational Supplement*, 15 February.

Harkin, J., Turner, G. and Dawn, T. (2001) *Teaching Young Adults* (London, Routledge-Falmer).

Harper, H. (1997) *Management in Further Education* (London, David Fulton).

Harris, S. and Hyland, T. (1995) Basic skills and learning support in further education, *Journal of Further and Higher Education*, 19(2), pp. 42–8.

Harrison, J. (1954) *The History of the Working Men's College, 1854–1954* (London, Routledge & Kegan Paul).

Harrison, R., Recve, F., Hanson, A. and Clarke, J. (eds) (2002) *Supporting Lifelong Learning – Volume 1: Perspectives on Learning* (London, Routledge-Falmer/Open University).

Hart, J. (1998) Report urges training overhaul, *Times Educational Supplement*, 30 October.

Hart, M. (1996) Educating cheap labour, in Raggatt, P., Edwards, R. and Small, N. (eds), *The Learning Society* (London, Routledge/Open University).

Hart, W.A. (1978) Against skills, *Oxford Review of Education*, 4(2), pp. 205–16.

Hartley, J., Trueman, M. and Lapping, C. (1997) The performance of mature and younger students at Keele University, *Journal of Access Studies*, 12(1), pp. 98–112.

Higgins, T. and Merson, C. (1995) GNVQs are good for you: it's official, *Education*, 24 November.

Higher Education Funding Council for England (1998) *Funding Higher Education in Further Education Colleges,* Report 98/59 (Bristol, HEFCE).

Higher Education Funding Council for England (2000) *Student Pioneers to Enrol on 40 Foundation Degree Courses* (London, Higher Education Funding Council for England).

Hill, D. (2000) New Labour's neo-liberal education policy, *Forum*, 42(1), pp. 8–11.

Hill, D. M. (2000) *Urban Policy and Politics in Britain* (Basingstoke, Macmillan).

Hillage, J., Uden, T., Aldridge, F. and Eccles, J. (2000) *Adult Learning in England; a review* (Brighton, Institute for Employment Studies).

Hillery, G.A. (1955) Definitions of community: areas of agreement, *Rural Sociology*, 20(2), 111–23.

Hillman, J. (1997) *University for Industry: Creating a National Learning Network* (London, Institute for Public Policy Research).

Hirst, P. H. (1974) *Knowledge and the Curriculum* (London, Routledge & Kegan Paul).

HMC (1995) *The [1995] Education 14–19 Conference* (Leicester, Headmasters' Conference).

Hobbes, T. (1651/1965) *Leviathan* (London, Dent/Everyman).

Hodgson, A. (ed.) (2000) *Policies, Politics and the Future of Lifelong Learning* (London, Kogan Page).

Hodgson, A. and Spours, K. (eds) (1997) *Dearing and Beyond: 14–19 Qualifications, Frameworks and Systems* (London, Kogan Page).

Hodgson, A. and Spours, K. (1999) *New Labour's Educational Agenda* (London, Kogan Page).

Hodkinson, P. (1996) Careership: The individual, choices and markets in the transition into work, in Avis, J., *et al.* (eds), op. cit.

Hodkinson, P., Sparkes, A. and Hodkinson, H. (1996) *Triumphs and Tears: Young People, Markets and the Transition from School to Work* (London, David Fulton).

Holland, R.F. (1980) *Against Empiricism: On Education, Epistemology and Value* (Oxford, Basil Blackwell).

Hook, S. and Learner, S. (2002) Economy held back by class divisions, *Times Educational Supplement*, 12 April.

Houghton, V. and Richardson, K. (eds) (1974) *Recurrent Education: A Plea for Lifelong Learning* (London, Ward Lock Educational).

Hughes, C. and Tight, M. (1998) The myth of the learning society, in Ranson, S. (ed.), op. cit.

Hughes, E.C. (1937) Institutional office and the person, *American Journal of Sociology*, 43, pp. 404–43.

Husen, T. (1974) *The Learning Society* (London, Methuen).

Hyland, T. (1979) Open education – a slogan examined, *Educational Studies*, 5(1), pp. 35–41.

Hyland, T. (1992) Moral vocationalism, *Journal of Moral Education*, 21(2), pp. 139–50.

Hyland, T. (1994) *Competence, Education and NVQs: Dissenting Perspectives* (London, Cassell).

Hyland, T. (1998) Exporting failure: The strange case of NVQs and overseas markets, *Educational Studies*, 24(3), pp. 369–80.

Hyland, T. (1999) *Vocational Studies, Lifelong Learning and Social Values* (Aldershot, Ashgate).

Hyland, T. (2000) Vocational education and training under the New Deal, *Journal of Vocational Education and Training*, 52(3), pp. 395–411.

Hyland, T. (2002) Third way values and post-school education policy, *Journal of Education Policy*, 17(2), pp. 245–58.

Hyland, T. and Johnson, S. (1998) Of cabbages and key skills, *Journal of Further and Higher Education*, 22(2), pp. 163–72.

Hyland, T. and Matlay, H. (1997) Small businesses, training needs and VET, *Journal of Education and Work*, 10(2), pp. 129–39.

Hyland, T. and Merrill, B. (1996) *The FE College and Its Communities* (Warwick University, Department of Continuing Education).

Hyland, T. and Merrill, B. (2001) Community, partnership and social inclusion in further education, *Journal of Further and Higher Education*, 25(3), pp. 353–64.

Hyland, T. and Musson, D. (2001) Unpacking the New Deal for Young People: promise and problems, *Educational Studies*, 27(1), pp. 55–67.

IJLE (1998) Editorial, *International Journal of Lifelong Education*, 17(2), p. 69.

ILT (2001) *ILT Newsletter No.6* (York, Institute for Learning and Teaching).

International Journal of Inclusive Education, 2(3), pp. 255–68.

Jackson, K. (1995) Popular education and the state: a new look at the community debate, in Mayo, M. and Thompson, J. (eds), *Adult Learning, Critical Intelligence and Social Change* (Leicester, NIACE).

Jarrett, J.L. (1991) *The Teaching of Values: Caring and Appreciation* (London, Routledge).

Jessup, F.W. (ed.) (1969) *Lifelong Learning* (Oxford, Pergamon Press).

Johnson, S. (1998) Skills, Socrates and the Sophists: learning from history, *British Journal of Educational Studies*, 46(2), pp. 201–13.

Johnston, R. (1988) 'Really Useful Knowledge' 1790–1850, memories in the 1980s, in Lovett, T. (ed.), *Radical Approaches to Adult Education* (London, Routledge).

Johnston, R. (1993) Can we serve communities in the market-place? in Brook, L. (ed.), *Serving Communities* (Bristol, Staff College and the Association of Colleges).

Jonathan, R. (1987) The Youth Training Scheme and core skills, in Holt, M. (ed.) *Skills and Vocationalism* (Milton Keynes, Open University Press).

Jonathan, R. (1997) *Illusory Freedoms: Liberalism, Education and the Market* (Oxford, Blackwell).

Kellner, P. (1998) Our mutual friends, *Times Educational Supplement*, 19 June.

Kennedy, H. (1997) *Learning Works: Widening Participation in Further Education* (Coventry, Further Education Funding Council).

Kenneth Richmond, W. (1945) *Education in England* (Harmondsworth, Penguin).

Kilpatrick, S., Bell, R. and Falk, I. (1999) The role of group learning in building social capital, *Journal of Vocational Education and Training*, 51(1), pp. 129–44.

Kingdom, J. (1992) *No Such Thing As Society? Individualism and Community* (Buckingham, Open University Press).

Kingston, P. (2001) Skilful Plan; *Education Guardian*, 16 October.

Knowles, M. (1970) *The Modern Practice of Adult Education* (New York, Association Press).

Knowles, M. (1979) Andragogy revisited, *Adult Education*, 30(1), pp. 52–3.

Kypri, P. and Clark, G. (1997) Furthering local economies, *Viewpoint*, No. 3, FEDA, pp 1–18.

Langford, G. (1985) *Education, Persons and Society – A Philosophical Enquiry* (London, Macmillan).

Lave, J. and Wenger, E. (2002) Legitimate peripheral participation in communities of practice, in Harrison, R., Reeve, F., Hanson, A. and Clarke, J. (eds), op. cit.

Lawson, K.H. (1998) *Philosophical Issues in the Education of Adults* (Nottingham University, Continuing Education Press).

Leadbetter, C. (1998) Head breaks the mould, *Times Education Supplement*, 26 June.

Leathwood, C. (1998) Irrational bodies and corporate culture: further education in the 1990s, *International Journal of Inclusive Education* 2(3), pp. 255–68.

Legge, D. (1982) *The Education of Adults in Britain* (Milton Keynes, Open University Press).

Leney, T., Lucas, N. and Taubman, D. (1998) *Learning Funding: The Impact of FEFC Funding – Evidence from Twelve FE Colleges* (London, University of London Institute of Education).

Levi, P. (1988) *The Wrench* (London, Abacus).

Levitas, R. (1998) *The Inclusive Society? Social Exclusion and New Labour* (London, Macmillan).

Levy, M., Oates, T., Hunt, M. and Dobson, F. (1989) *A Guide to WBL Terms: Definitions and Commentary on Terms for WBL in Vocational Education and Training* (Bristol, FE Staff College).

Lovett, T. (1975) *Adult Education, Community Development and the Working Class* (London, Ward Lock).

LSC (2001a) *Learning and Skills Council: Strategic Framework to 2004 – Corporate Plan* (Coventry, Learning and Skills Council).

LSC (2001b) *Skills and Enterprise Update* (Coventry, Learning + Skills Council).

LSC (2001c) *LSC to Lead on Modern Apprenticeships* (Coventry, Learning + Skills Council).

Lucas, N. (1993) Serving the community: community colleges in the USA, in Brook, L. (ed.) (1993), op. cit.

Lucas, N. (1999) Incorporated colleges: beyond the further education funding council's model, in Green, A. and Lucas, N. (eds) (1999a) op. cit.

Lucas, N. (2000) Hopes, contradictions and challenges: lifelong learning and the further education sector, in Hodgson, A. (ed.) (2000), op. cit.

Lucas, N. (2001) In the shadows, *Education Guardian*, 16 October.

Lucas, N., McDonald, J. and Taubman, D. (1999) *Learning to Live with It: the impact of FEFC funding, further evidence from fourteen colleges* (London, National Association of Teachers in Further and Higher Education).

McClure, R. (2000) Recurrent Funding, in Smithers, A. and Robinson, P. (eds), op. cit.

McCullough, G. (1989) *The Secondary Technical School: A Usable Past?* (London, Falmer).

McGinty, J. and Fish, J. (1993) *FE in the Marketplace* (London, Routledge).

MacIver, R.M. and Page, C.H. (1961) *Society: An Introductory Analysis* (London, Macmillan).

Maclure, S. (1973) *Educational Documents* (London, Methuen).

Maclure, S. (1991) *Missing Links – The Challenge to Further Education* (London, Policy Studies Institute).

Macpherson, C.B. (1964) *The Political Theory of Possessive Individualism* (Oxford, Oxford University Press).

Marsick, V.J. and Watkins, K.E. (2002) Envisioning new organisations for learning, in Reeve, F., Cartwright, M. and Edwards, R. (eds), op. cit.

Martin, I. (1987) Community education: towards a theoretical analysis, in Allen, G., Bastiani, J., Martin, I. and Richards, K. (eds), *Community Education: an agenda for reform* (Milton Keynes, Open University Press).

Martin, I. (1996) Community education: the dialectics of development, in Fieldhouse, R. (ed.), *A History of Modern British Adult Education* (Leicester, NIACE).

Martin, I. (1999) Connotations of community: implications for practice, in Merrill, B. (ed.), *Concepts of Community: Key Issues for the FE Sector* (London, FEDA).

Matza, D. (1964) *Delinquency and Drift* (Berkeley, John Wiley & Sons).

Mayes, T. (2002) The technology of learning in a social world, in Harrison, R. *et al.* (eds), op. cit.

Mayo, M. (1995) Towards a critical review, in Mayo, M. and Thompson, J. (eds), *Adult Learning, Critical Intelligence and Social Change* (Leicester, NIACE).

Mee, G. and Wiltshire, H. (1978) *Structure and Performance in Adult Education* (London, Longman).

Meighan, R. (1981) *A Sociology of Educating* (London, Holt, Rinehart & Winston).

Merrill, B. (1999) *Gender, Change and Identity: Mature Women Students in Universities* (Aldershot, Ashgate).

Merrill, B. (2000) *The Further Education College and its Communities* (London, FEDA).

Merrill, B. *et al.* (2000) *The FE College and its Communities* (London, FEDA).

Mezirow, J. (1983) A critical theory of adult learning and education, in Tight, M. (ed.), *Adult Learning and Education* (London, Routledge).

Milner, H. (1998) The broker and the catalyst, *Adults Learning*, 9(5), pp. 15–17.

Ministry of Education [Percy Report] (1945) *Higher Technological Education* (London, His Majesty's Stationery Office).

Morris, E. (2001) Ask the bosses, *Education Guardian*, 16 October.

MSC (1977) *Training for Skills* (Sheffield, Manpower Services Commission).

Musgrave, P.W. (1970a) The definition of technical education, 1860–1910, in Musgrave, P.W. (ed.), *Sociology, History and Education* (London, Methuen).

Musgrave, P.W. (1970b) Constant factors in the demand for technical education, 1860–1960, in Musgrave, P.W. (ed.), op. cit.

NACETT (1998) *Fast Forward for Skills* (London, National Advisory Council for Education and Training Targets).

NATFHE (1992) *The Community College* (London, National Association of Teachers in Further and Higher Education).

NCC (1990) *Education for Citizenship* (York, National Curriculum Council).

NCE (1993) *Learning To Succeed: Report of the National Commission on Education* (London, Heinemann).

NCVQ (1992) *Response to Consultation on GNVQs* (London, National Council for Vocational Qualifications).

Neary, M. (1999) Youth, training and the politics of 'Cool', in Hill, D., McLaren, P., Cole, M. and Rikowski, G. (eds), *Postmodernism in Educational Theory* (London, Tufnell Press).

NIACE (2001) *The Social, the Cultural and the Economic Case for Lifelong Learning* (Leicester, National Institute for Adult Continuing Education).

NIACE (2002) *Two Steps Forward, One Step Back* (Leicester, National Institute of Adult Continuing Education).

Nicholls, A. (1995) *Schools and Colleges: collaborators or competitors in the education system?* (London, Schools Guidance Council).

NTO (2001) *Foundation and Advanced Modern Apprenticeships: Key Operating Principles* (London, National Training Organisation National Council).

Ormerod, P. (1994) *The Death of Economics* (London, Faber & Faber).

Owen, G. (1999) Further education, its communities and economic regeneration, in Merrill, B. (ed.), *Concepts of Community: Key Issues for the FE Sector* (London, FEDA).

Parkinson, C. and Carter, A. (1999) *Perceptions of Local/Regional Partners,* Report for the University of Warwick FEDA Project Colleges and their Communities.

Peters, T. (1987) *Thriving on Chaos* (New York, Knopf).

Pirsig, R. (1974) *Zen and the Art of Motorcycle Maintenance* (London, Corgi).

Poole, R. (1990) Morality, masculinity and the market, in Sayers, S. and Osborne, P. (eds), *Socialism, Feminism and Philosophy* (London, Routledge).

Pound, T. (1998) Forty years on: the issue of breadth in the post-16 curriculum, *Oxford Review of Education*, 24(2), pp. 16–17.

Powell, B. and Buffton, J. (1993) The community profile as a key to growth and equity, in Brook, L. (ed.), *Serving Communities* (Bristol, Staff College and the Association of Colleges).

Prais, S. (1995) *Productivity, Education and Training: an international perspective* (Cambridge, Cambridge University Press).

Pratt, J. (2000) The emergence of the colleges, in Smithers, A. and Robinson, P. (eds), op. cit.

QCA (2000) *Citizenship Post-16 – Letter to QCA* (London, Qualifications and Assessment Authority).

QCA (2001a) *Curriculum 2000 Review* (London, Qualifications and Curriculum Authority).

QCA (2001b) *Introduction to Qualifications* (London, Qualifications and Curriculum Authority).

Raffe, D. (1993) Tracks and pathways: differentiation in education and training and their relation to the labour market, paper presented at the *First Conference of the European Research Network on Transitions in Youth Training* (Barcelona, Spain).

Ranson, S. (1994) *Towards the Learning Society* (London, Cassell).

Ranson, S. (ed.) (1998) *Inside the Learning Society* (London, Cassell).

Ranson, S. (1999) For citizenship and the remaking of civil society, in Merrill, B. (ed.), *Concepts of Community: Key Issues for the FE Sector* (London, FEDA).

Rees, G., Gorard, S., Fevre, R. and Furlong, J. (2000) Participation in the learning society: history, place and biography, in Coffield, F. (ed.), *Differing Visions of the Learning Society* (Bristol, The Policy Press).

Reeve, F., Cartwright, M. and Edwards, E. (eds) (2002) *Supporting Lifelong Learning – Volume 2: Organizing Learning* (London, Routledge-Falmer/ Open University).

Reeves, F. (1995) *The Modernity of Further Education* (Wolverhampton, Bilston College Publications/Education Now).

Reinharz, S. (1992) *Feminist Methods in Social Research* (New York, Oxford University Press).

Richardson, W. and Gumbley, N. (1995) *Foundation Learning in the Work-Based Route* (London, Institute of Education), Working Paper No. 4.

Rikowski, G. (1998) Only Charybdis: The Learning Society Through Idealism, in Ranson, S. (ed.), op. cit.

Rikowski, G. (1999) Education, capital and the transhuman, in Hill, D., McLaren, P., Cole, M. and Rikowski, G. (eds) (1999), *Postmodernism in Educational Theory: Education and the Politics of Human Resistance* (London, Tufnell Press).

Rikowski, G. (2000a) The 'Which Blair' Project: Giddens, the third way and education, *Forum*, 41(2), pp. 4–7.

Rikowski, G. (2000b) *The Battle in Seattle* (London, Tufnell Press).

Robbins, L. (1963) *Higher Education: Report of the Committee* (London, Her Majesty's Stationery Office).

Robertson, D. (1999) The University for Industry – a flagship for demand-led learning or another doomed supply-side intervention?, *Journal of Education and Work*, 11(1), pp. 5–22.

Robson, J. (1998) A profession in crisis: status, culture and identity in the further education college, *Journal of Vocational Education and Training*, 50(4), pp. 585–607.

Rozema, D. (2001) The polemics of education, *Journal of Philosophy of Education*, 35(2), pp. 237–54.

Russell, B. (1946) *History of Western Philosophy* (London, Allen & Unwin).

Russell, L. (1973) *Adult Education: A plan for development.* Report by a Committee of Inquiry for the Secretary of State for Education and Science, HMSO.

Sanderson, M. (1999) *Education and Economic Decline in Britain, 1870 to the 1990s* (Cambridge, Cambridge University Press).

Scheffler, I. (1973) *Reason and Teaching* (London, Routledge & Kegan Paul).

Schofield, H. (1972) *The Philosophy of Education: An Introduction* (London, Allen and Unwin).

Schuller, T. and Field, J. (1998) Social capital, human capital and the learning society, *International Journal of Lifelong Education*, 17(4), pp. 226–35.

Schuller, T. and McGarry, J. (eds) (1979) *Recurrent Education and Lifelong Learning* (London, Kogan Page).

Scott, P. (1996) *The Meanings of Mass Higher Education* (Milton Keynes, Open University Press).

Seagraves, L. *et al.* (1996) *Learning in Smaller Companies* (University of Stirling, Education Policy and Development).

Selwyn, N. (2000) The National Grid for Learning: Panacea or Panopticon?, *British Journal of Sociology of Education*, 21(2), pp. 243–55.

SENDA (2001) *Special Education Needs Disability Act 2001* (http://www.legislation.hmso.gov.uk/acts2).

Shattock, M. (2000) Governanace and management, in Smithers, R. and Robinson, P. (eds), op. cit.

Sherlock, P. (1999) Modern apprenticeship and national traineeship – raising standards: speech to *Training for Young People, Skills for the Millennium Conference* (Leicester, Training and Enterprise National Council).

Sieminski, S. (1993) The 'flexible' solution to economic decline, *Journal of Further and Higher Education*, 17(1), pp. 92–100.

Simon, B. (1969) *The Two Nations and the Education System, 1780–1870* (London, Lawrence & Wishart).

Singley, M.K. and Anderson, J.R. (1989) *The Transfer of Cognitive Skill* (Cambridge, MA, Harvard University Press).

Skilbeck, M., Connell, H., Lowe, N. and Tait, K. (1994) *The Vocational Quest* (London, Routledge).

Skills and Enterprise Network (1997) *Modern Apprenticeships – A Success Story* (London, Department for Education and Employment).

Smith, R. (1997) The education of autonomous citizens, in Bridges, D. (ed.), *Education, Autonomy and Democratic Citizenship* (London, Routledge).

Smithers, A. (1993) *All Our Futures: Britain's Education Revolution* (London, Channel 4 'Dispatches' Report on Education).

Smithers, A. and Robinson, P. (1993) *Changing Colleges: Further Education in the Market Place* (London, Council for Industry and Higher Education).

Smithers, A. and Robinson, P. (eds) (2000) *Further Education Re-Formed* (London, Falmer).

Standish, P. (1997) Heidegger and the technology of further education, *Journal of Philosophy of Education*, 31(3), pp. 439–59.

Steele, T. (1997) Marginal occupations and adult education, cultural studies and social renewal, *Scottish Journal of Adult and Continuing Education,* 4 (1).

Stephens, M.D. (1990) *Adult Education* (London, Cassell).

Strain, M. (1998) Towards an economy of lifelong learning: reconceptualising relations between learning and life, *British Journal of Educational Studies*, 46(3), pp. 264–77.

Strain, M. and Field, J. (1998) On the myth of the learning society, in Ranson, S. (ed.), op. cit.

Suttles, G. (1972) *The Social Construction of Communities* (Chicago, University of Chicago Press).

Symes, C. and McIntyre, J. (eds) (2000) *Working Knowledge: the New Vocationalism and Higher Education* (Buckingham, Open University Press).

Tam, H. (1998) *Communitiarianism: A New Agenda for Politics and Citizenship* (Basingstoke, Macmillan).

Tarrant, J. (2001) The ethics of post-compulsory education and training in a democracy, *Journal of Further and Higher Education*, 25(3), pp. 369–78.

Taubman, D. (2000) Staff relations, in Smithers, A. and Robinson, P. (eds), op. cit.

Taylor, A.J. (1972) *Laissez-Faire and State Intervention in Nineteenth Century Britain* (London, Macmillan).

Thomas, L. (2001) *Widening Participation in Post-Compulsory Education* (London, Continuum).

Thomson, A. (1997) Student numbers in FE grow by 16%, *Times Educational Supplement*.

Thomson, A. (2002) 'Postcode' premium is not enough, *Times Higher Education Supplement*, 22 February.

Tight, M. (1998) Lifelong Learning: Opportunity or Compulsion?, *British Journal of Educational Studies*, 46(3), pp. 25–26.

Tomlinson, J. (1996a) *Inclusive Learning: Principles and Recommendations* (Coventry, Further Education Funding Council).

Tomlinson, J. (1996b) *Inclusive Learning: Report of the Learning Difficulties and/or Learning Disabilities Committee* (London, The Stationery Office).

Tönnies, F. (1955) *Community and Association* (translated by C.P. Loomis) (London, Routledge & Kegan Paul).

Training Agency (1990) *Enterprise in Higher Education* (Sheffield, Training Agency).

Tressell, R. (1914/1993) *The Ragged Trousered Philanthropists* (London, Flamingo).

Trowler, P. (1998) *Education Policy* (Eastbourne, Gildredge Press).

Trusted, J. (1987) *Moral Principles and Social Values* (London, Routledge & Kegan Paul).

TUC (1947) *Annual Conference Report* (London, Trades Union Congress).

Tuckett, A. (2002) Older, but not wiser, *Times Educational Supplement*, 10 May.

Twining, J. (2001a) Joining it all up, *Educa*, No.212, April, p. 8.

Twining, J. (2001b) Give the LSC a chance, *Educa*, No.215, Sept, pp. 8–9.

Twining, J. (2001c) The shape of things to come?, *Educa*, No.216, Oct., pp. 8–9.

Twining, J. (2002a) 14–19 reform: some worries, *Educa*, No.221, March, pp. 8–9.

Twining, J. (2002b) Visions and market failure, *Educa*, No.222, April, pp. 8–10.

Tysome, T. (2001) Challenge 'too huge' for LSC?, *Times Higher Education Supplement*, 9 November.

Tysome, T. (2002a) LSC: let's blur the boundaries, *Times Higher Education Supplement*, 5 April.

Tysome, T. (2002b) Lifelong learning suffers a setback, *Times Higher Education Supplement*, 10 May.

University of Huddersfield (2001) *A New Kind of Partnership Between Further and Higher Education* (University of Huddersfield, School of Education and Professional Development).

Unwin, L. (2000) 'Flower arranging's' off but floristry is on, in Green, A. and Lucas, N. (eds), *FE and Lifelong Learning: Realigning the Sector for the Twenty-first Century* (London, Institute of Education, University of London).

Unwin, L. and Wellington, J. (2001) *Young People's Perspectives on Education, Training and Employment* (London, Kogan Page).

Venables, P.F.R. (1955) *Technical Education* (London, Bell).

Vygotsky, L.S. (1978) *Mind in Society* (Cambridge, MA, Harvard University Press).

Warnock, M. (1977) *Schools of Thought* (London, Faber & Faber).

Wenger, E. (2002) Communities of practice and social learning systems, in Reeve, F., Cartwright, M. and Edwards, E. (eds), op. cit.

West, L. (1996) *Beyond Fragments* (London, Taylor & Francis).

White, J. (1997) *Education and the End of Work* (London, Cassell).

Whitfield, D. (2000) The third way for education: privatisation and marketisation, *Forum*, 42(2), pp. 82–5.

Wilds, E.H. and Lottich, K.V. (1970) *The Foundations of Modern Education* (New York, Holt, Rinehart & Winston).

Wilkinson, R.H. (1970) The gentleman ideal and the maintenance of a political elite, in Musgrave, P.W. (ed.) *Sociology, History and Education* (London, Methuen).

Williams, R. (1988) *Keywords* (London, Fontana).

Willmott, P. (1986) *Social Networks, Informal Care and Public Policy* (London, Policy Studies Institute).

Winch, C. (1995) Education needs training, *Oxford Review of Education*, 21(3), pp. 315–25.

Winch, C. (2000) *Education, Work and Social Capital* (London, Routledge).

Wotjas, O. (2002) Smarter way for a nation to learn, *Times Higher Education Supplement*, 29 March.

Wright Mills, C. (1970) *The Sociological Imagination* (Harmondsworth, Penguin).

Wright, P. (1989) The ghosting of the inner city, in McDowell, L., Sarre, P. and Hammett, C. (eds), *Divided Nation: Social and Cultural Change in Britain* (London, Hodder & Stoughton).

Wringe, C. (1991) Education, schooling and the world of work, in Corson, D. (ed.), op. cit.

Wymer, K. (1996) *Further Education and Democracy* (Bilston, Bilston College Publications/Education Now).

Young, M. (1998) Post-compulsory education for a learning society, in Ranson, S. (ed.), op. cit.

Young, M. (1999) Reconstructing qualifications for further education: towards a system for the twenty-first century, in Green, A. and Lucas, N. (eds), op. cit.

Young, M.F.D. (1998) *The Curriculum of the Future* (London, Falmer).

Young, M. and Spours, K. (1998) 14–19: legacy, opportunities and challenges, *Oxford Review of Education*, 24(1), pp. 83–97.

Young, M. and Willmott, P. (1957) *Family and Kinship in East London* (London, Routledge & Kegan Paul).

Zuboff, S. (1988) *In the Age of the Smart Machine: The Future of Work and Power* (New York, Basic Books).

Index